## DATE DUE

| | | | |
|---|---|---|---|
| | | | |
| | | | |
| | | | |
| | | | |
| | | | |
| | | | |
| | | | |
| | | | |
| | | | |
| | | | |
| | | | |
| | | | |
| | | | |
| | | | |
| | | | |
| | | | |
| | | | |
| | | | |
| | | | PRINTED IN U.S.A. |

**PREP Publishing**
1110½ Hay Street
Fayetteville, NC 28305
(910) 483-6611

Library of Congress Cataloging-in-Publication Data

Real-resumes for medical jobs / Anne McKinney, editor.
        p.  cm. -- (Real-resumes series)
     ISBN  978-1475093704;  1475093705
    1. Résumés (Employment)  2. Medical personnel--Vocational guidance. I. McKinney, Anne, 1948- II. Series.

    R690 .R39 2001
    610.69--dc21                                           2001018562
                                                              CIP


Printed in the United States of America

Third printing 2004

# By PREP Publishing

*Business and Career Series:*

RESUMES AND COVER LETTERS THAT HAVE WORKED

RESUMES AND COVER LETTERS THAT HAVE WORKED FOR MILITARY PROFESSIONALS

GOVERNMENT JOB APPLICATIONS AND FEDERAL RESUMES

COVER LETTERS THAT BLOW DOORS OPEN

LETTERS FOR SPECIAL SITUATIONS

RESUMES AND COVER LETTERS FOR MANAGERS

REAL-RESUMES FOR TEACHERS

REAL-RESUMES FOR STUDENTS

REAL-RESUMES FOR CAREER CHANGERS

REAL-RESUMES FOR SALES

REAL ESSAYS FOR COLLEGE & GRADUATE SCHOOL

REAL-RESUMES FOR FINANCIAL JOBS

REAL-RESUMES FOR COMPUTER JOBS

REAL-RESUMES FOR MEDICAL JOBS

*Judeo-Christian Ethics Series:*

SECOND TIME AROUND

BACK IN TIME

WHAT THE BIBLE SAYS ABOUT...Words that can lead to success and happiness

A GENTLE BREEZE FROM GOSSAMER WINGS

BIBLE STORIES FROM THE OLD TESTAMENT

*Fiction:*

KIJABE...An African Historical Saga

# Table of Contents

Welcome to the Real-Resumes Series. The Real-Resumes Series is a series of books which have been developed based on the experiences of real job hunters and which target specialized fields or types of resumes. As the editor of the series, I have carefully selected resumes and cover letters (with names and other key data disguised, of course) which have been used successfully in real job hunts. That's what we mean by "Real-Resumes." What you see in this book are *real* resumes and cover letters which helped real people get ahead in their careers.

The Real-Resumes Series is based on the work of the country's oldest resume-preparation company known as PREP Resumes. If you would like a free information packet describing the company's resume preparation services, call 910-483-6611 or write to PREP at 1110½ Hay Street, Fayetteville, NC 28305. If you have a job hunting experience you would like to share with our staff at the Real-Resumes Series, please contact us at preppub@aol.com or visit our website at http://www.prep-pub.com.

The resumes and cover letters in this book are designed to be of most value to people already in a career change or contemplating a career change. If we could give you one word of advice about your career, here's what we would say: Manage your career and don't stumble from job to job in an incoherent pattern. Try to find work that interests you, and then identify prosperous industries which need work performed of the type you want to do. Learn early in your working life that a great resume and cover letter can blow doors open for you and help you maximize your salary.

This book is dedicated to the career advancement of medical professionals. We hope the superior samples will help you manage your career as you use the great resumes and cover letters shown in **Real-Resumes for Medical Professionals.**

As the editor of this book, I would like to give you some tips on how to make the best use of the information you will find here. Because you are considering a job change, you already understand the concept of managing your career for maximum enjoyment and self-fulfillment. The purpose of this book is to provide expert tools and advice so that you *can* manage your career. Inside these pages you will find resumes and cover letters that will help you find not just a job, but the type of work you want to do.

**Overview of the Book**

Every resume and cover letter in this book actually worked. And most of the resumes and cover letters have common features: all are one-page, all are in the chronological format, and all resumes are accompanied by a companion cover letter. The book is divided into three parts. **Part One** provides some advice about job hunting. Step One begins with a discussion of why employers prefer the one-page, chronological resume. In Step Two you are introduced to the direct approach and to the proper format for a cover letter. In Step Three you learn the 14 main reasons why job hunters are not offered the jobs they want, and you learn the six key areas employers focus on when they interview you. Step Four gives nuts-and-bolts advice on how to handle the interview, send a follow-up letter after an interview, and negotiate your salary. At the end of Part One, you'll find advice about how to research and locate the companies and organizations to which you want to send your resume.

Since the cover letter plays such a critical role in a career change, **Part Two** of the book is entitled Cover Letters for Medical Jobs. You will learn from the experts how to format your cover letters and you will see suggested language to use in particular career-change situations. It has been said that "A picture is worth a thousand words" and, for that reason, you will see examples of effective cover letters used by real individuals to advance in the medical and change functional areas. Part Two ends with Sample Cover Letters for Medical Jobs.

Parts One and Two lead up to the most important part of the book, which is Real-Resumes for Medical Jobs—**Part Three.** In this section you will see people in varying stages of change. In Section I of Part Three, you discover resumes and cover letters used by students seeking to enter the medical field. If you wonder how to show off clinical rotations or internships, you will find answers and suggestions in Section I. In Section II of Part Three, you find the resumes and cover letters of Administrators and Support Staff. The medical professionals in Section II include people such as medical secretary, dean of health sciences, and medical office manager. Section III contains resumes and cover letters of Experienced Medical Professionals, and in this section you will find numerous types of nurses. Finally, in Section IV you will see resumes and cover letters of Other Medical Professionals. Professionals such as cytotechnologist, medical doctor, and pharmaceutical sales representative are in this final section of Part Three.

Whatever your goal, and whatever your circumstances, you'll find resumes and cover letters that will "show you the ropes" in terms of successfully conducting a job hunt. Bear in mind that you can learn a lot from any of the resumes in this book. There are resumes of student nurses, nursing professionals, doctors, and many other types of medical professionals in nearly all areas of medicine. Whatever your career goal, chances are good that this book will provide you with helpful samples of resumes and cover letters to use in your job hunt.

Before you proceed further, think about why you picked up this book.

- Are you dissatisfied with the type of work you are now doing?
- Would you like to change the type of work you are doing within the medical field?
- Are you satisfied with your industry but not with your niche or function within it?
- Do you want to transfer your skills to a new area?
- Even if you have excelled in your field, have you "had enough?" Would you like the stimulation of a new challenge?
- Are you aware of the importance of a great cover letter but unsure of how to write one?
- Are you preparing to launch a first career in the medical field?
- Have you been downsized, or do you anticipate becoming a victim of downsizing?
- Do you need expert advice on how to plan and implement a job campaign that will open the maximum number of doors?
- Do you want to make sure you handle an interview to your maximum advantage?
- Would you like to master the techniques of negotiating salary and benefits?
- Do you want to learn the secrets and shortcuts of professional resume writers?

The "direct approach" is the style of job hunting most likely to yield the maximum number of job interviews.

## Using the Direct Approach

As you consider the possibility of a job hunt or career change, you need to be aware that most people end up having at least three distinctly different careers in their working lifetimes, and often those careers are different from each other. Yet people usually stumble through each job campaign, unsure of what they should be doing. Whether you find yourself voluntarily or unexpectedly in a job hunt, the direct approach is the job hunting strategy most likely to yield a full-time permanent job. The direct approach is an active, take-the-initiative style of job hunting in which you choose your next employer rather than relying on responding to ads, using employment agencies, or depending on other methods of finding jobs. You will learn how to use the direct approach in this book, and you will see that an effective cover letter is a critical ingredient in using the direct approach.

Using references in a skillful fashion in your job hunt will inspire confidence in prospective employers and help you "close the sale" after interviews.

## Lack of Industry Experience Not a Major Barrier to Entering New Field

"Lack of experience" is often the last reason people are not offered jobs, according to the companies who do the hiring. If you are job hunting, you may be glad to learn that even experienced professionals often are selling "potential" rather than experience in a job hunt. Companies look for personal qualities that they know tend to be present in their most effective professionals, such as communication skills, initiative, persistence, organizational and time management skills, and creativity. Frequently companies are trying to discover "personality type," "talent," "ability," "aptitude," and "potential" rather than seeking actual hands-on experience, so your resume should be designed to aggressively present your accomplishments. Attitude, enthusiasm, personality, and a track record of achievements in any type of work are the primary "indicators of success" which employers are seeking, and you will see numerous examples in this book of resumes written in an all-purpose fashion so that the professional can approach various industries and companies.

## The Art of Using References in a Job Hunt

You probably already know that you need to provide references during a job hunt, but you may not be sure of how and when to use references for maximum advantage. You can use references very creatively during a job hunt to call attention to your strengths and make yourself "stand out." Your references will rarely get you a job, no matter how impressive the names, but the way you use references can boost the employer's confidence in you and lead to a job offer in the least time. You should ask from three to five people, including people who have supervised you, if you can use them as a reference during your job hunt. You may not be able to ask your current boss since your job hunt is probably confidential. A common question in resume preparation is: "Do I need to put my references on my resume?" No, you don't. And even if you create a page of references at the same time that you prepare your resume, you don't need to mail your references page with the resume and cover letter. The potential employer is not interested in your references until he meets and gets interested in you, so the earliest you need to have references ready is at the first interview. An excellent attention-getting technique is to take to the first interview not just a page of references (giving names, addresses, and telephone numbers) but an actual letter of reference written by someone who knows you well and who preferably has supervised or employed you. A professional way to close the first interview is to thank the interviewer, shake his or her hand, and then say you'd like to give him or her a copy of a letter of reference from a previous employer. Hopefully you already made a good impression during the interview, but you'll "close the sale" in a dynamic fashion if you leave a letter praising you and your accomplishments. For that reason, it's a good idea to ask employers during your final weeks in a job if they will provide you with a written letter of recommendation which you can use in future job hunts. Most employers will oblige, and you will have a letter that has a useful "shelf life" of many years. Such a letter often gives the prospective employer enough confidence in his opinion of you that he may forego checking out other references and decide to offer you the job in the next few days. Whom should you ask to serve as references? References should be people who have known or supervised you in a professional, academic, or work situation. References with big titles, like school superintendent or congressman, are fine, but remind busy people when you get to the interview stage that they may be contacted soon. Make sure the busy official recognizes your name and has instant positive recall of you! If you're asked to provide references on a formal company application, you can simply transcribe names from your references list. In summary, follow this rule in using references: If you've got them, flaunt them! If you've obtained well-written letters of reference, make sure you find a polite way to push those references under the nose of the interviewer so he or she can hear someone other than you describing your strengths. Your references probably won't ever get you a job, but glowing letters of reference can give you credibility and visibility that can make you stand out among candidates with similar credentials and potential!

With regard to references, it's
best to provide the names
and addresses of people
who have supervised you
or observed you
in a work situation.

The approach taken by this book is to (1) help you master the proven best techniques of conducting a job hunt and (2) show you how to stand out in a job hunt through your resume, cover letter, interviewing skills, as well as the way in which you present your references and follow up on interviews. Now, the best way to "get in the mood" for writing your own resume and cover letter is to select samples from the Table of Contents that interest you and then read them. A great resume is a "photograph," usually on one page, of an individual. If you wish to seek professional advice in preparing your resume, you may contact one of the professional writers at Professional Resume & Employment Publishing (PREP) for a brief free consultation by calling 1-910-483-6611.

## Part One: Some Advice About Your Job Hunt

### What if you don't know what you want to do?

Your job hunt will be more comfortable if you can figure out what type of work you want to do. But you are not alone if you have no idea what you want to do next! You may have knowledge and skills in certain areas but want to get into another type of work. What *The Wall Street Journal* has discovered in its research on careers is that most of us end up having at least three distinctly different careers in our working lives; it seems that, even if we really like a particular kind of activity, twenty years of doing it is enough for most of us and we want to move on to something else!

That's why we strongly believe that you need to spend some time figuring out **what interests you** rather than taking an inventory of the skills you have. You may have skills that you simply don't want to use, but if you can build your career on the things that interest you, you will be more likely to be happy and satisfied in your job. Realize, too, that interests can change over time; the activities that interest you now may not be the ones that interested you years ago. For example, some professionals may decide that they've had enough of clinical nursing and want a job providing inservice training or developing training programs, even though they have earned a reputation for being an excellent charge nurse. We strongly believe that interests rather than skills should be the determining factor in deciding what types of jobs you want to apply for and what directions you explore in your job hunt. Obviously one cannot be a doctor without a medical degree or a medical office manager without appropriate knowledge and skills; but a medical professional can embark on a next career as a pharmaceutical sales representative or medical equipment sales representative if he/she has a strong interest in that type of work and can provide a resume that clearly demonstrates past excellent performance in *any* field and *potential* to excel in another field. As you will see later in this book, "lack of exact experience" is the last reason why people are turned down for the jobs they apply for.

> Figure out what interests you and you will hold the key to a successful job hunt and working career. (And be prepared for your interests to change over time!)

### How can you have a resume prepared if you don't know what you want to do?

You may be wondering how you can have a resume prepared if you don't know what you want to do next. The approach to resume writing which PREP, the country's oldest resume-preparation company, has used successfully for many years is to develop an "all-purpose" resume that translates your skills, experience, and accomplishments into language employers can understand. What most people need in a job hunt is a versatile resume that will allow them to apply for numerous types of jobs. For example, you may want to apply for a job in pharmaceutical sales but you may also want to have a resume that will be versatile enough for you to apply for jobs in other industries. Leaving the resume "all-purpose" and letting the cover letter focus on the exact type of position is a recipe for success in preparing your resume and cover letter.

> "Lack of exact experience" is the last reason people are turned down for the jobs for which they apply.

Based on 20 years of serving job hunters, we at PREP have found that **an all-purpose resume** and **specific cover letters tailored to specific fields** is often your best approach to job hunting rather than trying to create different resumes for different occupational areas. Usually, you will not even need more than one "all-purpose" cover letter, although the cover letter rather than the resume is the place to communicate your interest in a narrow or specific field. An all-purpose resume and cover letter that translate your experience and accomplishments into plain English are the tools that will maximize the number of doors which open for you while permitting you to "fish" in the widest range of job areas.

**Your resume will provide the script for your job interview.**

When you get down to it, your resume has a simple job to do: Its purpose is to blow as many doors open as possible and to make as many people as possible want to meet you. So a well-written resume that really "sells" you is a key that will create opportunities for you in a job hunt.

This statistic explains why: The typical newspaper advertisement for a job opening receives more than 245 replies. And normally only 10 or 12 will be invited to an interview.

But here's another purpose of the resume: it provides the "script" the employer uses when he interviews you. If your resume has been written in such a way that your strengths and achievements are revealed, that's what you'll end up talking about at the job interview. Since the resume will govern what you get asked about at your interviews, you can't overestimate the importance of making sure your resume makes you look and sound as good as you are.

*Your resume is the "script" for your job interviews. Make sure you put on your resume what you want to talk about or be asked about at the job interview.*

**So what is a "good" resume?**

Very literally, your resume should motivate the person reading it to dial the phone number you have put on the resume. (If you are relocating, that's one reason you should think about putting a local phone contact number on your resume, if possible, when your contact address is several states away; employers are much more likely to dial a local telephone number than a long-distance number when they're looking for potential employees.)

If you have a resume already, look at it objectively. Is it a limp, colorless "laundry list" of your job titles and duties? Or does it "paint a picture" of your skills, abilities, and accomplishments in a way that would make someone want to meet you? Can people understand what you're saying?

*The one-page resume in chronological format is the format preferred by most employers.*

**How long should your resume be?**

One page, maybe two. Usually only people in the academic community have a resume (which they usually call a *curriculum vitae*) longer than one or two pages. Remember that your resume is almost always accompanied by a cover letter, and a potential employer does not want to read more than two or three pages about a total stranger in order to decide if he wants to meet that person! Besides, don't forget that the more you tell someone about yourself, the more opportunity you are providing for the employer to screen you out at the "first-cut" stage. A resume should be concise and exciting and designed to make the reader want to meet you in person!

**Should resumes be functional or chronological?**

Employers almost always prefer a chronological resume; in other words, an employer will find a resume easier to read if it is immediately apparent what your current or most recent job is, what you did before that, and so forth, in reverse chronological order. A resume that goes back in detail for the last ten years of employment will generally satisfy the employer's curiosity about your background. Employment more than ten years old can be shown even more briefly in an "Other Experience" section at the end of your "Experience" section. Remember that your intention is not to tell everything you've done but to "hit the high points" and especially impress the employer with what you learned, contributed, or accomplished in each job you describe.

**Once you get your resume, what do you do with it?**

You will be using your resume to answer ads, as a tool to use in talking with friends and relatives about your job search, and, most importantly, in using the "direct approach" described in this book.

***When you mail your resume, always send a "cover letter."***

A "cover letter," sometimes called a "resume letter" or "letter of interest," is a letter that accompanies and introduces your resume. Your cover letter is a way of personalizing the resume by sending it to the specific person you think you might want to work for at each company. Your cover letter should contain a few highlights from your resume—just enough to make someone want to meet you. Cover letters should always be typed or word processed on a computer—never handwritten.

*Never mail or fax your resume without a cover letter.*

**1. Learn the art of answering ads.**

There is an "art," part of which can be learned, in using your "bestselling" resume to reply to advertisements.

Sometimes an exciting job lurks behind a boring ad that someone dictated in a hurry, so reply to any ad that interests you. Don't worry that you aren't "25 years old with a certification in critical care" like the ad asks for. Employers will always make compromises in their requirements if they think you're the "best fit" overall.

***What about ads that ask for "salary requirements?"***

What if the ad you're answering asks for "salary requirements?" The first rule is to avoid committing yourself in writing at that point to a specific salary. You don't want to "lock yourself in."

***There are two ways to handle the ad that asks for "salary requirements."***

First, you can ignore that part of the ad and accompany your resume with a cover letter that focuses on "selling" you, your abilities, and even some of your philosophy about work or your field. You may include a sentence in your cover letter like this: "I can provide excellent personal and professional references at your request, and I would be delighted to share the private details of my salary history with you in person."

*What if the ad asks for your "salary requirements?"*

Second, if you feel you must give some kind of number, just state a range in your cover letter that includes your medical, dental, other benefits, and expected bonuses. You might state, for example, "My current compensation, including benefits and bonuses, is in the range of $30,000-$40,000."

***Analyze the ad and "tailor" yourself to it.***

When you're replying to ads, a finely-tailored cover letter is an important tool in getting your resume noticed and read. On the next page is a cover letter which has been "tailored to fit" a specific ad. Notice the "art" used by PREP writers of analyzing the ad's main requirements and then writing the letter so that the person's background, work habits, and interests seem "tailor-made" to the company's needs. Use this cover letter as a model when you prepare your own reply to ads.

Date

Exact Name of Person
Exact Title
Exact Name of Company
Address
City, State, Zip

Dear Exact Name of Person (or Dear Sir or Madam if answering a blind ad):

With the enclosed resume, I would like to express my interest in exploring employment opportunities with your organization. An experienced Registered Nurse, I am in the process of permanently relocating to Arizona with my husband, and I offer a strong background in most areas of nursing.

After earning my Associate of Nursing degree *magna cum laude*, I quickly gained experience as a Charge Nurse while also working in surgical intensive care and other intensive environments at Mercer Hospital in Mercer, GA. Subsequently at a different hospital in Georgia, I gained experience in working with pelvic and cervical traction patients.

Since 1994, I have worked as an R.N. in Houston, TX, and I have provided quality nursing care at two different hospitals. For nearly eight years, I worked as an Emergency Department Registered Nurse and frequently handled triage duty. Most recently I have worked as a Charge Nurse in addition to providing quality care to orthopedic and neurosurgical patients. I also work with medical overflow patients as well as with general surgical and nephrology patients.

During my considerable experience in hospital environments, I have become accustomed to working with patients of all ages, from newborns to the very elderly. I can provide outstanding references at the appropriate time, and I would enjoy an opportunity to meet with you in person if you feel you can use my considerable knowledge and expert nursing skills. If we do meet in person, you will see that I am an R.N. who is committed to providing quality patient care in a caring and safe manner. Thank you in advance for your time.

Sincerely,

Aimee Lackland

Employers are trying to identify the individual who wants the job they are filling. Don't be afraid to express your enthusiasm in the cover letter!

## 2. Talk to friends and relatives.

Don't be shy about telling your friends and relatives the kind of job you're looking for. Looking for the job you want involves using your network of contacts, so tell people what you're looking for. They may be able to make introductions and help set up interviews.

About 25% of all interviews are set up through "who you know," so don't ignore this approach.

## 3. Finally, and most importantly, use the "direct approach."

The "direct approach" is a strategy in which you choose your next employer.

More than 50% of all job interviews are set up by the "direct approach." That means you actually send a resume and a cover letter to a company you think might be interesting to work for.

### *To whom do you write?*

In general, you should write directly to the *exact name* of the person who would be hiring you: say, the vice-president of marketing or data processing. If you're in doubt about to whom to address the letter, address it to the president by name and he or she will make sure it gets forwarded to the right person within the company who has hiring authority in your area.

### *How do you find the names of potential employers?*

You're not alone if you feel that the biggest problem in your job search is finding the right names at the companies you want to contact. But you can usually figure out the names of companies you want to approach by deciding first if your job hunt is primarily geography-driven or industry-driven.

In a **geography-driven job hunt,** you could select a list of, say, 50 companies you want to contact **by location** from the lists that the U.S. Chambers of Commerce publish yearly of their "major area employers." There are hundreds of local Chambers of Commerce across America, and most of them will have an 800 number which you can find through 1-800-555-1212. If you and your family think Atlanta, Dallas, Ft. Lauderdale, and Virginia Beach might be nice places to live, for example, you could contact the Chamber of Commerce in those cities and ask how you can obtain a copy of their list of major employers. Your nearest library will have the book which lists the addresses of all chambers.

In an **industry-driven job hunt,** and if you are willing to relocate, you will be identifying the companies which you find most attractive in the industry in which you want to work. When you select a list of companies to contact **by industry,** you can find the right person to write and the address of firms by industrial category in *Standard and Poor's, Moody's,* and other excellent books in public libraries. Many Web sites also provide contact information.

Many people feel it's a good investment to actually call the company to either find out or double-check the name of the person to whom they want to send a resume and cover letter. It's important to do as much as you feasibly can to assure that the letter gets to the right person in the company.

At the end of Part One, you will find some advice about how to conduct library research and how to locate organizations to which you could send your resume.

*What's the correct way to follow up on a resume you send?*

There is a polite way to be aggressively interested in a company during your job hunt. It is ideal to end the cover letter accompanying your resume by saying, "I hope you'll welcome my call next week when I try to arrange a brief meeting at your convenience to discuss your current and future needs and how I might serve them." Keep it low key, and just ask for a "brief meeting," not an interview. Employers want people who show a determined interest in working with them, so don't be shy about following up on the resume and cover letter you've mailed.

It pays to be aware of the 14 most common pitfalls for job hunters.

## STEP THREE: Preparing for Interviews

But a resume and cover letter by themselves can't get you the job you want. You need to "prep" yourself before the interview. Step Three in your job campaign is "Preparing for Interviews." First, let's look at interviewing from the company's point of view.

*What are the biggest "turnoffs" for companies?*

One of the ways to help yourself perform well at an interview is to look at the main reasons why companies *don't* hire the people they interview, according to companies that do the interviewing.

Notice that "lack of appropriate background" (or lack of experience) is the *last* reason for not being offered the job.

*The 14 Most Common Reasons Job Hunters Are Not Offered Jobs* (*according to the companies who do the interviewing and hiring*):

1.  Low level of accomplishment
2.  Poor attitude, lack of self-confidence
3.  Lack of goals/objectives
4.  Lack of enthusiasm
5.  Lack of interest in the company's business
6.  Inability to sell or express yourself
7.  Unrealistic salary demands
8.  Poor appearance
9.  Lack of maturity, no leadership potential
10. Lack of extracurricular activities
11. Lack of preparation for the interview, no knowledge about company
12. Objecting to travel
13. Excessive interest in security and benefits
14. Inappropriate background

Department of Labor studies have proven that smart, "prepared" job hunters can increase their beginning salary while getting a job in *half* the time it normally takes. (4½ months is the average national length of a job search.) Here, from PREP, are some questions that can prepare you to find a job faster.

*Are you in the "right" frame of mind?*

It seems unfair that we have to look for a job just when we're lowest in morale. Don't worry *too* much if you're nervous before interviews. You're supposed to be a little nervous, especially if the job means a lot to you. But the best way to kill unnecessary fears about job hunting is through 1) making sure you have a great resume and 2) preparing yourself for the interview. Here are three main areas you need to think about before each interview.

### Do you know what the company does?

Don't walk into an interview giving the impression that, "If this is Tuesday, this must be General Motors."

Research the company before you go to interviews.

Find out before the interview what the company's main product or service is. Where is the company heading? Is it in a "growth" or declining industry? (Answers to these questions may influence whether or not you want to work there!)

Information about what the company does is in annual reports as well as newspaper and magazine articles. Just visit your nearest library and ask the reference librarian to guide you to materials on the company. Internet searches will yield valuable information. At the end of Part One you will find many suggestions about how to research companies.

### Do you know what you want to do for the company?

Before the interview, try to decide how you see yourself fitting into the company. Remember, "lack of exact background" the company wants is usually the last reason people are not offered jobs.

Understand before you go to each interview that the burden will be on you to "sell" the interviewer on why you're the best person for the job and the company.

### How will you answer the critical interview questions?

Anticipate the questions you will be asked at the interview, and prepare your responses in advance.

Put yourself in the interviewer's position and think about the questions you're most likely to be asked. Here are some of the most commonly asked interview questions:

Q: *"What are your greatest strengths?"*
A: Don't say you've never thought about it! Go into an interview knowing the three main impressions you want to leave about yourself, such as "I'm hard-working, loyal, and an imaginative cost-cutter."

Q: *"What are your greatest weaknesses?"*
A: Don't confess that you're lazy or have trouble meeting deadlines! Confessing that you tend to be a "workaholic" or "tend to be a perfectionist and sometimes get frustrated when others don't share my high standards" will make your prospective employer see a "weakness" that he likes. Name a weakness that your interviewer will perceive as a strength.

Q: *"What are your long-range goals?"*
A: If you're interviewing with a small rural hospital, don't say you want to work for a Veterans Hospital eventually! Say your long-range goal is to be *with* the company, contributing to its goals and success.

Q: "What motivates you to do your best work?"
A: Don't get dollar signs in your eyes here! "A challenge" is not a bad answer, but it's a little cliched. Saying something like "troubleshooting" or "solving a tough problem" is more interesting and specific. Give an example if you can.

*Q: "What do you know about this company?"*

A: Don't say you never heard of it until they asked you to the interview! Name an interesting, positive thing you learned about the company recently from your research. Remember, company executives can sometimes feel rather "maternal" about the company they serve. Don't get onto a negative area of the company if you can think of positive facts you can bring up. Of course, if you learned in your research that the company's sales seem to be taking a nose-dive, or that the company president is being prosecuted for taking bribes, you might politely ask your interviewer to tell you something that could help you better understand what you've been reading. Those are the kinds of company facts that can help you determine whether you want to work there or not.

Go to an interview prepared to tell the company why it should hire you.

*Q: "Why should I hire you?"*

A: "I'm unemployed and available" is the wrong answer here! Get back to your strengths and say that you believe the organization could benefit by a loyal, hard-working cost-cutter like yourself.

In conclusion, you should decide in advance, before you go to the interview, how you will answer each of these commonly asked questions. Have some practice interviews with a friend to role-play and build your confidence.

## STEP FOUR: Handling the Interview and Negotiating Salary

Now you're ready for Step Four: actually handling the interview successfully and effectively. Remember, the purpose of an interview is to get a job offer.

A smile at an interview makes the employer perceive of you as intelligent!

### Eight "do's" for the interview

According to leading U.S. companies, there are eight key areas in interviewing success. You can fail at an interview if you mishandle just one area.

1. Do wear appropriate clothes.
   You can never go wrong by wearing a suit to an interview.

2. Do be well groomed.
   Don't overlook the obvious things like having clean hair, clothes, and fingernails for the interview.

3. Do give a firm handshake.
   You'll have to shake hands twice in most interviews: first, before you sit down, and second, when you leave the interview. Limp handshakes turn most people off.

4. Do smile and show a sense of humor.
   Interviewers are looking for people who would be nice to work with, so don't be so somber that you don't smile. In fact, research shows that people who smile at interviews are perceived as more intelligent. So, smile!

5. Do be enthusiastic.
   Employers say they are "turned off" by lifeless, unenthusiastic job hunters who show no special interest in that company. The best way to show some enthusiasm for the employer's operation is to find out about the business beforehand.

6. Do show you are flexible and adaptable.

An employer is looking for someone who can contribute to his organization in a flexible, adaptable way. No matter what skills and training you have, employers know every new employee must go through initiation and training on the company's turf. Certainly show pride in your past accomplishments in a specific, factual way ("I saved my last employer $50.00 a week by a new cost-cutting measure I developed"). But don't come across as though there's nothing about the job you couldn't easily handle.

7. Do ask intelligent questions about the employer's business.

An employer is hiring someone because of certain business needs. Show interest in those needs. Asking questions to get a better idea of the employer's needs will help you "stand out" from other candidates interviewing for the job.

8. Do "take charge" when the interviewer "falls down" on the job.

Go into every interview knowing the three or four points about yourself you want the interviewer to remember. And be prepared to take an active part in leading the discussion if the interviewer's "canned approach" does not permit you to display your "strong suit." You can't always depend on the interviewer's asking you the "right" questions so you can stress your strengths and accomplishments.

Employers are seeking people with good attitudes whom they can train and coach to do things their way.

**An important "don't": Don't ask questions about salary or benefits at the first interview.**
Employers don't take warmly to people who look at their organization as just a place to satisfy salary and benefit needs. Don't risk making a negative impression by appearing greedy or self-serving. The place to discuss salary and benefits is normally at the second interview, and the employer will bring it up. Then you can ask questions without appearing excessively interested in what the organization can do for you.

**"Sell yourself" before talking salary**
Make sure you've "sold" yourself before talking salary. First show you're the "best fit" for the employer and then you'll be in a stronger position from which to negotiate salary.

Interviewers sometimes throw out a salary figure at the first interview to see if you'll accept it. Don't commit yourself. You may be able to negotiate a better deal later on. Get back to finding out more about the job. This lets the interviewer know you're interested primarily in the job and not the salary.

**Now...negotiating your salary**
You must avoid stating a "salary requirement" in your initial cover letter, and you must avoid even appearing **interested** in salary before you are offered the job.

Don't appear excessively interested in salary and benefits at the interview.

**Never** bring up the subject of salary yourself. Employers say there's no way you can avoid looking greedy if you bring up the issue of salary and benefits before the company has identified you as its "best fit."

When the company brings up salary, it may say something like this: "Well, Mary, we think you'd make a good candidate for this job. What kind of salary are we talking about?"

Never name a number here, either. Give the ball back to the interviewer. Act as though you hadn't given the subject of salary much thought and respond something like this: "Ah, Mr. Jones, salary. . .well, I wonder if you'd be kind enough to tell me what salary you had in mind when you advertised the job?" Or ... "What is the range you have in mind?"

Don't worry, if the interviewer names a figure that you think is too low, you can say so without turning down the job or locking yourself into a rigid position. The point here is to negotiate for yourself as well as you can. You might reply to a number named by the interviewer that you think is low by saying something like this: "Well, Mr. Lee, the job interests me very much, and I think I'd certainly enjoy working with you. But, frankly, I was thinking of something a little higher than that." That leaves the ball in your interviewer's court again, and you haven't turned down the job, either, in case it turns out that the interviewer can't increase the offer and you still want the job.

*Salary negotiation can be tricky.*

**Last, send a follow-up letter.**
Finally, send a letter right after the interview telling your interviewer you enjoyed the meeting and are certain (if you are) you are the "best fit" for the job. The people interviewing you will probably have an attitude described as either "professionally loyal" to their companies or "maternal and proprietary" if the interviewer also owns the company. In either case, they are looking for people who want to work for *that* company in particular. The follow-up letter you send might be just the deciding factor in your favor if the employer is trying to choose between you and someone else.

A sample follow-up letter is shown on page 24. Be sure to modify the model letter according to your particular skills and interview situation.

*A follow-up letter can help the employer choose between you and another qualified candidate.*

## Researching companies and locating employers

Figuring out the names of the organizations to which you want to mail your resume is part of any highly successful job campaign. Don't depend on only answering the ads you read in printed or electronic form, waiting for the ideal job to appear in **newspapers or magazines,** many of which are published online. If you are geographically oriented and need to find work in a particular city or town, check out the Sunday advertisements in the classified sections which suit you best, such as "administrative" or "professional" or "technical." Also aggressively research possible employers. Here is some information which you can use in researching the names of organizations for which you might be interested in working.

In electronic and printed form, most libraries have a variety of information available on various organizations throughout the U.S. and worldwide. If your local library has computers, you will probably have access to a vast network of information. Many printed materials might be available only for use in the reference room of the library, but some items may be checked out. Listed below are some of the major sources to look for, but be sure and check at the reference desk to see if there are any resources available in a printed or online form related to the specific types of companies you wish to investigate.

### The Worldwide Chamber of Commerce Directory
Most chambers of commerce annually produce a "list of major employers" for their market area (or city). Usually the list includes the name, address, and telephone number of the employer along with information about the number of people employed, kinds of products and services produced, and a person to contact about employment. You can obtain the "list of major employers" in the city where you want to work by writing to that chamber. There is usually a small charge.

The *Worldwide Chamber of Commerce Directory* is an alphabetical listing of American and foreign chambers of commerce. It includes:

> All U.S. Chambers of Commerce (with addresses and phone numbers)
> American Chambers of Commerce abroad
> Canadian Chambers of Commerce
> Foreign Chambers of Commerce in principal cities worldwide
> Foreign Embassies and Consulates in the U.S.
> U.S. Consulates and Embassies throughout the world

### Standard and Poor's Register of Corporations, Directors, and Executives

Standard and Poor's produce three volumes annually with information concerning over 77,000 American corporations. They are:

Volume 1—**Corporations.** Here is an alphabetical listing of a variety of information for each of over 77,000 companies, including:

- name of company, address, telephone number
- names, titles, and functions of several key officers
- name of accounting firm, primary bank, and law firm
- stock exchange, description of products or services
- annual sales, number of employees
- division names and functions, subsidiary listings

Volume 2—**Directors and Executives.** This volume lists alphabetically over 70,000 officers, directors, partners, etc. by name. Information on each executive includes:

- principal business affiliation
- business address, residence address, year of birth
- college and year of graduation, fraternal affiliation

Volume 3—**Index.**

### Moody's Manuals

Moody's Manuals provide information about companies traded on the New York and American Stock Exchanges and over the counter. They include:

### Moody's Industrial Manual

Here, Moody's discusses detailed information on companies traded on the New York, American, and regional stock exchanges. The companies are listed alphabetically. Basic information about company addresses, phone numbers, and the names of key officers is available for each company listed. In addition, detailed information about the financial and operating data for each company is available. There are three levels of detail provided:

**Complete Coverage.** Companies in this section have the following information:

- *financial information* for the past 7 years (income accounts, balance sheets, financial and operating data).
- *detailed description of the company's business* including a complete list of subsidiaries and office and property sites.
- *capital structure information,* which includes details on capital stock and long-term debt, with bond and preferred stock ratings and 2 years of stock and bond price ranges.
- *extensive presentation of the company's last annual report.*

**Full Measure Coverage.** Information on companies in this section includes:

- *financial information for the past 7 years* (income accounts, balance sheets, financial and operating data).
- *detailed description of company's business,* with a complete list of subsidiaries and plant and property locations.
- *capital structure information,* with details on capital stock and long term debt, with bond and preferred stock ratings and 2 years of stock and bond price changes.

**Comprehensive Coverage.** Information on companies in this section includes:

- *5 years of financial information* on income accounts, balance sheets, and financial and operating ratios.
- *detailed description of company's business,* including subsidiaries.
- *concise capital structure information,* including capital stock and long term debts, bond and preferred stock ratings.

### Moody's OTC Manual

Here is information on U.S. firms which are unlisted on national and regional stock exchanges. There are three levels of coverage: complete, full measure, and comprehensive (same as described above). Other Moody's manuals include: *Moody's Public Utility Manual, Moody's Municipal and Government Manual,* and *Moody's Bank and Finance Manual.*

### Dun's Million Dollar Directory

Three separate listings (alphabetical, geographic, and by products) of over 120,000 U.S. firms. There are three volumes:

Volume 1—The 45,000 largest companies, net worth over $500,000.

Volume 2—The 37,000 next largest companies.

Volume 3—The 37,000 next largest companies.

### U.S. industrial directories

Ask your librarian to guide you to your library's collection of industrial directories. Almost every state produces a manufacturing directory, for example, and many libraries maintain complete collections of these directories. You may find information on products and the addresses and telephone numbers of industrial companies.

### Thomas' Register of Manufacturers

16 volumes of information about manufacturing companies.

Volumes 1-8—Alphabetical listing by product.

Volumes 9-10—Alphabetical listing of manufacturing company names, addresses, telephone numbers, and local offices.

Volumes 11-16—Alphabetical company catalog information.

## Information About Foreign Companies

If you'd like your next job to be overseas or with an international company, you can find much helpful information in the library. You approach these companies in the same way as you would approach U.S.-based companies.

### Directory of Foreign Manufacturers in the U.S.

Alphabetical listing of U.S. manufacturing companies which are owned and operated by parent foreign firms. The information provided includes the name and address of the U.S. firm, the name and address of the foreign parent firm, and the products produced.

### Directory of American Firms Operating in Foreign Countries

Alphabetical listing of the names, addresses, chief officers, products, and country operated in of U.S. firms abroad.

### International Firms Directory

This lists foreign corporations.

### Hoover's Handbook of World Business

This lists corporations in Asia and Europe.

### Principal International Businesses

This is a comprehensive directory of international businesses.

## Information Available From The Internet

Information about companies is also available through the Internet. You can use all the search engines to help you in your search for company information and company website addresses. It is not the purpose of this book to recommend websites by name, but you can type in "jobs" or "employment" or "careers" as a key word using any search engine and you will be introduced to organizations that will allow you to post your resume online. You can also usually find an organization's website by typing in the following website addresses, just substituting the name of the company you want to find, such as "mayoclinic," for "organizationname":

> http://www.organizationname.com
> http:/www.organizationname.org
> http://www.organizationname.net

However, sometimes finding what you are looking for takes trial and error. For example, if you wanted to find Hewlett Packard's website, you would find it either by typing in "Hewlett Packard" as a key word or by typing in http://www.HP.com. Not all website addresses are perfectly obvious, straightforward, or intuitive, but the search engines usually perform in an excellent fashion when you type in key words in a trial-and-error "surfing" or fact-finding mode.

Many people are aware of the importance of having a great resume, but most people in a job hunt don't realize just how important a cover letter can be. The purpose of the cover letter, sometimes called a **"letter of interest,"** is to introduce your resume to prospective employers.

## "A Picture Is Worth a Thousand Words."

As a way of illustrating how important the cover letter can be, we have chosen to show you on the next two pages the cover letter and resume of an experienced nursing professional who is seeking a new challenge. She has found herself in a situation in which she wishes to apply for a newly created position in the hospital where she is currently employed. You will see clearly from the documents on the next page that she is approaching her job hunt in an intelligent fashion. Although she has the experience and credentials for the position, she has decided to "take no chances" in aggressively presenting herself. Because she knows that (1) the job is being advertised in numerous print media and (2) she has worked for her current employer for fewer than two years, she realizes that she must apply for the position in the same way as everyone else: with a resume and cover letter which enthusiastically express her talents, experience, and skills.

## The Resume and Cover Letter are "Companion Documents."

You will see on the next two pages that the cover letter gives you a chance to "get personal" with the person to whom you are writing whereas the resume is a more formal document. Even if the employer doesn't request a cover letter, we believe that it is *always* in your best interest to send a cover letter with your resume. In the case of Carmen Santiago, whose resume and cover letter you will see on the next two pages, the cover letter provides an opportunity to say how much she wants the job. The aim of this book is to show you examples of cover letters and resumes designed to blow doors open so that you can develop your own resumes and cover letters and increase the number of interviews you have.

**A cover letter is an essential part of a career change.**

Please do not attempt to implement a career change without a cover letter such as the ones you see in Part Two and in Part Three of this book. A cover letter is the first impression of you, and you can influence the way an employer views you by the language and style of your letter.

# Your cover letter and resume are "companion" documents.

Date

Mr. Gordon Peebles
Nurse Recruiter
Waylon University Hospital
Waylon, TX

**Experienced nurse seeking to advance within the hospital currently employing her**

Although this individual already works at the hospital which is attempting to fill a newly created position, she knows that her current employer is not aware of all her talents, certifications, and aptitude for the position. Here's a tip: when applying for internal openings, don't sacrifice any formality in your approach. Make sure you have a great cover letter and resume in order to compete for the job as aggressively as the "outside" candidates.

Dear Mr. Peebles:

With the enclosed resume, I would like to express my interest in the position as Clinical Educator—Cardiac Service Line, which you recently advertised in the Waylon Times.

As you will see from my resume, I offer extensive training, certifications, and experience related to critical care and cardiac patients along with experience in developing and providing inservice training for other medical professionals. I began my medical career as an LPN in 1990 and then completed my Bachelor of Science in Nursing in 1992. From 1992-96 I worked in the Georgia University Medical Center in the Medical/Surgical/Trauma Intensive Care Unit. In that job I worked in a vibrant teaching and research hospital, and I gained extensive ICU experience in a 500-bed facility which contained a Level I Trauma Center.

I joined the U.S. Army in 1996 and served my country as a Captain while working in the Medical/Surgery/Coronary Care Unit of one of the Army's largest medical centers. As a Charge Nurse and Intensive Care Nurse, I was extensively involved in training and development. I worked on a team with another RN and three medical technicians in developing a training program which became an integral part of a five-week training program. I also spearheaded orientation for ICU specialists and was commended for developing and implementing training which "produced rock-solid clinicians." I was described as an "outstanding educator" in teaching the Critical Care Course, and I revised and updated three ICU orientation/education packets and produced training which was praised for "arming orientees with the latest practice standards."

You will notice from my resume that I earned and have maintained since 1994 the C.C.R.N. certification in critical care. On my own initiative, I have aggressively pursued training opportunities related to the clinical management of the cardiac surgery patient. I enjoy sharing my knowledge with other medical professionals as well as with families and patients.

I have been with the Waylon Medical Center since 2000, and I have served as Charge Nurse, Preceptor, and Resource Person. I am eager to serve Waylon Medical Center as its Clinical Educator – Cardiac Service Line, and I respectfully request an opportunity to speak with you in person about this position. Thank you for your time.

Sincerely,

Carmen Santiago

# CARMEN SANTIAGO, C.C.R.N.

1110½ Hay Street, Fayetteville, NC 28305   •   preppub@aol.com   •   (910) 483-6611

**OBJECTIVE**  To contribute to a medical environment that can use a highly motivated individual known for resourcefulness and personal initiative who offers extensive critical care and cardiac experience along with a proven ability to develop and implement inservice and staff training activities.

**EDUCATION**  **Certificate of Training in Critical Care;** obtained my **C.C.R.N.** in 1994, and complete 100 hours annually in order to maintain this certification.
**Continuing training, 1990-present:** Completed multiple training activities related to *Critical Care and EKG Interpretation* sponsored by MED-ED, an AACN-approved provider; received a Certificate of Training from the U.S. Army for completing specialized training in *Clinical Management of the Cardiac Surgery Patient;* completed training sponsored by the Georgia Nurses Association entitled *Multiple Trauma in the 21st Century.* Completed other training including these courses:

Multisystem Organ Failure: A Pathophysiologic Approach     Critical Care Crisis
Critical Care Essentials                                   Critical Care Challenges
What's New in Critical Care                                Intra-Aortic Balloon Pumping
Current Diagnosis and Treatment of Tachyarrhythmias

**Bachelor of Science in Nursing,** University of Georgia, Atlanta, GA, 1992.
**Diploma in Practical Nursing,** Greyson Practical Nursing Program, Greyson, GA, 1990.
Completed **Officer Training School,** U.S. Army, Ft. Benning, GA, 1996.

**CERTIFICATIONS**  Registered Nurse **(R.N.),** currently licensed in NC and GA.; previously certified as an **L.P.N.** Critical Care Registered Nurse **(C.C.R.N.),** certified since 1994.

**EXPERIENCE**  **REGISTERED NURSE & CHARGE NURSE.** Waylon Medical Center, Waylon, GA (2000-present.)  Became Charge Nurse after six months; schedule 12 nurses.

**CHARGE NURSE & INTENSIVE CARE NURSE.** U.S. Army, Womack Army Hospital, Ft. Bragg, NC (1996-2000). In the Medical/Surgical/Coronary Care Unit of one of the Army's largest medical centers, provided skilled critical care nursing in a 100-bed facility while also supervising other RNs and technicians during a 12-hour shift. Advanced to the rank of Captain.
**Training and development:**
- Developed a training module which became an integral part of a five-week training program; worked on a team with another RN and three medical technicians in developing this training program. Spearheaded orientation for seven ICU specialists and was commended for developing and implementing training which "produced rock-solid clinicians."
- Revised/updated three ICU orientation/education packets, and produced training which was praised for "arming orientees with the latest practice standards."
- Was described as an "outstanding educator" in teaching the Critical Care Course.

**Quality nursing:**
- Implemented the nursing process for critically ill patients in a 12-bed intensive care/observation status unit; planned and managed patient/nursing care activities; prepared nursing reports. On a formal performance evaluation, was praised for providing "ingenious tailored care for respiratory patients" and was described as a "clinical expert."

**R.N. MEDICAL/SURGICAL/TRAUMA INTENSIVE CARE UNIT.** Georgia University Medical Center, Atlanta, GA (1992-96). In a vibrant teaching and research hospital associated with the Georgia Tech Medical School, gained extensive ICU experience in a 500-bed facility which contained a Level I Trauma Center.

**Other experience:** Worked as an LPN in a nursing home and in rural Georgia hospitals.

**Addressing the Cover
Letter:** Get the exact
name of the person to
whom you are writing. This
makes your approach
personal.

**First Paragraph:** This
explains why you are
writing.

**Second Paragraph:** You
have a chance to talk
about whatever you feel is
your most distinguishing
feature.

**Third Paragraph:** You
bring up your next most
distinguishing qualities and
try to
sell yourself.

**Fourth Paragraph:** Here
you have another
opportunity to reveal
qualities or achievements
which will impress your
future employer.

**Final Paragraph:** He asks
the employer to contact
him. Make sure your
reader knows what the
"next step" is.

**Alternate Final
Paragraph:** It's more
aggressive (but not too
aggressive) to let the
employer know that you
will be calling him or her.
Don't be afraid to be
persistent. Employers are
looking for people who
know what they want to
do.

Date

Mrs. Samantha Smith
Administrative Director, Radiology Department
Sneeds Mayo Medical Center
1102 Kenton Road
Sneedsville, LA 23001

Dear Mrs. Smith:

With the enclosed resume, I would like to make you aware of my qualifications for the position of Radiology Staff Nurse, specifically my background as a radiology nurse with more than nine years of service to Sneeds Mayo Medical Center, and the extensive list of certifications and credentials with which I have supplemented that experience.

I am currently excelling as a Staff Registered Nurse in the Emergency Department, where my primary duty is to serve as Triage Nurse. I interview presenting patients, assigning a triage category and prioritizing the placement of patients into the appropriate treatment areas based on the nature and severity of the patient's condition. I monitor the condition of patients in the waiting area, and upgrade or downgrade their assigned triage categories based on changes in patient condition.

Although I am highly regarded within the Emergency Department, and can provide excellent references at the appropriate time, it is my desire to return to Radiology, where I previously served with distinction. As you will see, I hold certifications in ACLS, BCLS, and PALS in addition to credentials which qualify me to administer a wide range of medications specific to radiology procedures, including nuclear medicines and special procedures.

My knowledge, my skills, and above all, my personal loyalty made me a strong asset to the Radiology Department in the past and would continue to do so in the future. I was proud to be a part of the growth and development of the radiology team during the nine years I served, and I would relish the opportunity to rejoin that team. I have a deep respect for the expertise and reputation of the radiology team headed by Dr. Evans, and it is my strong desire to be of service to Dr. Quixote and the other team members.

Sincerely,

Larry French

Date

Exact Name of Person
Title or Position
Name of Company
Address (number and street)
Address (city, state, and zip)

Dear Exact Name of Person: (or Sir or Madam if answering a blind ad)

    With the enclosed resume, I would like to express my interest in exploring employment opportunities with your organization and make you aware of my versatile skills and abilities which could complement your goals.

    As you will see from my enclosed resume, I earned my B.S. from Michigan State University where I maintained a 3.5 GPA. During my senior year I worked as many as 50 hours a week as a Research Assistant and Tutor in the university's chemistry lab.

    In my most recent job as a middle school science and math teacher, I refined my communication, organizational, and time management skills while organizing and directing numerous projects. On my own initiative, I planned the school's first science fair as well as a Christmas play and a musical. Earlier while serving in the U.S. Army for four years, I was handpicked for supervisory positions ahead of my peers and commended for my effective leadership style.

    Both my management experience in the military and my teaching experience have helped me refine my verbal and written communication skills. I am highly regarded for my ability to persuade, motivate, and lead, and I am certain I could utilize those skills and talents in order to positively impact a company's bottom line.

    If you can use a proven performer with an ability to work well with others, I hope you will contact me to suggest a time when we might talk to discuss your needs. Single and available for worldwide relocation, I would cheerfully travel as frequently as your needs require. I can provide excellent references at the appropriate time.

Sincerely,

Julie M. Vogel

CC: Dr. Nathan Rogers

Date
Three blank spaces

Address

Salutation
One blank space

Body

One blank space

Signature

cc: Indicates you are sending a copy of the letter to someone

Date

Exact Name of Person
Title or Position
Name of Company
Address (number and street)
Address (city, state, and zip)

Dear Exact Name of Person: (or Dear Sir or Madam if answering a blind ad)

**Changing Careers into
the pharmaceutical
sales field**
In this letter, a store
manager is seeking to
transfer her strong
bottom-line orientation
and impressive
accomplishments in
boosting sales and profit
into a new industry. She
is primarily interested in
the pharmaceutical
industry, and the letter is
designed to acquaint
pharmaceutical
companies with her
knowledge of the
territory she would be
covering as well as with
her fine personal and
professional reputation.
She is hoping that the
company will be willing to
train a highly motivated
producer who has
excelled in another
industry.

I would appreciate an opportunity to talk with you soon about how I could contribute to your organization through my excellent sales, communication, and customer service skills. I am responding to your advertisement for a Pharmaceutical Sales Representative. I am very knowledgeable of the Dallas, TX, area and offer an outstanding personal and professional reputation in the community.

As you will see from my enclosed resume, I have been highly successful in sales and operations management with a major corporation. Beginning as a Customer Service Manager, I was promoted to manage stores with increasing sales volumes of $7 million, $8.5 million, and $11.5 million annually. In my current position, I have raised total sales by 20%, and profit levels by 25% through my aggressive sales orientation.

Although I am held in high regard by my employer and can provide outstanding references at the appropriate time, I have decided that I would like to apply my sales, customer service, and communication skills within the pharmaceutical sales field. I am certain that my sales ability and strong bottom-line orientation would be ideally suited to pharmaceutical sales. As a store manager, I have become very familiar with a wide range of pharmaceutical products as I have provided oversight of store merchandising, vendor relations, and product mix. I interact with pharmacists and other healthcare professionals with regard to the range of pharmaceutical products carried by the store.

With a B.S.B.A. degree, I possess an educational background which complements my sales and management experience. My highly developed communication skills, assertive personality, and time-management ability have allowed me to effectively manage as many as 100 employees. I offer a reputation as a forceful yet tactful salesperson who is able to present ideas as well as products in a powerful and convincing fashion.

I can assure you that this is a very deliberate attempt on my part to transition into the pharmaceutical sales field, and I hope you will call or write me soon to arrange a brief meeting to discuss your current and future needs and how I might serve them. Thank you in advance for your time.

Sincerely,


Gloria Pena

Date


BY FAX TO: Human Resources Department
910-483-2439
Reference Job Code XYZ 9034

Dear Sir or Madam:

With the enclosed resume, I would like to make you aware of my interest in employment as a Pharmaceutical Healthcare Representative with Johnson & Johnson. I believe you are aware that Walter Freeman, one of your Healthcare Representatives, has recommended that I talk with you because he feels that I could excel in the position as Pharmaceutical Healthcare Representative.

As you will see from my enclosed resume, I offer proven marketing and sales skills along with a reputation as a highly motivated individual with exceptional problem-solving abilities. Shortly after joining my current firm as a Mortgage Loan Specialist, I was named Outstanding Loan Officer of the month through my achievement in generating more than $20,000 in fees.

I believe much of my professional success so far has been due to my highly motivated nature and creative approach to my job. For example, when I began working for my current employer, I developed and implemented the concept of a postcard that communicated a message which the consumer found intriguing. The concept has been so successful that it has been one of the main sources of advertisements in our office, and the concept has been imitated by other offices in the company.

In addition to my track record of excelling in the highly competitive financial services field, I gained valuable sales experience in earlier jobs selling copying equipment and sleep systems. I also applied my strong leadership and sales ability in the human services field when I worked in adult probation services. I am very proud of the fact that many troubled individuals with whom I worked told me that my ability to inspire and motivate them was the key to their becoming productive citizens.

If you can use a creative and motivated self-starter who could enhance your goals for market share and profitability, I hope you will contact me to suggest a time when we could meet in person to discuss your needs and goals and how I could meet them. I can provide strong personal and professional references at the appropriate time.

Yours sincerely,



Cheri Garcia

Date

Exact Name of Person
Title or Position
Name of Company
Address (number and street)
Address (city, state, and zip)

**Follow-up Letter**

A great follow-up letter
can motivate the
employer
to make the job offer,
and the salary offer may
be influenced by the
style and tone of your
follow-up
letter, too!

Dear Exact Name:

I am writing to express my appreciation for the time you spent with me on December 9, and I want to let you know that I am sincerely interested in the position of Registered Nurse and Charge Nurse which we discussed.

I feel confident that I could skillfully interact with your hospital's fine staff, and I would cheerfully relocate to Tennessee, as we discussed.

As you described to me what you are looking for in the person who fills this position, I had a sense of "déjà vu" because my current employer was in a similar position when I went to work for his neurological practice. He needed someone to come in and be his "right arm" and take on an increasing amount of his management responsibilities so that he could be freed up to do other things. I have played a key role in the growth and profitability of his practice, and he has come to depend on my sound advice as much as well as my proven ability to "cut through" huge volumes of work efficiently and accurately. Since this is one of the busiest times of the year in his practice, I feel that I could not leave during that time. I could certainly make myself available by mid-January.

Although I have enjoyed being a part of a prominent neurological practice, I am eager to return to a hospital environment. It would be a pleasure to work for your well-known and prestigious medical center, and I am confident that I could contribute significantly not only through my clinical and administrative background but also through my strong qualities of loyalty, reliability, and trustworthiness. I assure you that I could quickly learn your style and procedures, and I feel certain that you will come to appreciate my strong administrative and patient relations skills.

Yours sincerely,

Jacob Evangelisto

# SECTION I.
# STUDENTS SEEKING TO ENTER THE MEDICAL FIELD

In this section, you will find resumes and cover letters of students who are trying to use a newly minted degree as their main tool for entering the world of work in the medical field.

By looking over the resumes and cover letters in this section, you will see examples which demonstrate how to show clinical rotations, when to reveal your grade point average (only if it's above a 3.3, usually!), and how to present your skills and knowledge in a creative fashion in order to "make up" for a lack of experience.

When you look at the resume of Mary Erkelen, you will notice that she has sections on her resume which include Computer Skills, Laboratory Knowledge, and Languages in addition to the "standard" sections such as Objective, Experience, Education, and Personal. George Coopland has a Training section which is separate from his Education section. Kathleen Gallagher has sections called Certifications & Training as well as Technical Skills. One of the "jobs" shown in the resume of Janet McCue is her "Student Teacher" experience, because she is seeking to utilize her medical and scientific knowledge by teaching biology in an educational institution. Laura Ann Feldhahn's resume demonstrates how to show off affiliations to best advantage. On several resumes, you will see how to professionally present experience as a Tutor and Mentor. For example, the resume of Carol Mace contains job titles including Engineering & Science Mentor as well as Chemistry & Calculus Tutor.

Students are often "selling" their potential to do a job they've actually never done before. In this section, you will see examples of how to market your talents and potential, even if you have limited or no experience in the field.

And how does one show clinical rotations on a resume? You will find some answers if you examine the resume of Joseph Edward Mullen, whose resume shows his fourth year clinical rotations and clerkships.

Have you ever been a waitress or intern? Allison Miller's resume in this section will give you some ideas about how to present such experience.

**Some advice to students...**
If senior professionals could give students a piece of advice about careers, here's what they would say: Manage your career and don't stumble from job to job in an incoherent pattern. Learn early in your working life that a great resume and cover letter can blow doors open for you and help you maximize your salary.

Date

Exact Name of Person
Title or Position
Name of Company
Address (no., street)
Address (city, state, zip)

Dear Sir or Madam:

Sometimes the Objective on a resume emphasizes personal qualities, as this one does. Why has she put Computer Skills and Laboratory Experience ahead of the Experience section? She feels that she wants to "hit" an employer early in her resume with her computer and laboratory knowledge, and she feels her experience is the least impressive thing she has to offer.

With the enclosed resume, I would like to formally apply for the position of Laboratory Technician which you recently advertised in *"The San Diego Times."*

As you will see from my resume, I earned a Bachelor of Science degree from the University of California majoring in Biological Sciences. While earning my degree I gained extensive "hands-on" experience in biology, physics, and chemistry labs.

Through my experience in those laboratories, I became familiar with a wide range of laboratory equipment. I am comfortable using the microscope, preparing slides, working with a cell-counting apparatus, utilizing an autoclave and incubator, and using an NMR Spectrometer. I have utilized loops and swabs to cultivate bacteria in petri dishes, and I am proficient in working with test tubes, pipettes, and measuring suction pipettes. With a reputation as a creative and hard-working young professional, I have constructed complex reflux apparatuses in order to obtain pure end products from a reaction.

You would find me to be a high-energy person who would enjoy contributing to your goals. I can provide outstanding personal, professional, and academic references upon your request.

I hope you will write or call me soon to suggest a time when we might meet in person to discuss your needs and how I might serve them. Thank you in advance for your time.

Yours sincerely,


Mary Erkelen

# MARY ERKELEN

1110½ Hay Street, Fayetteville, NC 28305  •  preppub@aol.com  •  (910) 483-6611

| | |
|---|---|
| **OBJECTIVE** | I want to contribute to an organization that can use an enthusiastic and high-energy young professional who offers excellent mathematical skills and computer knowledge along with "hands-on" laboratory experience. |
| **COMPUTER SKILLS** | Experienced in using IBM/IBM-compatible and Macintosh computer systems with software including Word, Quicken, and Windows; rapidly master new hardware and software. |

**LABORATORY KNOWLEDGE**

- Gained extensive laboratory knowledge in biology, chemistry, and physics.
- In laboratory settings, have aided with medical procedures including blood work, anesthesia, animal euthanasia, as well as prep for surgery and x-ray.
- Have learned how to prepare slides; was instructed in using lighting and magnification and both the oil/non-oil viewing of the slides.
- Have created chemical compounds and analyzed them using chemical, reflux, cooling, heating, and evaporation techniques.
- Have utilized gel electrophoresis to determine sample contents; have become skilled in titration experiments to determine amount of substance in a solution.

**EDUCATION**

Earned **Bachelor of Science** (B.S.) degree with a major in **Biological Sciences**, University of California, Irvine, CA, 2000.

- Excelled in course work in genetics, cell biology, parasitology, psychobiology, molecular biology, and ecology as well as chemistry and organic chemistry.
- Completed five biology labs, five chemistry labs, and two physics labs.

In high school, was an honors student and excelled in advanced physics, chemistry, and calculus as well as three years of both Spanish and German.

**LANGUAGES**

Speak German and Spanish; can read/write both languages with moderate proficiency.

**EXPERIENCE**

**BIOLOGY STUDENT/LABORATORY TECHNICIAN.** University of California, Irvine, CA (1998-2000). Gained insight into laboratory operations while performing as a student in biology, chemistry, and physics labs in the process of earning my B.S. degree; completed in four years a rigorous degree program which many students take five years to finish.

- While earning my degree, worked as a Receptionist/Administrative Assistant at the University of California's Human Resources Department.
- Also worked in a sales job at Pet Haven, a pet store; frequently explained to customers how to use medications we sold; cared for dogs, cats, mice, rats, and snakes.

**VETERINARY ASSISTANT.** University City Veterinary Clinic, San Diego, CA (1997).
At a busy clinic, aided the vet in procedures which included prepping the animals for surgery by shaving/sterilizing the area, assisting with surgeries including spays and ovariohysterectomies, and performing minor surgeries for broken legs and internal injuries; also assisted in taking x-rays.

- Collected and prepared samples and created slides which I viewed under the microscope to determine presence of parasites; used a combination chemical/centrifuge technique to check blood samples for feline leukemia.
- Mastered the use of the fecal float method.

**PERSONAL**

Am a very creative person who enjoys the research, analysis, and problem solving that goes on in a laboratory. Have been fortunate in having a strong academic family background which has given me feelings of security, stability, and confidence. Enjoy horseback riding.

Date

Exact Name of Person
Title or Position
Name of Company
Address (no., street)
Address (city, state, zip)

## BIOLOGY GRAD WITH LABORATORY EXPERIENCE

Dear Exact Name of Person: (or Dear Sir or Madam if answering a blind ad.)

If you have worked in a family-owned business, don't discount the skills and knowledge you obtained by working there. Notice that the Experience section on Mr. Coopland's resume is comprised entirely of jobs he performed in his family's motel business. Even though he is seeking a job in the scientific field, his work experience in another field helped him gain valuable experience that potential employers will appreciate.

I would appreciate an opportunity to talk with you soon about how I could contribute to your organization through my education in biology and experience in small business management.

As you will see from my enclosed resume, I will receive my bachelor's degree in Biology from The University of South Carolina at Columbia in December. I have completed more than 300 hours as a Lab Technician in biology, chemistry, and organic chemistry labs at USC and earlier while studying Organic Chemistry at Bradley University.

Through my experience in helping build a family-owned business to increased profitability, I have gained valuable exposure to bookkeeping and finance, customer service, maintenance and groundskeeping, and public relations. During the past eight years, beginning while I was still in high school and part-time throughout my college years, I have been involved in making decisions and advanced with the business as profits increased at a 20% growth rate over the last five years.

I am a fast learner with knowledge of several languages. Through my adaptability, friendly personality, and initiative I have always been able to quickly earn the respect and admiration of people from employees, to peers, to members of the public.

I hope you will welcome my call soon to arrange a brief meeting at your convenience to discuss your current and future needs and how I might serve them. Thank you in advance for your time.

Sincerely yours,

George Coopland

Alternate last paragraph:
I hope you will call or write me soon to suggest a time convenient for us to meet and discuss your current and future needs and how I might serve them. Thank you in advance for your time.

# GEORGE COOPLAND

1110½ Hay Street, Fayetteville, NC 28305    •    preppub@aol.com    •    (910) 483-6611

---

**OBJECTIVE**

To contribute to an organization through my education in biology, my experience in small business management, as well as my exposure to public relations, customer service, and financial/accounting functions.

**EDUCATION**

**Bachelor's degree in Biology**, The University of South Carolina at Columbia, SC, December 2001.
Studied Organic Chemistry, Bradley University, Bradley, SC.

**TRAINING**

Completed 100 hours as a Lab Technician in university laboratory settings such as:
    Chemistry lab and biology lab — USC-SC
    Organic chemistry lab — Bradley University

**EXPERIENCE**

*Gained experience in all phases of small business operations and made important contributions to the growth of a family-owned motel, Days Inn, Columbia, SC, in this track record of advancement:*
**MANAGER.** (2000-present). Refined my managerial skills and learned to oversee the work of others while becoming familiar with the financial aspects of taking care of the company's bookkeeping activities.

- Quickly learned the details of handling financial activities and prepared the daily figures for the accountants and wrote checks to pay various operating expenses.
- Was praised for my decision-making skills and ability to develop ideas which led to increased profitability and smoother daily operations.
- Made suggestions which helped ease the transition to a new name after the motel had operated as the Columbia Motor Inn for several years.
- Refined my interpersonal communication skills dealing with a wide range of customers and employees.
- Have been recognized as a key figure in the motel's record of annual increases in income—over the past five years the business has seen a 20% increase.

**DESK CLERK** and **REPAIRMAN.** (1999). Advanced to take on a more public and active role in day-to-day operations as a front-desk clerk responsible for providing helpful and courteous service to customers and handling large sums of money.

- Maintained the swimming pool which included seeing that the proper chemical balances were reached and that the pool was clean and safe to use.
- Displayed my versatility by doing painting, roofing, and minor electrical repairs on air conditioning systems and TVs which resulted in extending the usefulness of appliances and reduced the need for outside repairs.

**MAINTENANCE WORKER/GROUNDSKEEPER.** (1996-98). While still in high school, began helping with building maintenance, minor repairs, and lawn maintenance.

*Highlights of other experience:* As a **Patient Care Volunteer** at the VA Hospital, Columbia, SC (1996), helped the nursing staff in emergency room care such as transporting patients and assisting in preliminary check-ups.

- Learned how to operate vital computer systems and hook up equipment such as heart monitors and blood sugar checking devices as well as preparing records.

**COMPUTERS**

Am proficient in using MS Word, WordPerfect, and Windows for word processing and recordkeeping. Excellent personal and professional references on request.

Date

Exact Name of Person
Exact Title
Exact Name of Company
Address
City, State, Zip

Dear Exact Name of Person: (or Dear Sir or Madam if answering a blind ad):

When you look at this resume, you see right away that this individual graduated with honors. Since she is entering a scientific field, she wants to acquaint potential employers with her skills related to various types of equipment. You will see that the first job on her resume is Biology Tutor. Employers will usually infer that only the top biology students could be tutors, so this creates a positive impression of her intellect and communication skills.

With the enclosed resume, I would like to make you aware of my education and background in the fields of science and medicine as well as my highly developed analytical, technical, and problem-solving skills and extensive laboratory experience.

As you will see, I have earned a Bachelor of Science in Biology with a minor in Chemistry from Ball State University, where I graduated with honors, maintaining a cumulative GPA of 3.5. For the past year, I have also worked as a tutor for first-year biology students, conducting individual sessions twice weekly and leading a classroom discussion with all sixteen of my students once per week.

In earlier positions as a Laboratory Technician and Medical Assistant, I honed my growing technical skills while using my knowledge of medical, biological, and laboratory theory and technique in a practical working environment. Experienced in taking vital signs and updating medical charts, performing phlebotomies, and conducting laboratory tests to include complete blood counts (CBCs) and drug screens, I am also proficient in the safe and accurate operation of most common laboratory equipment.

If you can use a skilled laboratory technician with highly-developed analytical and technical skills, I hope you will welcome my call soon when I try to arrange a brief meeting to discuss your goals and how my background might serve your needs. I can provide outstanding references at the appropriate time.

Sincerely,

Kathleen Gallagher

Alternate Last Paragraph:
I hope you will write or call me soon to suggest a time when we might meet to discuss your needs and goals and how my background might serve them. I can provide outstanding references at the appropriate time.

# KATHLEEN GALLAGHER

1110½ Hay Street, Fayetteville, NC 28305   •   preppub@aol.com   •   (910) 483-6611

**OBJECTIVE**

To benefit an organization that can use an articulate and intelligent young professional with exceptional technical and analytical skills who offers a strong educational background and experience with scientific and medical testing in laboratory and medical clinic environments.

**EDUCATION**

**Bachelor of Science** in **Biology** with a minor in Chemistry, Ball State University, Muncie, IN, 2001; **graduated with honors**, maintaining a **3.5 cumulative GPA**.

- Recognized for academic performance by my induction into Beta Beta Beta National Honor Society for Biology majors and the State Science Club.
- President of the Indian Trail Head Start Parent Committee.
- Studied a wide range of challenging courses related to science and medicine, including:

| | | |
|---|---|---|
| Cellular and Molecular Biology | Principles of Genetics | Microbiology |
| General Chemistry I & II | Comparative Anatomy | Radiation |
| Organic Chemistry I & II | Animal Development | Trigonometry |
| Histology & Microtechniques | Principles of Biology | Biochemistry |
| Vertebrate Physiology | Medical Terminology | Psychology |
| Analytical Chemistry | Child & Adolescent Development | |

**CERTIFICATIONS & TRAINING**

Certified in CPR and First Aid through the Indiana Community Action Program.
Familiar with OSHA guidelines and regulations, as well as the use and proper disposal of chemicals, specimens, and instruments; skilled at recording and maintaining data.

**TECHNICAL SKILLS**

Skilled in the use of the following types of laboratory equipment:

| | | |
|---|---|---|
| gel electrophoresis plates | autoclave | digital & manual scales |
| chemical fume hoods | centrifuge | spectrometer |
| electron & dissecting microscopes | pH meters | micropipettes and large pipettes |

**EXPERIENCE**

**BIOLOGY TUTOR.** Ball State University, Muncie, IN (2000-01). Provided instruction and assistance to first-year students in the Biology program, teaching Principles of Biology and Zoology in one-on-one sessions and in a weekly classroom discussion.

- Provided tutoring for 16 students in twice-weekly sessions addressing the problems of the individual student; led a weekly classroom discussion attended by all my students.

**LABORATORY TECHNICIAN** and **RECEPTIONIST.** Alpha Plasma Center, Muncie, IN (1999). Admitted donors to the center, recording vital signs (height, weight, temperature, and blood pressure) and performing a complete blood count (CBC) on each donor before they were allowed to donate plasma.

- Assisted the on-site physician with performing physicals; trained other laboratory technicians/receptionists in center policies and donor admission/approval procedures.

**MEDICAL ASSISTANT.** Primary Care Plus, Muncie, IN (1997-98). Provided a variety of medical and laboratory assistance at this local urgent care center; recorded patients' vital signs and assisted physicians and physician's assistants.

- Performed eye and ear screens, drug screens, and EKGs as well as performing phlebotomy and blood work to include CBCs; assisted in performing x-rays.

**COMPUTERS**

Familiar with operating systems and software including Windows and Microsoft Office.

**PERSONAL**

Excellent personal and professional references are available upon request.

Date

Exact Name of Person
Exact Title
Exact Name of Company
Address
City, State, Zip

Dear Exact Name of Person: (or Dear Sir or Madam if answering a blind ad):

With the enclosed resume, I would like to make you aware of my interest in teaching biology at your school. I have earned my B.S. in Biology Teaching and recently completed a highly successful student teaching assignment at a high school in Wyeth, GA. I was commended by the teacher who supervised me for my exceptional creativity and for my willingness to tackle and follow through on difficult assignments.

My interest in teaching biology developed while I was serving my country in the U.S. Army, where I was trained as a Laboratory Technician. In order to gauge the depth of my interest in the field, I became a Volunteer with the Red Cross at an Army hospital. When I decided to leave military service and enter the civilian work force, I explored opportunities for earning my Biology Teaching degree and I chose Bainbridge College. You will notice from my resume that I worked nearly 30 hours a week in a demanding job throughout my college career.

Because I am slightly older than the average college graduate, I feel I have a degree of maturity which could be most beneficial in a high school classroom. Since I was myself the first person in my family to graduate from college, I am confident that I could be a powerful motivator to youth who are unsure of their goals in life. I am a highly motivated individual and I believe in leading by example.

If you can use a well-trained individual who offers outstanding communication skills along with a proven ability to work well with others, I hope you will contact me to suggest a time when we might meet to discuss your goals. I can provide outstanding references at the appropriate time.

Sincerely,

Janet McCue

# JANET McCUE

1110½ Hay Street, Fayetteville, NC 28305 • preppub@aol.com • (910) 483-6611

**OBJECTIVE**   To offer my strong desire to teach and work with young people by applying my degree in the science field as well as my creativity, motivational skills, knowledge of computer operations, and practical experience with a variety of laboratory procedures.

**EDUCATION**   **Bachelor of Science, Biology Teaching,** Bainbridge College, Bainbridge, GA, 2001.
- Named to the Chancellor's List in recognition of academic achievements in maintaining a GPA of 3.8 or higher.
- Excelled in specialized coursework including:

  | | | |
  |---|---|---|
  | methods of teaching | analytical chemistry | histology |
  | anatomy and physiology | medical terminology | biochemistry |
  | probability and statistics | human development | Spanish |
  | computers in education — emphasis on Lotus 1-2-3, Word, Report Card | | |

- Held membership in the Science Club.

**EXPERIENCE**   **STUDENT TEACHER.** Georgia Board of Education, Wyeth, GA (2001). Instructed a diverse student population at Wyeth High School while teaching Biology I and Biology II to ninth through 12th grade students.
- Applied active learning techniques while motivating students to participate in class activities and open themselves to learning.
- Implemented positive classroom management strategies to encourage proper behavior and respect for others.
- Utilized planning and organizational skills in carrying out classroom support activities including completing interesting and thorough lesson plans as well as preparing test materials and monitoring testing.
- Earned the teacher's respect for my true concern for the students, willingness to tackle hard assignments, and ability to follow through on any project taken on.
- Displayed creativity and initiative in the development of informative bulletin boards.

**CASHIER.** Taco Bell, Bainbridge, GA (1997-00). Refined time management skills and displayed a high level of self-motivation while working 30 hours a week.
- Known for my dedication to providing high quality customer service, was entrusted with training new employees and setting an example for them to follow.

**LABORATORY ASSISTANT.** The American Red Cross, Germany (1995-96). As a volunteer in the chemistry department lab of a U.S. Army hospital in Germany, logged in and separated blood specimens and then ran them through the SMA-18 machine which analyzed specimens for 18 separate chemical tests.
- Assisted in drawing blood from patients and doing electrolyte testing.

*Highlights of earlier experience as a LABORATORY TECHNICIAN, U.S. Army:*
- Processed urine specimens for military personnel throughout the Pacific while screening for illegal substances including heroin, cocaine, barbiturates, and amphetamines.
- Conducted drug screening procedures at a facility which supported Army, Navy, and Air Force personnel based in the Philippines, Japan, Korea, and Hawaii.
- Assisted a doctor doing research on high blood pressure and the effects of high altitude.

**PERSONAL**   Am an open water-certified SCUBA diver; received Red Cross certification in CPR and life-saving techniques. Offer empathy for the problems and tough choices facing young people.

Date

Exact Name of Person
Exact Title
Exact Name of Company
Address
City, State, Zip

**CHEMISTRY GRAD WITH RESEARCH ASSISTANT EXPERIENCE**

This young chemistry graduate offers some experience as a research assistant. It's not often that one can graduate and have experience in one's field, but this fortunate individual found a summer and part-time job that helped her refine her technical skills while she was completing her degree.

Dear Exact Name of Person: (or Dear Sir or Madam if answering a blind ad):

With the enclosed resume, I would like to make you aware of my exceptional technical abilities as well as my background as a motivated and experienced chemist who offers experience in research and development, troubleshooting, and quality assurance for a variety of latex polymer compounds.

As you will see from my resume, I have a Bachelor of Science in Chemistry from Drake University in Des Moines, IA. In addition to exceptional computer skills, I am also experienced in the operation of numerous state-of-the-art laboratory apparatuses, including HPLC, Nuclear Magnetic Resonance (NMR), MS-GC, IR, and UV-VIS, as well as Gas Chromatography and other tests used for identification purposes.

While completing my education, I excelled as a Research Assistant at a large international chemical company. As a member of the Applications team, I have performed quality assurance, testing, and evaluation of various latex polymers used in commercial paint applications and made several successful presentations related to projects to which I was assigned. My supervisors lauded me for displaying "initiative and creativity" in problem-solving, and I have met or exceeded all of my individual performance goals.

I am in the process of permanently relocating to my home state of California in order to be closer to family and friends. I feel that there is a good "fit" between my knowledge and skills and your company's needs. I hope you will welcome my call soon, when I try to arrange a brief meeting to discuss your goals and how my background might serve your needs. Thank you in advance for your time and professional courtesies.

Sincerely,


Laura Ann Feldhahn

# LAURA ANN FELDHAHN

1110½ Hay Street, Fayetteville, NC 28305　　•　　preppub@aol.com　　•　　(910) 483-6611

**OBJECTIVE**

I want to contribute to an organization that can use an experienced young chemist with exceptional technical, communication, and organizational skills who offers a background in research and development, production, and quality assurance.

**EDUCATION**

**Bachelor of Science** in **Chemistry**, Drake University, Des Moines, IA, 2001.
- Received the Outstanding Graduate Research Award for 2000.

Completed three years towards my Bachelor of Science in Chemistry at Iowa State University prior to transferring to Drake University.
- Awarded a scholarship after being named Miss Iowa State University, 1998; was selected as representative to the Miss Iowa State Scholarship Pageant.

**TECHNICAL & COMPUTER SKILLS**

Experienced in the operation of various state-of-the-art laboratory instrumentation used for chemical analysis, such as **HPLC**, **Nuclear Magnetic Resonance (NMR)**, **MS-GC**, **IR**, and **UV-VIS**. In addition, am computer-literate and familiar with many popular operating systems and software, including Windows 95 & 98; Microsoft Word, Excel, PowerPoint, and Access; Local Area Networks (LAN) and Internet applications; WordPerfect; Quattro Pro.

**AFFILIATIONS**

Member, Student Chemist's Society.
Serve on the Rules and Procedures Site Safety Committee (SOP).
Oversee Quality Control for the Environmental Chamber.

**EXPERIENCE**

**RESEARCH ASSISTANT.** UCAR Emulsion Systems (Union Carbide), Des Moines, IA (Summers and part-time during college (1998-2001). Based on the recommendation of the Chairman of the Department of Chemistry, was selected for this job performing research and development, formulation, troubleshooting, and product improvement for numerous developmental latex polymers used in commercial paint applications.
- Functioned as a resource to the Applications team during the development of both the low VOC semigloss and Branched Ester Ethylene Vinyl Acetate (BEEVA) projects.
- Prepared presentations on Ethylene Vinyl Accil, using Microsoft PowerPoint.
- Assessed raw materials for cost efficiency and to identify and implement improvements in product performance; evaluated the Total Solids, Glass Transition, and MFT for various latex polymer formulations.
- Completed detailed evaluations of commercial paint products in order to benchmark products against current performance objectives.
- Served on Y2K team for the Applications and CTCH areas, inventorying and evaluating all equipment to determine vulnerability to Y2K-related failures.
- Described as "an integral part of the Applications team," was cited in an appraisal for displaying "a great deal of initiative and creativity."

**ASSISTANT TO THE RESEARCH CHEMIST.** Iowa State University, Des Moines, IA (Summers, 1996-97). Assisted in researching compounds containing fluorine.
- Utilized chemical compounds containing carbon-fluoride linkages as building blocks in the construction of larger molecules; performed Nuclear Magnetic Resonance (NMR) and Gas Chromatography testing for identification purposes.

**PERSONAL**

Excellent personal and professional references are available upon request.

Date

Exact Name of Person
Title or Position
Name of Company
Address (number and street)
Address (city, state, and zip)

Dear Exact Name of Person: (or Sir or Madam if answering a blind ad.)

With the enclosed resume, I would like to initiate the process of being considered for employment within your organization. I am a May 2001 graduate of the College of Notre Dame with an excellent scientific education along with superior technical writing skills, experience in laboratory analysis and instrumental analysis, and knowledge of medicinal chemistry.

While earning my B.S. in Chemistry, I excelled in courses including Medicinal Chemistry, which focused on modern pharmaceuticals, and Instrumental Analysis. I am skilled in operating equipment and devices including fluorescence spectrometers, atomic mass spectrometers, UV/VIS molecular absorption spectrometers, high performance liquid chromatography (HPLC), gas chromatography (GC), as well as IR/Raman spectrometers, NMR, and FTIR.

At college, I was a popular tutor of Chemistry and Calculus, and I acted as a Mentor for 11 Engineering and Science students. During the summers while earning my college degree, I worked in technical environments which taught me much about teamwork. In the summer of 1998, I worked on an assembly line assembling, inspecting, and packing electrical control panels. In the summer of 1997, I worked as a Procedure Writer for an electric company, where I developed and revised Defense Waste Processing Operations Procedures with special emphasis on chemical processing procedures. In the summer of 1996, I worked as a Production Assistant.

You would find me in person to be a warm and congenial individual who relates well to others and who offers excellent communication skills. While mentoring other Engineering and Science students, I frequently mediated disputes and trained students to utilize conflict management techniques. Known for my natural leadership skills, I served as President of my sorority and led the sorority to a major membership increase. At the same time, however, I take my greatest pleasure in performing analytical tasks ranging from analyzing drinking water to agricultural samples.

If you can use a sharp and astute young chemistry graduate who offers excellent analytical and communication skills, I hope you will contact me to suggest a time when we might meet in person. I am flexible and able to relocate according to your needs. Thank you in advance for your time.

Yours sincerely,


Carol Mace

# CAROL MACE

1110½ Hay Street, Fayetteville, NC 28305　　•　　preppub@aol.com　　•　　(910) 483-6611

**OBJECTIVE**　　To contribute to an organization that can use a dedicated young professional with an excellent scientific education along with superior technical writing skills, experience in laboratory analysis and instrumental analysis as well as some knowledge of medicinal chemistry.

**EDUCATION**　　Earned **B.S. degree in Chemistry,** College of Notre Dame, Belmont, CA, 2001.
- Recipient of the U.S. Achievement Academy Collegiate Award; nominated by faculty.
- Authored a senior paper entitled *"The Effects of Proton Conductivity."*
- Coursework included Medicinal Chemistry which focused on modern pharmaceuticals.
- Coursework also included Instrumental Analysis, and my skills include operating:

| | |
|---|---|
| Fluorescence Spectrometers | UV/VIS Molecular Absorption Spectrometers |
| IR/Raman Spectrometers | High Performance Liquid Chromatography (HPLC) |
| NMR | FTIR |
| Atomic Mass Spectrometer | Gas Chromatography (GC) |

- Am skilled in utilizing chart recorders and multimeters.
- Elected **President** of my sorority, Zeta Phi Beta, and led sorority to a major increase in membership while becoming recognized as a vibrant and enthusiastic leader.

**COMPUTERS**　　Highly proficient with Excel, MS Word, PowerPoint, WordPerfect, Lotus, and ZPlot.

**EXPERIENCE**　　**ENGINEERING & SCIENCE MENTOR** and **CHEMISTRY & CALCULUS TUTOR.** College of Notre Dame's Program for Educational Enrichment and Retention, Belmont, CA (2000-01). Earned a reputation as an articulate communicator and inspiring young leader while introducing first-year engineering and science students to different opportunities in the PEER Program.
- Taught students to solve problems; tutored students in calculus and chemistry.
- Utilized my natural tact and ability to develop consensus while mediating disputes among students; trained the students themselves in conflict management techniques.
- Mentored 11 engineering and science students who looked to me as their "Team Leader."

**SALES ASSOCIATE.** Volume Services, Belmont, CA (1998-99). Was frequently commended for my ability to handle the public in a gracious manner while selling food and drinks during home games at the College of Notre Dame; handled various administrative tasks including controlling an inventory of perishable items and other supplies.
- Developed balance sheets for different food stands; supervised the contract groups and vendors who operated the stands; gained experience in financial management and financial control while developing balance sheets.

**Other experience (summers):**
**PRODUCTION ASSISTANT.** Cutler-Hammer, San Diego, CA (summer 1998). Assembled, inspected, and packed various sizes of electrical control panels while ensuring that the production line was always stocked with needed supplies.

**PROCEDURE WRITER.** Electric River Company, Elkton, CA (summer 1997). Developed and revised Defense Waste Processing Operations Procedures with special emphasis on chemical processing-related procedures; edited procedures to ensure they addressed human factors; conducted research for data critical to success of the procedures.

**PRODUCTION ASSISTANT.** Black & Decker, San Diego, CA (summer 1996). Tested commutators for power drills, and ensured they were heat and wear resistant.

Date

Exact Name of Person
Title or Position
Name of Company
Address (no., street)
Address (city, state, zip)

**DOCTOR OF PHARMACY
WITH NUMEROUS
CLINICAL ROTATIONS**

After earning his degree
with extensive academic
honors, this young
professional is now
ready to market his
skills and communicate
the clinical rotations and
clerkships which helped
him refine his skills.

Dear Exact Name of Person: (or Dear Sir or Madam if answering a blind ad.)

With the enclosed resume, I would like to make you aware of my desire to utilize my Doctor in Pharmacy degree for the benefit of your organization.

In the process of completing my Doctor of Pharmacy degree, I excelled in several fourth year clinical rotations which enhanced my clinical knowledge and management abilities. After completing a rotation in geriatrics, I was specially requested to return for a second rotation by the medical professionals with whom I worked. You will also see that I completed two rotations at pharmacies in New York as well as a clinical rotation at the Veterans Administration Hospital.

You would find me in person to be an outgoing individual who prides myself on my ability to remain poised in all customer service situations. I can provide outstanding personal and professional references, and I would cheerfully relocate and travel extensively according to your needs.

I hope you will call or write me soon to suggest a time convenient for us to meet and discuss your current and future needs and how I might serve them. Thank you in advance for you time.

Sincerely yours,

Joseph Edward Mullen

# JOSEPH EDWARD MULLEN

1110½ Hay Street, Fayetteville, NC 28305  •  preppub@aol.com  •  (910) 483-6611

**OBJECTIVE**      I want to contribute to an organization that can use a skilled health care professional who offers an extensive background as a pharmacist along with a strong bottom-line orientation.

**EDUCATION**     **Doctor of Pharmacy**, Daemen College School of Pharmacy, Amherst, NY, 2001.
- Graduated *magna cum laude*.
- Elected officer in Phi Delta Chi Pharmacy Fraternity; inducted into Pre-Med-Allied Health Honor Society; Epsilon Pi Eta Honor Society; Phi Eta Sigma Honor Society.
- Named to Dean's List, President's List; awarded Presidential Scholarship.
- Member of Phi Delta Chi Pharmacy Fraternity; Christian Pharmacist Fellowship.
- Active in student life and community organizations: participated in annual Phi Delta Chi fundraiser for Daemen Creek Elementary School and battered women's shelter; as a tutor at Boose Creek Elementary School; participated in health fair.

**EXPERIENCE**    **FOURTH YEAR CLINICAL ROTATIONS & CLERKSHIPS:**
- **Geriatrics (two rotations):** Methodist Retirement Community, Amherst, NY and Southeastern General Hospital, Adlee, NY, Jan-June 2001. Gained knowledge of geriatric patients.

- **Community Pharmacy:** Revco Drugs, Amherst, NY, Dec 2000. Gained experience in all aspects of the operation of a community pharmacy; learned techniques related to receiving and processing Rx orders; dispensing and checking prescriptions; counseling patients; and billing third party payers.

- **Ambulatory Medicine:** Merck Permanente, Amherst, NY, Nov 1999. Worked closely with physicians and mid-level practitioners and provided clinical pharmacy services; refined my skills in basic physical assessment; drug utilization reviews; and clinical pharmacy practice including patient chart reviews, interpretation of lab results, development of drug regiments, patient counseling, and kinetics service.

- **Drug Information:** Daemen College Drug Information Center, Sep 1999. Received requests for information concerning drugs and drug therapy from physicians, pharmacists, and nurses; searched primary, secondary, and tertiary sources for information, to include computerized databases and online sources; compiled information into concise answers.

- **Community Pharmacy:** Rite Aid, Adlee, NY, Aug 1998. Gained experience in all aspects of the operation of a community pharmacy; completed a school project in which data was collected and counseling given to patients concerning drug-drug interactions.

- **Internal Medicine:** Veteran's Administration Hospital, Amherst, NY, Jun 1998. Monitored inpatients on a general medicine ward; member of a medical team consisting of an attending physician, a medical resident, an intern, and a student. Monitored patients through attending rounds, medical charts, and computerized databases.

**PERSONAL**      Outstanding references. Completed 16 hours of training in primary compounding.

Exact Name of Person
Exact Title
Exact Name of Company
Address
City, State, Zip

## HEALTH CARE MANAGEMENT GRAD

Dear Exact Name of Person (or Dear Sir or Madam if answering a blind ad):

With the enclosed resume, I would like to make you aware of my interest in exploring employment opportunities with your organization and introduce you to my background and credentials related to your goals.

With classic credentials including the Harvard Business School, this top executive has worked for only two companies. She is seeking a new challenge that will further test her ability to optimize efficiency and maximize profitability.

As you will see from my resume, I recently completed my B.S. degree in Health Care Management from Berry College, where I also obtained a minor in Business Administration. In a two-month internship related to my degree, I gained knowledge of the health care delivery system while working with medical records, insurance recertification, insurance claims, and data entry in a specialized pediatric center. I also excelled in a part-time job in the medical community as a Medical Administrative Assistant.

Prior to college graduation, I was recruited for my current position as an Insurance Agent by a company founded in 1874, and I have obtained my Life and Health License. I am excelling in all aspects of my job and have especially enjoyed the customer service and community involvement. I am familiar with CPT-4/ICD-9 Coding for Medicare and Medicaid reimbursements, and I am knowledgeable of both medical and insurance terminology.

My desire to become involved in the Health Care Management field began when I was a youth, as I always gravitated toward jobs which involved helping others. From the time I was 14 years old until I was 23, I worked in the hospitality industry as a waitress and waitstaff manager, and I always became the individual selected to handle the most difficult customer problems.

My husband and I are in the process of relocating permanently to the Washington, DC/Maryland area, and I am seeking an organization which can make use of my education in health care management as well as my practical, hands-on experience related to the insurance industry and medical practices. I can provide excellent references at the appropriate time. If your organization is committed to quality customer care and needs a committed and well-educated young individual to join your team, I hope you will contact me to suggest a time when we might talk. My husband and I are frequently in the Maryland/Washington area to locate housing, so I could make myself available at your convenience to meet with you.

Yours sincerely,

Allison Miller

# ALLISON MILLER

1110½ Hay Street, Fayetteville, NC 28305　　•　　preppub@aol.com　　•　　(910) 483-6611

---

**OBJECTIVE**　　I want to contribute to an organization that can use a resourceful young professional who offers strong problem-solving and customer service skills along with experience in sales, office administration, budgeting and accounting, as well as the management of people and operations.

**EDUCATION**　　**Bachelor of Science (B.S.) degree in Business Administration and Health Care Management,** Berry College, Tucson, AZ, May 2001.
- Excelled academically with a 3.3 GPA.
- Persisted in obtaining my college degree despite frequent relocations with my husband; completed extensive coursework toward the degree at Tucson College, Tucson, AZ.
- Business coursework included Principles of Marketing, Economics, Accounting, Managerial Finance, Statistics, and many other courses.

Graduated from Walkersville High School, Walkersville, MD, 1997.
- Played field hockey and was active in drama.
- Was **Volunteer Counselor** for 6th and 8th graders; received numerous letters of appreciation.

**EXPERIENCE**　　**INSURANCE AGENT.** Independent Order of Foresters of Ontario, Canada, Tucson, AZ (May 2001-present). Was recruited by this organization which has been in existence since 1874; the organization is committed to the philosophy of "members helping members" and offers insurance services, financial planning, benevolent assistance, and other services.
- After obtaining my Life and Health License, was assigned a customer base of 500 accounts; vigorously prospect for new accounts at schools and community events.

**MEDICAL ADMINISTRATIVE ASSISTANT.** Tucson Imaging Center, Tucson, AZ (2000-01). Resigned from this part-time position because I sought full-time hours; began with Tucson Imaging Center as a nighttime receptionist and then moved to days.
- Received superior evaluations of my performance in all areas; demonstrated my ability to handle multiple tasks and to produce top-quality results under tight deadlines.
- Trained the nighttime receptionist after I was asked to move to a daytime schedule.
- Worked with the Director of Marketing on marketing projects which increased revenue.
- Handled daily deposits; was responsible for resolving claims; handled billing and posted accounts receivable and accounts payable.
- Became knowledgeable of insurance coding and billing; refined my knowledge of medical terminology as well as Coding CPT-4/ICD-9 for Medicare and Medicaid reimbursements.
- Handled insurance billing and reviewed insurance denials; worked with insurers to resolve issues related to payment and eligibility.

**INTERN.** Pediatric Developmental Center, Tucson, AZ (1999-00). Excelled in a two-month internship while completing my college degree; gained knowledge of the health care delivery system while working with medical records, insurance recertification, insurance claims denial, and data entry.

**WAITRESS & WAIT STAFF MANAGER.** Various restaurants in Baltimore, MD; Frederick, MD; and Missouri. Began working when I was 14 years old and worked in the hospitality industry for nearly 10 years, while earning both my high school diploma and college degree.
- For Coconut Alley in Frederick, MD, trained and scheduled a staff of 15 employees.

**COMPUTERS**　　Proficient with Microsoft Windows, PowerPoint, Excel, Quicken 2000, other software.

MEDICAL BILLING CERTIFI-
CATION WITH NURSING
EXPERIENCE

Here is an example of a
resume in which the
previous work
experience has nothing
in common with the
degree program.

Dear Sir or Madam:

With the enclosed resume, I would like to make you aware of my background as an enthusiastic young professional with an education in Medical Billing who offers proven skills related to medical office administration, records management, and medical billing which have been tested in busy hospital environments.

Recently, I have been excelling as a Night Auditor for several different hotels while pursuing my diploma in Medical Billing. Using Microsoft Excel, I generated revenue and expense reports as well as reconciling daily receipts to ensure that all funds are accounted for. I have been recognized by these employers as an enthusiastic, reliable worker who adheres to a high work standard while providing exceptional customer service.

Earlier, I served with distinction as a Medical Corpsman in the U.S. Navy. While assisting nursing professionals and physicians in busy hospital environments, I performed a number of medical and administrative functions, including patient screening, updating and maintenance of patient medical records, phlebotomy, and patient billing. I completed inpatient registration of new clients, screening the patient and creating a file containing their medical history and major complaint. While serving as Medical Receptionist in the Medical Clinic, it was also my responsibility to obtain patient insurance information, file insurance claims, perform patient education, and provide administrative and clerical support to the office.

As you will see from my enclosed resume, I have recently completed a diploma program in Medical Billing from an accredited correspondence school, which included course work in Medical Terminology, Medical Claims Procedures, and CPT/ICD-9 coding. I have also received a diploma in Medical Science and graduated from the U.S. Navy's three-month Medical Corpsman School, completing courses in a variety of medical disciplines. I feel that my strong combination of education and practical experience would make me a valuable addition to any medical office.

Highly regarded by my previous employers, I can provide outstanding letters of recommendation at the appropriate time. I assure you in advance that I have an excellent reputation and would quickly become an asset to your organization.

Sincerely,

Gerald Faich

# GERALD FAICH

1110½ Hay Street, Fayetteville, NC 28305   •   preppub@aol.com   •   (910) 483-6611

---

**OBJECTIVE**

To benefit an organization that can use an enthusiastic, reliable young professional with strong communication and organizational skills who offers an education in medical billing and experience in medical office administration, patient screening, billing, and auditing.

**EDUCATION**

Completed **Certification in Medical Billing** through an accredited correspondence course, 2001. Courses included:

| | |
|---|---|
| Medical Terminology | Anatomy and Physiology |
| Procedural Coding | Diagnostic Coding |
| Medical Claims Procedures | CPT/ICD-9 Coding |

Earned diploma from a Screener's course in Medical Science, Great Lakes, IL, 1999.
Graduated from the U.S. Navy Medical Corpsman School, a three-month program which included courses in:

| | |
|---|---|
| Venipuncture and Phlebotomy | Medical Records Management |
| Patient Screening and Assessment | Medical Office Administration |

**COMPUTERS**

Familiar with popular computer systems and software including Windows , Microsoft Word, and Microsoft Excel. Have quickly mastered new software, including a variety of proprietary systems specific to the military and to the medical profession.

**EXPERIENCE**

**NIGHT AUDITOR.** Various locations throughout Fargo, IL (2000-present). Have served with distinction, working simultaneously as Night Auditor and "Manager on Duty" for several different hotels while completing my education in Medical Billing.

- Generated daily revenue and expense reports in Microsoft Excel and reconciled daily receipts to ensure that all funds were accounted for; handled large volumes of cash.
- Supervised the night shift hotel staff while performing customer service, bookkeeping, and guest check-in.
- Personally credited with increasing total revenue at one hotel by seven percent.
- Recognized by my employers as an enthusiastic, reliable worker who adheres to a high work standard and excels at customer service; can provide letters of recommendation.

**NURSING ASSISTANT.** U.S. Navy, Great Lakes, IL (1996-00). After completing extensive military training in various medical disciplines, served as a Hospital Corpsman; assisted nurses and physicians, providing patient care in busy hospital environments.

- Performed patient screening and initial assessment for more than 100 patients per week; utilized extensive knowledge of medical terminology and abbreviations.
- Completed patient registration, verifying insurance information and utilizing the DEERS military dependent eligibility system; gained valuable experience in medical billing.
- Updated and maintained medical records for more than 1,000 patients, documenting all medical visits, treatments, and changes to patients' medical history.
- Served as a Medical Receptionist at the Medical Clinic; answered phones, scheduled appointments, screened patients, and pulled, updated, maintained, and filed charts.
- Operated a computer, utilizing a variety of proprietary software specific to military medical environments to prepare reports, patient histories, and other documents.
- Conducted patient education related to subjects such as side effects of prescribed medication and proper home care procedures for patients being released.

**PERSONAL**

Enthusiastic individual with a results-oriented attitude. Outstanding references.

Date

Exact Name of Person
Exact Title
Exact Name of Company
Address
City, State, Zip

Dear Exact Name of Person (or Dear Sir or Madam if answering a blind ad):

With the enclosed resume, I would like to make you aware of my strong educational background in science and medicine, my highly developed analytical and problem-solving skills, and my extensive laboratory experience.

As you will see, I am currently completing a Bachelor of Science degree in Natural Sciences with a concentration in Biology from Wright State University. In addition to the rigorous course load of my degree program and my teaching responsibilities, I have taken on courses from the biotechnology program, which have provided me with the opportunity to develop cutting edge knowledge and learn to operate state-of-the-art laboratory equipment. While learning the fundamentals of DNA manipulation, I have used micropipettes, centrifuges, thermocyclers, and gel electrophorens apparatuses. I have studied techniques of DNA cloning, restriction digestion, transformation, plasmid isolation, bacterial culturing, and gel electrophorens. During a one-year project, I assisted on work involving the cloning of microbial resistant genes from the clinical isolation of *Klebsiella pneumoniae*.

If you can use an educated professional with highly developed analytical and technical skills who offers a strong background in laboratory testing, I look forward to hearing from you soon to suggest a time when we might meet to discuss your needs. I can assure you in advance that I have an excellent reputation and would rapidly become a valuable addition to your organization.

Sincerely,


Elka Westervelt

A career in nursing is ahead of this young professional, and she is using her resume to show off her medical skills, office skills, certifications, license, honors, education, and experience. The cover letter gives her a chance to add the "warmth" and "personality" that can sometimes be lacking in a resume.

# ELKA WESTERVELT

1110½ Hay Street, Fayetteville, NC 28305 • preppub@aol.com • (910) 483-6611

**OBJECTIVE**    To benefit an organization that can use an articulate and intelligent young professional with exceptional technical and analytical skills who offers a strong educational background in scientific and medical testing in laboratory environments.

**EDUCATION**    Completing a **Bachelor of Science degree in Natural Sciences**, with a concentration in Biology, Wright State University, Dayton, OH. Will receive degree in May 2001.
Have studied a wide range of difficult courses related to science and medicine, including:

| | | |
|---|---|---|
| Cellular and Molecular Biology | Techniques in Microbiology | Genetics |
| Radiation Biology | Comparative Anatomy | Chemistry I |
| Integrated Zoology | Calculus w/Analytic Geometry | Chemistry II |
| General Physics I, II, & III | Anatomy & Physiology I & II | Botany |
| Ecology and Evolution | Elementary Statistics | Spanish I & II |
| Animal Development | Intro. To Computer Science | |
| Vertebrate Physiology | Special Problems (lab assignments) | |

Completed 52 hours of **field experience teaching science** to local high school students.

**TECHNICAL
SKILLS**    Excelled in a number of additional courses from the biotechnology program, developing skills in the following areas:

- Fundamentals of DNA manipulation using state-of-the-art equipment such as micropipettes, centrifuges, thermocyclers, and gel electrophorens apparati.
- Techniques of DNA cloning, restriction digestion, transformation, plasmid isolation, bacterial culturing, and gel electrophorens.
- Spent a year on work involving the cloning of microbial resistant genes from clinical isolation of *Klebsiella pneumoniae*.

**EXPERIENCE**    **TELEMARKETER.** Big Starr Telemarketing, Dayton, OH (Summers 1998, 1999, 2000). During summer break, demonstrated my exceptional verbal communication and listening skills while excelling in this stressful telephone direct sales environment.

- Quickly developed a rapport with customers, uncovered their objections, and used product knowledge and persuasion to close the sale.
- Provided direct marketing sales and support, presenting customers with the benefits and advantages of various products offered by the company.

**CUSTODIAN.** North High School, Dayton, OH (1997). In a part-time job while in college, performed general maintenance, cleaning, and landscaping services in order to beautify and prepare the school's interior, exterior, and grounds for the fall enrollment.

**SEWING MACHINE OPERATOR.** D& D Jeans, Dayton, OH (1996-1997). Worked in this commission-based position in a busy clothing production plant.

**COOK** and **CASHIER.** Burger King, Dayton, OH (1994-1996). Honed my skills in teamwork and time management while cooking and providing customer service for this local branch of the large national fast food chain.

- Was frequently called upon to accept the additional responsibility of training new employees due to my patience and exceptional communication skills.
- Provided customer service, taking food orders and operating a cash register.

**PERSONAL**    Excellent personal and professional references are available upon request.

**NURSING GRAD WITH CLINICAL ROTATIONS**

The resume shows off internships which have helped her gain valuable knowledge.

Dear Sir or Madam:

I would appreciate an opportunity to talk with you soon about how I could contribute to your organization through my formal education as a Registered Nurse as well as through my outstanding personal qualities.

As you will see from my resume, I completed several clinical rotations while earning my nursing degree; these gave me hands-on experience in medical-surgical nursing, newborn and maternal care nursing, and psychiatric nursing. In every situation, I was commended for my excellent communication skills and ability to deal professionally with doctors, nurses, patients, administrators, and other personnel.

Extremely active as a student, I was involved in the Nursing Students Association and was an elected delegate to the National Student Nurses Association Conference in New York. I have always been regarded as an outgoing individual with an ability to relate well to people on all levels.

You would find me in person to be a congenial individual who always strives to do my best in all situations. I am a mature individual who raised two children before embarking on my lifelong dream of becoming a nurse. I can provide outstanding personal and professional references.

I hope you will call or write me soon to suggest a time convenient for us to meet and discuss your current and future needs and how I might serve them. Thank you in advance for your time.

Sincerely,


Ragina Raftery

# RAGINA RAFTERY

1110½ Hay Street, Fayetteville, NC 28305  •  preppub@aol.com  •  (910) 483-6611

---

**OBJECTIVE**

To contribute to an organization that can use a Registered Nurse with excellent judgment and decision-making skills who offers a strong desire to make a significant contribution to medical, surgical, and patient care activities.

**EDUCATION**

**Associate of Applied Science degree in Nursing,** Averett College, Danville, VA, 2000
Completed Rape Crisis Intervention Volunteer Training, January 1999

**RN LICENSE**

Valid until February 13, 2003.

**CERTIFICATIONS**

Certified Nursing Assistant I and II; CPR Certified.

**MEDICAL SKILLS**

- Am trained in patient assessment, medication administration, catheterizations, sterile dressing changes, charting, and patient education.
- Skilled in using IV pumps, CPM (continuous passive motion) machine, and AccuChek.

**OFFICE SKILLS**

- Computer knowledgeable.
- Skilled in using office machines including faxes, copiers, printers, and typewriters.

**EXPERIENCE**

*1998-2001—While earning my nursing degree, have excelled in the following clinical rotations:*
*Medical-Surgical Nursing Clinical Rotation*: Danville Medical Center, Danville, VA. Provided total patient care while administering medications, assisting with activities of daily living including body mechanics, nutrition, and safety.
- Took vital signs; made dressing changes.
- Learned tracheotomy suctioning techniques.
- Applied sterile dressings and handled tube feedings.

*Maternal and Newborn Nursing*: Danville Medical Center, Danville, VA. Attended mothers through labor and delivery of infants.
- Became proficient in relaxation techniques during labor.
- Became a breast-feeding specialist.
- Completed one rotation in Neonatal ICU.
- Cared for critically ill newborns as well as healthy newborns.

*Psychiatric Nursing*: Danville Hospital, Danville, VA. Was commended for my compassionate attitude and my excellent communication skills while working in the adult unit.

*1996-98: While earning my nursing degree, also worked part-time for LOMAC, Danville, VA*: As **TREASURER**, was proudly associated with this fine organization and played a key role in the daily business operation of the day program for autistic adults; LOMAC is a nonprofit organization funded by the county which has evolved into the County Mental Health Day Program of today.
- Worked closely with the Board of Directors and was accountable to the board.
- Was responsible for more than $70,000 per year in cash and disbursements.

**HONORS**

- Member, Nursing Students Association, Averett College
- Delegate, National Student Nurses Association Conference in New Orleans

Date

Exact Name of Person
Exact Title
Exact Name of Company
Address
City, State, Zip

Dear Exact Name of Person (or Dear Sir or Madam if answering a blind ad):

With the enclosed resume, I would like to make you aware of my desire to explore employment as a Registered Nurse.

As you will see, I will shortly graduate with an Associate's degree in Nursing and am seeking employment in the San Diego area, where my extended family is from. While earning my degree, I excelled in numerous clinical rotations and internships. I have worked in med-surg, ortho/neuro, labor and delivery, long-term care, psychiatric, and substance abuse environments.

I have taken the time to work actively in student organizations, and I have held numerous elected offices in student nursing associations. I can provide outstanding personal and professional references.

If you can use an educated professional with highly developed analytical and technical skills, I hope you will contact me to suggest a time when we might meet to discuss your present and future needs. I can assure you in advance that I have an excellent reputation and would rapidly become a valuable addition to your organization.

Sincerely,

Andrew Reese

# ANDREW REESE

1110½ Hay Street, Fayetteville, NC 28305   •   preppub@aol.com   •   (910) 483-6611

**OBJECTIVE**

I want to contribute to an organization that can use a skilled young nursing professional who offers proven management and leadership skills.

**CERTIFICATIONS**

Certified Nurse Aide II.
CPR Certification.

**LICENSES**

Will take the NCLEX-RN in June 2001.

**EDUCATION**

Associate Degree in Nursing (ADN) degree, Drexel University, Philadelphia, PA; will graduate May 2001. **Current GPA 3.89.**
- Named to President's List; inducted into Phi Theta Kappa Honor Society.
- Will pursue Bachelor of Science in Nursing in my spare time after receiving RN license.
- Graduated from Chambers Senior High School, Philadelphia, PA, 1995.
- Extensive management and leadership training as a U.S. Army professional, 1995-98.

**EXPERIENCE**

**NURSING INTERN & NURSING STUDENT.** Drexel University, Philadelphia, PA (1998-present). Have excelled academically, in clinical rotations, and in leadership positions with the Pennsylvania Association of Nursing Students (PANS) and the Drexel Association of Nursing Students (ANS).

*Clinical Rotations*: Have received the highest-possible evaluations of my performance in these clinical rotations:
- **Med/Surg:** Raleigh Memorial Hospital, Fall 2000 and 2001. Refined skills in patient care and administered oral medications; provided advanced care in Fall 1999.
- **Ortho/Neuro:** Philadelphia Medical Center, Spring 1999. Administered parenteral and IV medications; expanded my assessment skills with adult patients.
- **Labor & Delivery/Newborn:** Philadelphia Medical Center, Summer 1999. Administered IVs; refined my assessment skills related to newborns and mothers.
- **Long-Term Care:** Carrol Nursing Home, Fall 1998. Administered medications and feedings via gastrostomy tubes; gained skills in long-term care geriatric nursing.
- **Psychiatric:** Hope Hospital, Fall 1998. Gained insights into psychiatric care.
- **Substance Abuse:** Blunt Avenue Clinic, Spring 1998. Learned about substance abuse nursing practices.

**Leadership in Professional Organizations:** Have been elected Breakthrough to Nursing Director in both the state (PANS) and the Drexel nursing associations.
- Awarded the PANS Nursing Scholarship at PANS Annual Convention, Oct 2000.
- For the Drexel Association of Nursing Students, supervised recruiting activities; achieved a 95% retention rate of second-year students while aggressively recruiting new first-year student members.
- For the Philadelphia Association of Nursing Students, am supervising membership recruitment and retention for all 78 nursing schools in Pennsylvania.
- Represented the state nursing association at the Pennsylvania State Legislature; have played a key role in planning the 2001 mid-year conference.

**MEDEVAC OPERATIONS MANAGER.** U.S. Army, Ft. Sill, OK (1995-98). For a medevac company at a large U.S. military base, was promoted to manage an average of seven people and up to 40 personnel while assuring the availability of 15 helicopters and medevac assets.

**PERSONAL**

Can provide outstanding references. Proven leadership and management skills.

Date

Exact Name of Person
Exact Title
Exact Name of Company
Address
City, State, Zip

NURSING GRAD WITH CNA
AND PHLEBOTOMY
INTERNSHIPS

The Objective of the
resume is a blend of all-
purpose and specific. He
mentions his specialized
knowledge of the
automotive industry as
well as his sales and
management skills which
are transferable to any
field.

Dear Exact Name of Person (or Dear Sir or Madam if answering a blind ad):

With the enclosed resume, I would like to acquaint you with my exceptional organizational and communication skills as well as my experience in Phlebotomy and as a Certified Nursing Assistant I & II.

A Certified Nursing Assistant, I have earned a certification in Phlebotomy from the American Society of Phlebotomy Technicians as well as a certification in Medical Terminology. Currently pursuing an Associate's degree in Nursing in the evenings at Carthage University, I expect to complete the requirements for the Licensed Practical Nurse program by June of 2000, and the Registered Nurse requirements in June of 2001.

In my most recent position, I worked a four-month internship in Phlebotomy at several area hospitals. Earlier in a four-month Certified Nursing Assistant Internship, I performed, cleaned, and maintained tracheostomies and catheters, inserted and cleaned feeding tubes, and assisted nurses in providing patient care.

While pursuing my nursing degree and working in the above positions, I simultaneously oversee the operation of J & D 24-hour Towing, a successful small business. I interview and hire all new employees, handle accounts payable and receivable, and process weekly payroll. In an earlier position with Quick Stop, I served as Assistant Manager in this convenience store chain. I feel that my versatile experience, supervisory skills, and education would make me a valuable addition to your organization.

If you can use a highly motivated professional with strong organizational and communication skills, I hope you will contact me to suggest a time when we might meet. I can assure you that I have an excellent reputation and would quickly become an asset to your organization.

Sincerely,

Young Sikh Sondheimer

# YOUNG SIKH SONDHEIMER

1110½ Hay Street, Fayetteville, NC 28305  •  preppub@aol.com  •  (910) 483-6611

**OBJECTIVE**    To contribute to an organization that can use a dedicated and hard-working medical professional with exceptional communication and organizational skills as well as certifications in Phlebotomy and as a Certified Nursing Assistant I & II.

**EDUCATION**    Completing **Associate's** degree in **Nursing** program at Carthage College, Kenosha, WA.
- Will complete the Licensed Practical Nurse requirements in June, 2001, and the Registered Nurse requirements in June, 2001.

Completed the Phlebotomy, Certified Nursing Assistant I & II, and Medical Terminology courses, Carthage College, Kenosha, WA, 1999.

**CERTIFICATION**    Certified in Phlebotomy, American Society of Phlebotomy Technicians, certificate XYZ123, 1999.

Certified Medical Assistant I & II, certificate #0922929, 1999.

Earned a certification in Medical Terminology, certificate #0923931, 1999.

**EXPERIENCE**    **COLLEGE STUDENT** and **SMALL BUSINESS OWNER.** J & D 24-hour Towing, Kenosha, WA (1996-present). Assumed ownership of his business after the death of my father; oversee all operational aspects of this successful towing company while simultaneously pursuing my Associate's degree in Nursing.
- Interview and hire all new employees; process weekly payroll and manage accounts payable/ accounts receivable.
- Update and maintain all licenses and permits.

*Completed the following internships while pursuing my Associate's degree in Nursing and simultaneously running a small business:*

**PHLEBOTOMY INTERNSHIP.** Veterans Administration Hospital, Kenosha, WA; Good Hope Hospital, Kenosha, WA; and Harnett Manor, Lillith, WA (1999). Completed this internship program while earning my certification in phlebotomy.
- Prepared patients for phlebotomy, sterilizing the venipuncture site and tying off the vein before drawing blood for laboratory testing and diagnosis.
- Retrieved records from the computer to determine what tests are to be performed.
- Maintained strict adherence to safety regulations and guidelines related to the handling and disposal of all blood products and related biohazards.

**INTERNSHIP, CERTIFIED NURSING ASSISTANT I & II.** Veterans Administration Hospital, Kenosha, WA; Good Hope Hospital, Kenosha, WA; and Harnett Manor, Lillith, WA (1998). Performed the duties of a CNA while completing a four-month internship; assisted nurses in providing patient care while pursuing my nursing degree.
- Performed tracheostomies and administered catheters; cleaned and maintained catheters and tracheostomy tubes; turned stroke and heart patients every two hours.

**ASSISTANT MANAGER.** Quick Stop, Kenosha, WA (1993-1996). Managed this busy location of the regional convenience store chain; oversaw all facets of operation, including human resources, inventory control and purchasing, loss prevention, and accounting.
- Supervised five employees; interviewed, hired, and trained all new personnel.
- Balanced cash registers and safe, tracking all discrepancies and recording overages, shortages, and sales figures on daily transaction logs.

**PERSONAL**    Excellent personal and professional references are available upon request.

Date


Exact Name of Person
Exact Title
Exact Name of Company
Address
City, State, Zip

Dear Exact Name of Person (or Dear Sir or Madam if answering a blind ad):

Here is another resume
of a technical
professional who has
clinical rotations to show
off.

    With the enclosed resume, I would like to make you aware of my background as an articulate young professional with exceptional communication, organization, and patient care skills who offers an educational background and clinical rotation experience in various occupational therapy environments.

    As you will see from my enclosed resume, I am currently excelling both academically and in clinical rotations while completing my Bachelor of Science degree in Occupational Therapy. Currently maintaining a **3.89 GPA**, I will graduate in May and test for certification as an Occupational Therapist Registered in September of 2002. I previously earned an Associate of Applied Science degree in Accounting and completed two years college course work in Biology before entering the Occupational Therapy program.

    I have excelled in clinical rotations at Charles Mental Health Center and at Northeastern Regional Rehabilitation Center, where I demonstrated my creativity, problem-solving ability, and therapeutic skills. In addition to preparing a multimedia in-service presentation for the Occupational Therapy department using Microsoft PowerPoint, I also designed and created a new adaptive tool for patients with hemiparesis. Currently, I am beginning a Pediatric Outpatient rotation.

    If you can use a dedicated, accomplished young professional with a strong desire to make a contribution in the field of Occupational Therapy, I look forward to hearing from you soon. I assure you in advance that I have an excellent reputation and would quickly become an asset to your organization.


Sincerely,



Deborah Lucas

# DEBORAH LUCAS

1110½ Hay Street, Fayetteville, NC 28305   •   preppub@aol.com   •   (910) 483-6611

---

**OBJECTIVE**    To offer my education and experience in Occupational Therapy to an organization that could benefit from the services of a creative and dedicated professional with exceptional communication, problem-solving, and patient care skills which have been tested in a variety of clinical environments.

**EDUCATION**    **Bachelor of Science in Occupational Therapy**, Hastings College, Hastings, NE; currently maintaining a **3.89 GPA**, will graduate May 2002.
- Named to the **President's Honor List** three times, for achieving a perfect **4.0 GPA** for the semester, and the **Dean's List**, for a **3.5 GPA** or better.
- Received the prestigious Thomas Foundation scholarship, a $16,000 award in recognition of my extensive hours of volunteer work.
- Completed two years of college-level course work towards a Bachelor of Science in Biology at Hastings College before entering the Occupational Therapy program, 1997-1999.

**Associate of Applied Science** degree in Accounting, Hastings Community College, Hastings, NE, 1996.

**CERTIFICATIONS**    Will test for Occupational Therapist Registered through the National Board for Certification in Occupational Therapy, September 18, 2002.

**AFFILIATIONS**    Member, American Student Occupational Therapy Association, 1997-present.
Treasurer, Phi Beta Lambda, 1997-1999.

**EXPERIENCE**    **OCCUPATIONAL THERAPY INTERN** and **STUDENT.** Hastings College, Hastings, NE (2000-present). Have excelled academically, in clinical rotations, and in leadership positions with the American Student Occupational Therapy Association.
*Clinical Rotations*: Have received the highest-possible evaluations of my performance and been praised for my creativity and problem solving while completing these clinical rotations:
**Pediatric Outpatient:** Caring Hands, Hastings, NE (Mar 2001-present). Apply my growing knowledge and exceptional care skills while providing occupational therapy to children.
**Rehabilitation:** Northeastern Regional Rehabilitation Center, Hastings, NE (Jan-Mar 2001). Demonstrated resourcefulness while further honing my patient care skills during this clinical rotation at a major regional rehabilitation center; performed patient assessment and evaluation in order to establish a plan of care.
**Mental Health:** Charles Mental Health Center, Hastings, NE (May-Aug 00). Gained valuable experience in helping clients with schizophrenia and bipolar disorder to develop problem-solving ability as well as social and communication skills; held a money management workshop and conducted weekly money management group meetings to help patients achieve a greater sense of personal responsibility.

**THERAPY ASSISTANT.** Titus Rehabilitation Hospital, Hastings, NE (1996-99). Performed more than 240 hours of volunteer work, assisting with patient activities under the supervision of an Occupational Therapist.

**ACCOUNTING CLERK** and **DATA ENTRY CLERK.** Kearns Guidance & Navigation Corporation, Charles, NE (1994-96). Started with this major defense contractor as a Data Entry Clerk and quickly advanced to a position of increased responsibility.

**PERSONAL**    Excellent personal and professional references are available upon request.

Date

Exact Name of Person
Exact Title
Exact Name of Company
Address
City, State, Zip

Dear Exact Name of Person: (or Dear Sir or Madam if answering a blind ad):

With the enclosed resume, I would like to make you aware of my education as a Physician's Assistant as well as my extensive experience in surgical environments as a Certified Surgical Technologist. I am interested in exploring employment with you as a Surgical Physician's Assistant.

As you will see from my resume, I completed my Associate of Science and earned a diploma as a Surgical Technologist, and I have worked as a Surgical Technologist at Malibu Regional Hospital. I am highly skilled in operating room procedures and am known for my dedication to providing the highest quality patient care. I am also skilled in interacting with staff and physicians and am known for my ability to establish and maintain effective working relationships with people at all levels.

While excelling in my full-time job, I have also excelled academically while completing the Physician Assistant Program at Pepperdine University. You will see from my resume that I have completed rotations in orthopedics, family practice, pediatrics, internal medicine, surgery, and obstetrics and gynecology. In 2001, I will be involved in rotations in vascular surgery, dermatology, urology, psychiatry, emergency medicine, and public health.

If you can use a dedicated young Physician Assistant who is highly experienced in surgical and medical environments, I hope you will contact me to suggest a time when we might meet in person to discuss your needs. I can provide outstanding references at the appropriate time.

Sincerely,


Su H. Chung

# SU H. CHUNG

1110½ Hay Street, Fayetteville, NC 28305  •  preppub@aol.com  •  (910) 483-6611

**OBJECTIVE**

To benefit an organization that can use a skilled young Physician Assistant dedicated to the highest standards of patient care who offers a background as a Certified Surgical Technologist along with extensive experience in surgical and medical environments.

**EDUCATION**

Completing **Physician Assistant Program,** Pepperdine University, Malibu, CA; degree to be awarded May 2002; have excelled academically; named to **President's List** and **Dean's List**; inducted into **Tri Beta Biological Honor Society.**

Completed **Associate of Science (A.S.) degree** and a **Diploma as a Surgical Technologist**, Malibu Technical College, Malibu, CA, 1998.
  • Elected President, Surgical Technology Club.

One year of college in general studies, Pacific Union College, Angwin, CA, 1994-95.

**CERTIFICATIONS & AFFILIATIONS**

Certified in Advanced Cardiac Life Support (ACLS).
AAPA: American Academy of Physician Assistants.
CAPA: California Academy of Physician Assistants.

**EXPERIENCE**

**CERTIFIED SURGICAL TECHNOLOGIST.** Malibu Regional Hospital, Malibu, CA (2000-present). Am known for my dedication to providing the highest quality patient care in the process of performing surgical assisting and surgical first-assisting.

**PHYSICIAN ASSISTANT ROTATIONS:** While completing Physician's Assistant School, have excelled in the following rotations:

**Orthopedics:** Alabaster Hospital, Malibu, CA . Performed assessment and treatment of trauma patients; handled reducing, casting, splinting of fractures; performed hardware removal, x-ray interpretation, surgical first-assisting, inpatient care, suturing, and handled operative orders and notes.

**Family Practice:** Heritage Family Practice, Malibu, CA. Was involved in inpatient rounds and care; took dictations; performed assessment, diagnosis, and treatment of a wide variety of conditions; performed routine gynecological exams.

**Pediatrics:** Malibu Public Health, Malibu, CA. Handled well-baby exams. Performed Denver II assessments along with assessment, diagnosis, and treatment of childhood illnesses. Provided school and sports physicals.

**Family Practice:** Langolier Medical Center, Langolier, CA. Handled the diagnosis and treatment of a wide variety of conditions while also performing office procedures such as toenail removal, steroid injections, sebaceous cyst incisions, and gynecological exams.

**Internal Medicine:** Alabaster Hospital, Malibu, CA. Was involved in the daily management and care of inpatients and ICU patients. Handled procedures including thoracentesis, abdominocentesis, joint aspiration, and lumbar puncture. Monitored ventilator patients and stress testing.

**Surgery:** Village Surgical Associates, Malibu, CA. Was involved in surgical first-assisting, suturing, performing daily rounds, and providing patient care.

**Obstetrics and Gynecology:** Alabaster Hospital, Malibu, CA. Handled routine OB-GYN assessment exams, vaginal/C-section deliveries, surgical first-assisting, and suturing.

**Rotations scheduled for 2002:**

| | | |
|---|---|---|
| **Vascular Surgery** | **Urology** | **Emergency Medicine** |
| **Dermatology** | **Psychiatry** | **Public Health** |

**PERSONAL**

Excellent personal and professional references are available upon request.

Date

Exact Name of Person
Exact Title
Exact Name of Company
Address
City, State, Zip

Dear Exact Name of Person (or Dear Sir or Madam if answering a blind ad):

The internships shown on the resume will help this young professional attract the notice of large veterinary organizations. She is also planning on sending this resume with her application to veterinary graduate schools.

With the enclosed resume, I would like to make you aware of a dedicated, experienced veterinary technician with exceptional communication and organizational skills and a background in internal medicine, emergency care, and pharmacy environments.

I am currently completing an internship at an animal hospital, performing the same duties that I had as a Veterinary Intern at Centre Veterinary Clinic, Danville, KY. In that position, I assisted the veterinarian in all phases of treatment, taking vital signs, drawing blood, administering medications, and performing other duties as needed.

I have also worked in an emergency care environment, as a Veterinary Technician for Centre Animal Hospital, where I learned to deal with stressful situations while caring for with sick or injured pets, interacting with pet owners who were upset, and assisting the veterinarian with emergency procedures.

I have earned an Associate of Applied Science in Veterinary Technology from Centre College, and am a Registered Veterinary Technician with the state of Kentucky. I feel that my education and experience in a variety of clinical environments will be an asset to your organization.

If you can use a compassionate veterinary technician with strong organizational and communication skills and a background in internal medicine, emergency care, and pharmacy environments, then I look forward to hearing from you soon to arrange a time when we might meet to discuss your needs. I can assure you in advance that I would quickly become a valuable addition to your organization.

Sincerely,

Shannon Henry

# SHANNON HENRY

1110½ Hay Street, Fayetteville, NC 28305 • preppub@aol.com • (910) 483-6611

---

**OBJECTIVE**

To benefit an organization that can use a dedicated and experienced veterinary technician with exceptional organizational and communication skills, a strong attention to detail, and a background in internal medicine, emergency care, and pharmacy environments.

**EDUCATION**

Associate of Applied Science degree in Veterinary Technology, Centre College, Danville, KY, 2001.
Graduated from Metzer High School, Danville, KY.

**CERTIFICATIONS**

Kentucky Registered Veterinary Technician #957.
Florida Board Certified Veterinary Technician #2004.

**EXPERIENCE**

**VETERINARY INTERN.** Centre Animal Hospital, Danville, KY (2001-present). Perform a wide variety of functions in this extremely busy veterinary clinic.
- Work in the pharmacy, dispensing medications and typing labels.
- Other duties are essentially the same as those I performed at Centre Veterinary Specialists.

**VETERINARY INTERN.** Centre Veterinary Specialists, Danville, KY (1998-00). Provided a number of services in support of the veterinarians in this practice which focuses on internal medicine and serves as an emergency care facility at nights and on weekends.
- Performed patient assessments, taking vital signs and communicating pertinent information to the veterinarian in an accurate and timely manner.
- Assisted the veterinarian in all phases of treatment.
- Made triage determinations, both physically and over the telephone.
- Operated radiography equipment, taking views and developing X-ray film.
- Drew blood and executed complete blood counts, including differentials; placed IV catheters.
- Administered medication including chemotherapy.
- Restrained animals appropriately to avoid injury to the patient or the care team.
- Interacted with and educated pet owners on issues related to surgical aftercare, diet and exercise, etc.

**VETERINARY INTERN.** Centre Animal Hospital, Danville, KY (1996-97). Rapidly performed patient assessments and assisted the veterinarian under stressful conditions in this busy animal emergency care facility.
- Assisted the veterinarian in emergency surgeries and other emergency procedures.
- Safely restrained and calmed injured animals so they could be treated without causing them further harm.
- Interacted with pet owners who were upset, calming them and quickly obtaining information vital to the appropriate treatment of the patient's emergency condition.

Other experience:
**SALES ASSOCIATE.** Yours Truly Cards & Gifts, Danville, KY (1995-96). Assisted customers in the selection and purchase of merchandise; responsible for cash handling and balancing cash receipts.

**PERSONAL**

Excellent personal and professional references are available upon request.

In this section, you will find resumes and cover letters of experienced medical professionals. If you are yourself an experienced medical professional, you will enjoy reading the career summaries of highly competent professionals in your field.

Experienced medical professionals whom you will meet in this section include a medical administrator who offers strong accounting experience. Office professionals are part of this section, including James Gray, whose resume shows a track record of promotion and accomplishment with a health care organization. An assistant director of nursing is among those whose resumes and cover letters are included.

If you are on the technical side, you may enjoy reading the resume of Martha Stewart, a physical therapy assistant. If you are an academician, the resume of Cecilia Scott will interest you, since she was a university instructor and dean of health sciences. Does home health hold any appeal for you? You will see a history of experience within a home health organization in the resume of Terri Alligood. Hospice case managers, registered nurses, psychiatric nurses, medical accounts managers, medical office managers, emergency medical technicians, medical secretaries and transcriptionists, mental health professionals, nursing home administrators, dental office managers, patient accounts representatives, and many others are represented in this section.

Experienced professionals are often still experimenting in their careers, and they have more freedom than older job hunters to try new fields and change careers. They are not "locked in" to one segment or functional area within the medical field. New certifications can lead to new opportunities!

Although most people have three distinctly different careers in their working lifetimes, you *could* have three different careers within the medical field if you want to. The medical field is a vast arena with many interesting types of work, and skills you gained in one area may transfer easily to other areas. And if you're in the medical field, you'll like this fact: the medical field is expected to be a growing source of jobs for at least the first two decades in the 21st century!

The section that follows is aimed at helping experienced professionals develop the tools to find the jobs which they really want to do.

Date

Dear Sir or Madam:

With the enclosed resume, I would like to make you aware of my interest in the position of Provider Relations Representative with Allied Health which you advertised in The Atlanta Sun. Although I am responding to that particular ad, I would be delighted to be considered for any other position within your organization in which you could utilize my expertise and knowledge.

As you will see from my resume, my background is tailor-made to your requirements, and I offer the Bachelor's degree as well as the experience in provider relations, marketing/contract negotiation, and managed care which you are seeking.

In my current position as Administrator with Georgia Regional Radiology, I oversee billing operations, financial reporting, and statistical analysis for a 21-doctor practice while supervising 26 employees. I am skilled at reading and interpreting managed care contracts as well as negotiating terms and fee structures for insurance companies, HMOs, and PPOs. As Coordinator for the Georgia Regional Physicians Alliance – a 25-doctor IPA, I also handle responsibilities which include negotiating managed care contracts as well as bulk purchasing contracts and providing educational forums for office managers from participating practices.

In a previous job as Assistant Controller with Atlanta Community Hospital, I supervised accounts payable, accounts receivable, payroll, and accounting while also assisting the Controller in preparing year-end financial work papers, Medicare cost report work papers, as well as operating and capital assets budgets.

I can assure you that I am a detail-oriented individual with excellent communication and negotiating skills, and I can provide excellent personal and professional references at the appropriate time. I hope you will contact me to suggest a time when we might meet to discuss your needs and how I might meet them. Thank you in advance for your time.

Yours sincerely,

Jennifer K. Maley

P.S. I will be out of town on vacation from 14 January until 23 January, but you may leave a message on my answering machine during that time, and I will contact you upon my return.

# JENNIFER K. MALEY

1110½ Hay Street, Fayetteville, NC 28305   •   preppub@aol.com   •   (910) 483-6611

**OBJECTIVE**
To offer a strong base of management and accounting experience to an organization that can benefit from my education, skills, and abilities.

**EDUCATION**
Completed 27 hours of **post-baccalaureate course work in Accounting**, Albany State University, Albany, GA.
**B.S., Political Science**, Georgia Southern University, Statesboro, GA, 3.55 GPA
**Georgia State University**, Atlanta, GA.
- Graduated ***magna cum laude* (3.8 GPA),** was named to Who's Who in American Junior Colleges, and held membership in Phi Theta Kappa national honor society.

**SPECIAL SKILLS**
Offer experience in both computerized and manual accounting systems with PC experience which includes Lotus, WordPerfect, and Microsoft Office including Word and Excel. Strong negotiating skills and extensive knowledge of managed care contracts.

**EXPERIENCE**
**ADMINISTRATOR.** Georgia Regional Radiology, Americus, GA (2001-present). Oversee billing operations, financial reporting, and statistical analysis for a 21-doctor practice while supervising 26 employees who include data entry clerks and front desk personnel, radiology technicians, medical transcriptionists, patient representatives, and a variety of clerks (payroll, accounts receivable, and accounts payable).
- Manage activities such as long-range planning, project development, marketing strategies, building projects, and the development of new business such as the addition of satellite offices.
- Read and interpret managed care contracts as well as negotiating terms and fee structures for insurance companies, HMOs, and PPOs.
- Coordinator for the Clarkston Regional Physicians Alliance, a 25-doctor IPA; responsibilities include negotiating managed care and bulk purchasing contracts as well as providing educational forums for office managers from participating practices.

**ASSISTANT CONTROLLER.** Atlanta Community Hospital, Atlanta, GA (1991-00). Supervised accounts payable, accounts receivable, payroll, and accounting.
- Assisted Controller in preparing year-end financial work papers, Medicare cost report work papers, as well as operating and capital assets budgets.
- Compiled data which was used to prepare financial statements for four medical office building corporations.
- Reconciled all general ledger accounts pertaining to Medicare reimbursements.
- Prepared monthly forecasts of revenues and expenses.

**TAX SUPERVISOR.** The Record Bar, Inc., Atlanta, GA (1989-91). Supervised and prepared corporate federal tax returns, 28 state returns, property tax listings and returns, and sales tax returns for each state where the corporation conducted business.
- Conducted quarterly audits of retail store inventories.
- Was promoted to this position on the basis of accomplishments as Supervisor of Sales Reporting from 1987-89: analyzed and distributed sales information for a 150-store retail chain; supervised four data entry clerks; reconciled general ledger accounts and corporate bank accounts; coordinated month-end journal entries; resolved sales-related problems.

**PERSONAL**
Am a detail-oriented professional who enjoys meeting challenges. Enjoy active pursuits which include scuba diving, training and showing horses, and training dogs.

Date

Exact Name of Person
Exact Title
Exact Name of Company
Address
City, State, Zip

Dear Exact Name of Person (or Dear Sir or Madam if answering a blind ad):

With the enclosed resume, I would like to make you aware of my reputation as an experienced, loyal, and highly motivated management and accounting professional with excellent communication, organizational, and motivational skills as well as a background in office management and accounting.

With First Health of Kentucky, my loyalty and dedication have been rewarded by advancement into positions of increasing responsibility. I started with the company as a registration clerk in the Emergency Room and quickly advanced to Assistant Supervisor, overseeing the activities of as many as 30 clerks, providing administrative, patient registration, and accounting services. In this position, I prepared weekly schedules for three rotating shifts of 30 employees while also providing counseling for marginal performers and conducting employee evaluations. I attended seminars on ICD-9 coding, and coded emergency room charts daily, entering them into the computer for billing.

You will also notice from my resume that I am experienced in the full range of accounting activities. Prior to my employment with First Health of Kentucky, I handled the accounting function for a furniture retailer, and in that capacity I was involved in accounts payable, cost accounting, shipping and freight reports, and inventory control.

Of course all of my jobs have involved customer service, and I offer strong customer service and public relations skills. I have frequently been commended for my gracious manner of dealing with the public and for my skill in troubleshooting difficult problems so that customer satisfaction is retained while safeguarding the company's bottom line goals.

I can provide outstanding references at the appropriate time, and I would appreciate an opportunity to talk with you in person about how my versatile skills and background could make a difference to your organization. I hope you will call and suggest a time when we might meet in person to discuss your needs and how I might serve them.

Sincerely,

James Gray

# JAMES GRAY

1110½ Hay Street, Fayetteville, NC 28305   •   preppub@aol.com   •   (910) 483-6611

**OBJECTIVE**     To benefit an organization that can use an experienced management and accounting professional with exceptional communication, organizational, and motivational skills who offers a background in office management and accounting.

**EDUCATION**     Graduated with a **Bachelor's degree** in **Business Administration, Magna Cum Laude**, with a 3.85 G.P.A.; Leighton University, Leighton, KY.
- Majored in **Accounting** with a minor in **Computer Programming.**

Have nearly completed the requirements for an **Associate's degree** in **Nursing**, Sandhills Community College, Leighton, KY; am only five courses short of this degree.
Completed **Associate's degree** in **Accounting**, Sandhills Community College, Leighton, KY.
Completed two years of course work in General Studies and Accounting, Wake Technical Community College and Wilson Technical Community College, Wake and Wilson, KY.

**CERTIFICATIONS**     Certified Nursing Assistant I, Kentucky certificate # 189773.
Licensed Notary Public for the state of Kentucky, commission expires 4/27/2006.

**AFFILIATIONS**     Member, Phi Kappa Phi national honor society.

**EXPERIENCE**     *With First Health of Kentucky at Moore Regional Hospital, have advanced in the following "track record" of increasing responsibilities:*
*2000-present:* **ADMISSIONS CLERK.** Leighton, KY. During the evening shift, operated the admissions office completely by myself, working without supervision since 2001; oversaw all aspects of the admissions process and assisted with billing and accounting.
- Coordinated with in-patient nursing supervisor and housing supervisor on matters pertaining to patient placement and availability of beds.
- Escorted patients to their rooms; ordered diagnostic testing for newly admitted patients.
- Quickly mastered the transition from the proprietary SMS computer system to a Windows-based system.
- On my own initiative, kept the office open until midnight in order to catch change-of-shift admissions and ensure that doctors would get paid for Emergency Room work-ups on D.R.G. if the E.R. counted as the first day of admission. This saved the hospital thousands of dollars in Medicare payments that would otherwise have been lost.

*1995-00:* **ADMISSIONS OFFICE CLERK.** Leighton, KY. Performed administrative, accounting, and clerical duties for the admissions office of this busy regional medical center.
- Processed inpatient registrations, took financial statements and ran credit checks on self-pay patients, and interviewed patients to acquire necessary information.
- Contacted insurance companies to verify patient coverage, get benefits information, and pre-certify inpatient services.
- Administered the Hill Burton Fund, completing applications for qualified patients.

*1990-94:* **ASSISTANT SUPERVISOR** and **EMERGENCY ROOM REGISTRATION CLERK.** Leighton, KY. Managed as many as 30 clerks in rotating shifts, providing direct supervision, administrative support, employee counseling and evaluation, and accounting services to the Emergency Department patient registration office.
- Coordinated patient registration efforts with billing office goals, ensuring that all patient information required by the billing department was complete and accurate.
- Coded emergency room charts daily and entered them into the computer for billing; attended seminars on ICD-9/CM coding.

Date

Exact Name of Person
Exact Title
Exact Name of Company
Address
City, State, Zip

Dear Exact Name of Person (or Dear Sir or Madam if answering a blind ad):

With the enclosed resume, I would like to acquaint you with my strong administrative, organizational, and problem-solving skills as well as my extensive background in nursing supervision and administration.

I have earned a Bachelor of Science in nursing from Kent State University, in addition to my Associate degree in Registered Nursing and Licensed Practical Nurse programs. I have been certified as an instructor in Basic Cardiac Life Support (BCLS), and have received my ANCC Gerontological Nurse Certification.

At Elderlodge of Kent, I was hired as an RN Supervisor and was quickly promoted to Assistant Director of Nursing/Staff Development. In this position, I support the Director of Nursing, supervising 75 Registered Nurses, Licensed Practical Nurses, and Certified Medical Assistants, coordinating and directing the day-to-day operations of the nursing department to insure that appropriate levels of direct care are provided to the Residents. I am responsible for assessing, selecting, and implementing training programs for the nursing staff and developing other programs to meet the needs of the facility's employees.

As you will see from my resume, I have worked at this level of responsibility for most of my nursing administration career. In previous positions at Village Green Care Center and Carrolton of Kent, my leadership and management skills were recognized, and I was either hired at the Assistant Director of Nursing level or quickly advanced to that level and beyond.

If you can use a highly educated, articulate professional with a strong background in nursing administration and long-term care environments, I hope you will contact me to suggest a time when we might meet to discuss your need. I can assure you that I have an excellent reputation and could quickly become a valuable asset to your organization.

Sincerely,

Sandra Bush

# SANDRA BUSH

1110½ Hay Street, Fayetteville, NC 28305  •  preppub@aol.com  •  (910) 483-6611

---

**OBJECTIVE**

To benefit an organization that can use a motivated, experienced administrator with strong organizational and problem-solving skills who offers a strong background of nursing supervision in long-term care environments.

**EDUCATION**

**Bachelor of Science in Nursing (BSN)**, Kent State University, Kent, OH.
**Associate degree, Registered Nursing (RN)**, Kent Community College, Kent, OH.
**Licensed Practical Nurse program (LPN)**, Kent Technical Community College, Kent, OH.
Registered Nurse License #ZXX106744 , Expires 12/31/03.
Basic Cardiac Life Support (BCLS) Instructor, Certificate #244869872, Expires 5/31/05.
ANCC Gerontological Nurse Certification, Certificate # 8900058-09, Expires 11/30/03.

**AFFILIATIONS**

Member, American Society of Long Term Care Nurses
Member, Ohio Nurses Association

**EXPERIENCE**

*At Elderlodge of Kent, was hired as an RN Supervisor, and was quickly promoted to Assistant Director of Nursing/Staff Development.*
*2000-present:* **ASSISTANT DIRECTOR OF NURSING.** Elderlodge of Kent, OH. Support the Director of Nursing, supervising a staff of 75 RNs, LPNs, and CNAs in order to coordinate and direct the day-to-day operations of the nursing department in this busy long-term care facility.
- Perform daily rounds of the Nursing Service Department.
- Develop, implement, and maintain an effective orientation program that quickly and effectively familiarizes nursing staff with the facility, its policies and procedures, and the job duties they will be expected to discharge.
- Work closely with the Director of Nursing to ensure that a sufficient number of Registered Nurses, Licensed Practical Nurses, and Certified Medical Assistants are available for each tour of duty, in order to maintain quality resident care.
- Assess, select, and implement in-service training and other programs to meet specific needs of the facility's employees.
- Assist the Director of Nursing in preparation of employee performance evaluations.
- Serve as Coordinator for resident assessment and care planning, compiling the Minimum Data Set for Nursing Home Resident Assessment and insuring the implementation of Resident Assessment Protocols and Triggers.

*1996-00:* **REGISTERED NURSE SUPERVISOR.** Observed and assessed the physical and emotional health of Residents, ensuring that direct nursing care was provided.
- Made rounds with physician; notified physician of changes in resident's condition.
- Reviewed nurse's notes and C.N.A. flow sheets to insure that all documentation was descriptive of the resident care being provided.
- Admitted, transferred, and discharged residents, completing all necessary paperwork.
- Monitored all operational areas; notified the Director of Nursing of any problem areas.
- Assisted charge nurse; monitored seriously ill residents and provided nursing care.

**ASSISTANT DIRECTOR OF NURSING.** Village Green Care Center, Kent, OH (1991-96). Performed essentially the same duties as the **Assistant Director of Nursing** position at Elderlodge; also performed some of the duties of an **RN Supervisor.**

**PERSONAL**

Outstanding personal and professional references are available upon request.

---

**CLINIC ASSISTANT DIRECTOR**

Dear Sir or Madam:

With the enclosed resume, I would like to make you aware of my background as an experienced licensed physical therapy assistant and supervisor with a high degree of professionalism, a strong work ethic, and a background of excellence in hand therapy, general orthopedics, wound care, and all aspects of direct patient care.

As you will see, I graduated with honors from the Associate degree program in Physical Therapy at Cary Technical Community College. I have supplemented my college education with numerous continuing education courses, covering a broad range of physical therapy topics.

At ProActive Therapy's busy clinic in Cary, I have played a key role through my special interest and expertise in hand therapy, and my leadership and contributions to their success have been rewarded through promotion to positions of increased responsibility. In my most recent position as Assistant Director, I supervised the clinic staff of 15 employees, including Licensed Physical Therapy Assistants, Physical Therapy Technicians, office staff, and Staff Therapist. Previously, as Senior Licensed Physical Therapy Assistant, I served as clinical preceptor for the Physical Therapy Assistant program at Cary Technical Community College, and mentored Medical Sciences students from local high schools.

Although I was highly regarded by this employer, and can provide outstanding references and letters of recommendation at the appropriate time, my husband and I are permanently relocating to the Asheville area. I feel that my strong combination of education, experience, and expertise in physical therapy would be a valuable addition to any organization.

If you can use a highly experienced licensed physical therapy assistant with a proven background in hand therapy, wound care, general orthopedics, and supervision, then I look forward to hearing from you soon, to arrange a time when we might meet to discuss your needs. I can assure you that I have an exceptional reputation and would quickly become a strong asset to your company.

Sincerely,

Martha Stewart

# MARTHA STEWART

1110½ Hay Street, Fayetteville, NC 28305   •   preppub@aol.com   •   (910) 483-6611

---

**OBJECTIVE**

To benefit an organization that can use an experienced licensed physical therapy assistant or supervisor with a high degree of professionalism, a strong work ethic, and a background of excellence in hand therapy, general orthopedics, aquatic therapy, and wound care.

**EDUCATION**

Graduated with honors from the Associate degree program in Physical Therapy, Cary Technical Community College, Cary , AL, 1990; named to President's List, 1990.

*Have completed numerous continuing education courses including:*

| | |
|---|---|
| Surgery & Rehabilitation of the Hand | Understanding Total Knee Replacement |
| Understanding Total Hip Replacement | Carpal Tunnel Syndrome |
| Temporomandibular Joint Dysfunction | Management of Soft-Tissue Injury |
| Neuro-Surgical Intervention of the Spine | Gleno-Humeral Complex |
| P. T. Evaluation & Treatment — Cervical Spin | Advances in Wound Care Management |
| P. T. Therapy Approach to Ob/Gyn | Aquatic Rehabilitation Systems |

**LICENSES**

Licensed Physical Therapy Assistant, License #601.

**AFFILIATIONS**

Member, American Physical Therapy Association

**EXPERIENCE**

*With ProActive Therapy, Inc., have been promoted to increasing responsibility by this busy Physical Therapy clinic while playing a key role within the organization due to my special interest and expertise in the area of hand therapy:*

*2001-present:* **ASSISTANT DIRECTOR.** Cary, AL.  Recognized for my leadership and contributions by my promotion to Assistant Director; continued to provide direct patient care and perform all of the duties of a **Licensed Physical Therapy Assistant**.

- Supervised a staff of 15, including Licensed Physical Therapy Assistants, Physical Therapy Technicians, office personnel, and a Staff Therapist.
- Developed and maintained monthly employee schedules, ensuring that the clinic was adequately staffed and coordinating vacation times and sick leave to avoid conflicts.
- Performed DME supply and ordering of medical supplies as well as inventory control.
- Assisted with continuing education and trained other staff members on OSHA and Medicare regulations in order to ensure compliance.

*1995-2001:* **SENIOR LICENSED PHYSICAL THERAPY ASSISTANT.**  Cary, AL. Advanced to this position after only two years with the clinic, accepting responsibilities while still staying focused on my primary task of direct patient care.

- Supervised 3 Licensed Physical Therapy Assistants and Physical Therapy Technicians.
- Served as clinical preceptor for the Physical Therapy Assistant program.
- Assisted with office duties, taking payments and processing insurance forms.
- Administered aquatic therapy, including pool activities for lumbar stabilization and rehabilitation of the upper and lower extremities; performed pool care and maintenance.
- Mentored local high school students in the medical sciences program.

*1990-1995:* **LICENSED PHYSICAL THERAPY ASSISTANT.** Winterville, KY.  Started with ProActive upon completion of my Associate's degree program; provided direct patient care to include general orthopedics, hand therapy, wound care, and home care training.

- Developed a special interest in hand rehabilitation; knowledgeable of flexor and extensor tendon repairs, RSD, work stimulation, and carpal tunnel.

**PERSONAL**

Outstanding personal and professional references are available upon request.

Date

Exact Name of Person
Exact Title
Exact Name of Company
Address
City, State, Zip

**DEAN OF HEALTH SCIENCES**

Dear Exact Name of Person (or Dear Sir or Madam if answering a blind ad):

With the enclosed resume, I would like to make you aware of my interest in joining your faculty in some administrative or teaching role.

As you will see from my resume, I became a tenured faculty member with the University of Johannesburg while also serving as Dean of Health Sciences. As a University Instructor, I lectured in several subjects which included Epidemiology, Public Health, Biochemistry, Pharmacology, Pharmaceutical Chemistry, and Environmental Health. I achieved tenured status in an unusually short time, and I earned a reputation as a popular teacher who could "translate" complex scientific and technical subjects into easily understood language and concepts.

As Dean of Health Sciences, I planned and implemented programs in Medicine, Environmental Health, Pharmacy, Radiography, and Medical Laboratory Technology. In addition to developing numerous budgets for the faculty, I coordinated the Accreditation Program for Registered Pharmacists including the establishment and supervision of the clinical rotations. I wore numerous "hats" at this university which included responsibilities for Student Affairs and curriculum development in addition to serving as External Examiner for the Faculty of Agriculture.

You will also see from my resume that my educational credentials are top notch. I received a scholarship to complete my Master of Science in Biochemistry at Ohio State University, was honored by being named a Hubert Humphrey Fellow by the U.S. Government, and then earned my Master of Public Health at Harvard University.

I can provide outstanding personal and professional references at the appropriate time, and I would be delighted to make myself available for a personal interview at your convenience. Thank you in advance for your professional courtesies.

Sincerely,

Cecilia Denton Scott

# CECILIA DENTON SCOTT

1110½ Hay Street, Fayetteville, NC 28305    •    preppub@aol.com    •    (910) 483-6611

---

**OBJECTIVE**     To benefit an organization that can use a dedicated professional and distinguished scholar with experience in university teaching along with knowledge and management skills related to public health, environmental health, scientific and pharmaceutical research, and medical laboratory technology.

**EDUCATION**     **Master of Public Health,** International Health, Harvard University, Boston, MA, 1993.
- Received a prestigious U.S. Government award as a Hubert Humphrey Fellow, 1992-93.

**Master of Science,** Biochemistry (on scholarship), Ohio State University, Columbus, OH, 1985.

**Bachelor of Science,** Biology/Chemistry, Ohio State University, 1980.

**Diploma of Education,** Post-Graduate, Ohio State University, 1989.

**EXPERIENCE**     **CASE ADMINISTRATOR.** New Brunswick Labour Relations Board, New Brunswick, Canada (2001-present). Am involved in processing a variety of applications and appeals under statutes which include the Labour Relations Act, Occupational Safety and Health Act, Employment Standards Act, and the Environmental Protection Act.

**GENERAL MANAGER.** Dusseldorf Development Co., Ltd., Johannesburg, South Africa (1995-01). Was recruited aggressively and resigned a tenured university position in order to take on this job managing the environmental and safety programs for a prestigious gold and diamond mining company with operations in the Hinterlands of South Africa; recruited, trained, and developed staff for jobs in remote locations.
- Provided technical expertise on proper environmental practices to ensure that the mining operations were in compliance with stipulated regulations.
- Aggressively instituted new safety and public health programs which decreased the incidence of malaria and other communicable diseases and which increased awareness of AIDS and sexually transmitted diseases.
- Was named a Member of the Board of Directors, and was extensively involved in budget preparation and decision making.

**UNIVERSITY INSTRUCTOR & DEAN OF HEALTH SCIENCES.** University of South Africa, Johannesburg, South Africa (1985-94). As a University Instructor who became a tenured faculty member, developed curriculum and lectured in several subjects which included Epidemiology, Public Health, Biochemistry, Pharmacology, Pharmaceutical Chemistry, and Environmental Health; as Dean of Health Sciences, planned and implemented programs in Medicine, Environmental Health, Pharmacy, Radiography, and Medical Laboratory Technology.
- Coordinated Accreditation Program for Registered Pharmacists to include establishing and supervising clinical field rotations; developed and managed budgets for the faculty.
- Member of the National Planning Team funded by the Pan African Health Organization; member of the Appointments Board responsible for professional recruitment.

**SENIOR LABORATORY TECHNICIAN.** University of Johannesburg (1981-85). For the Faculty of Natural Science, administered laboratory programs for students, coordinated and directed research experiments including research related to indigenous plants for pharmaceutical properties; also procured laboratory materials and equipment and maintained effective control of inventory.

**PERSONAL**     Outstanding references on request. Strong analytical, planning, and administrative skills.

Exact Name of Person
Title or Position
Name of Company
Address (number and street)
Address (city, state, and zip)

## HOME HEALTH CARE REGIONAL DIRECTOR

Dear Exact Name of Person: (or Dear Sir or Madam if answering a blind ad.)

You will see a steady progression of advancement in the resume of this home health care professional. Her industry is expanding, and she is using this resume and cover letter as "fishing bait" to catch the best job.

With the enclosed resume, I would like to indicate my interest in your organization and my desire to explore employment opportunities.

As you will see from my enclosed resume, I am an experienced home health care manager currently excelling as Regional Director of 12 branch offices with 35 administrative personnel reporting to me. Although I am held in high regard by my current employer and can provide excellent references at the appropriate time, I am attracted to your company because of its #1 ranking in the home health care industry.

I hope you will welcome my call soon to arrange a brief meeting at your convenience to discuss your current and future needs and how I might serve them. Thank you in advance for your time.

Sincerely yours.

Terri Alligood

Alternate last paragraph:
I hope you will call or write me soon to suggest a time convenient for us to meet and discuss your current and future needs and how I might serve them. Thank you in advance for your time.

# TERRI ALLIGOOD

1110½ Hay Street, Fayetteville, NC 28305 • preppub@aol.com • (910) 483-6611

**OBJECTIVE**  To offer my strong background in health care management to an organization that can use a mature professional known for leadership and self-motivation as well as analytical and problem-solving abilities which enhance my practical nursing and patient care skills.

**EXPERIENCE**  *Advanced in administrative roles with Comprehensive Home Health Care, Atlanta, GA:*
**REGIONAL DIRECTOR.** (2000-present). Oversee operational areas including patient management, regulatory affairs, corporate planning and development, and financial management of 12 branch offices and a work station; manage 35 people in 12 locations.
- Coordinated each office's accounts receivable issues and concerns while working with the accounts receivable supervisor.
- Assisted in the development of and then managed Quality Assurance and Risk Management programs as well as policy and programs in all operating areas.
- Ensured compliance with applicable federal, state, and local laws, regulations, and rules.

**ASSISTANT ADMINISTRATOR** and **DIRECTOR OF PROFESSIONAL SERVICES (DPS).** (1995-00). Continued to function as DPS after earning a promotion to assist the administrator in overseeing activities in each branch office and ensuring that staff members received adequate training and supervision.

**DIRECTOR OF PROFESSIONAL SERVICES.** (1990-95). Held responsibility for managing both clinical and operational activities in the Augusta branch office.

**HOME HEALTH NURSE** and **HOSPITAL COORDINATOR.** (1985-90). Provided home health care to patients while keeping primary care staff informed of the disposition of their patients when they received hospital care; received updates from hospital staff on our patients and developed contacts with their physicians.

**STAFF REGISTERED NURSE.** Numerous locations in SC (1981-85). Ensured that general medical and surgical patients received total nursing care; assessed physical and mental health and recorded information on patient charts; implemented treatment plans.

**EDUCATION**  **Bachelor of Science in Nursing degree,** Orion State University, Orion, MT, 1983; 3.9 GPA.
**Associate's degree in Nursing,** Sandhills Community College, Carthage, NC, 1981; with honors.

**LICENSES**  Received Home Health Nurse certification from the American Nurses' Credentialing Center, October 1995
Licensed Registered Nurse in Georgia, certification number 123245
Licensed Registered Nurse in South Carolina, license number 34578

**AFFILIATIONS**  American Nurse's Association, 1992-present
Georgia Association for Home Care Intermediary Relations Committee, 1995-present
Georgia Association for Home Care Ethics Subcommittee, 1997-01
Georgia Association for Home Care Provider Services Committee, 1996-01

**AWARDS**  Award for Academic Excellence in Nursing, May 2001
Award for Academic Excellence, April 2000
Georgia "Great 100 Nurses," October 2000
Hanni Schultz Memorial Award for Academic Excellence, May 2000

**PERSONAL**  Am results oriented. Have an enthusiastic, caring manner which makes others comfortable. Feel that I offer a well-rounded background of clinical and managerial skills.

Date

Exact Name of Person
Title or Position
Name of Company
Address (number and street)
Address (city, state, and zip)

**HOSPICE CASE MANAGER**     Dear Exact Name of Person:  (or Dear Sir or Madam if answering a blind ad.)

Can you use an articulate and knowledgeable medical professional who offers a reputation as an enthusiastic and energetic individual who excels in communicating with others whether contributing to team efforts, instructing and mentoring other medical professionals, or educating patients and family members?

You will see from my enclosed resume that I offer a solid background of experience as a nursing professional who has often been called on to instruct, educate, and teach. Currently excelling as a Case Manager in Hospice, I manage a case load of up to 21 terminally ill patients, providing supportive care, patient assessment, and education. I joined the staff of San Diego Area Medical Center as a Registered Nurse, and then worked as a Psychiatric Nurse from November of 2000 until I was promoted into my current position.

Although I am highly regarded by my present employer and can provide outstanding references at the appropriate time, I have decided to permanently relocate back to my native Canada. I am interested in exploring career options with companies in the area that can use a highly skilled, dedicated medical professional.

I offer experience in the nursing field, along with knowledge of medical facility operations including case management, data entry, and records management which combine to make me a well-rounded professional. With my enthusiastic and energetic approach and reputation as a compassionate and caring individual, I am certain that I offer a blend of skills, experience, and knowledge which would make me a valuable addition to any organization searching for a versatile and adaptable mature professional.

I hope you welcome my call soon when I try to arrange a brief meeting to discuss your needs and how I might help you. Thank you in advance for your time.

Sincerely,

Samuel Jackson

Alternate last paragraph:
I hope you will call or write me soon to suggest a time convenient for us to meet and discuss your current and future needs and how I might serve them.  Thank you in advance for your time.

# SAMUEL JACKSON

1110½ Hay Street, Fayetteville, NC 28305    •    preppub@aol.com    •    (910) 483-6611

| | |
|---|---|
| **OBJECTIVE** | To offer a combination of experience, education, and strong well-defined personal strengths to an organization that can benefit from my knowledge of the medical field as well as from my communication, teaching, and decision-making skills. |
| **EDUCATION & TRAINING** | Completed a three-year program leading to a **Diploma in Nursing,** Seneca College, Montreal, Quebec, Canada, 1995.<br><br>Began a training program in January 2002 with Comprehensive Home Health Care, San Diego, CA; earning certification to provide home health care on a case-by-case basis. |
| **EXPERIENCE** | **San Diego Area Medical Center, San Diego, CA:**<br>**CASE MANAGER, HOSPICE.** (2001-present). Manage a case load of as many as 21 terminally ill patients, handling admissions processing, patient assessment, and education as well as performing home visits to care for the patient. |

  - Instruct patients and their family members on matters related to pain management, medications and their side effects, and disease process.
  - Conduct weekly meetings (attended every two week by the physician) with the patient's care team to discuss care and treatment of the patient.
  - Provide supportive care and counseling during home visits to terminally ill patients.

**PSYCHIATRIC NURSE.** (2000-01). Transferred from a ward with from five to 10 patients, was selected to provide nursing care for anywhere from four to 12 patients.
Demonstrated the ability to work independently and respond to challenges and change on a demanding ward where communication and interaction were especially important.

**REGISTERED NURSE.** (1998-00). Supervised an L.P.N. and a Patient Care Assistant (P.C.A.) while handling nursing assessments, patient care, and case management for an average patient load of from four to eight at any time.

  - Provided care support which included IV and LAB therapy as well as medication education for patients.
  - Gained experience in patient administration support such as data entry and records management.
  - Implemented a system of checking doctor's orders for accuracy and to prevent errors and then trained other personnel on how to apply this information.
  - Contributed my knowledge and mentoring skills as a preceptor for nursing students.

**REGISTERED NURSE.** Sunnybrook Hospital, Toronto, Ontario, Canada (1996-98). Cited for my communication skills and ability to deal with patients and their families with compassion and concern, provided patient care including dispensing medications through I.V. therapy and oral injections.

  - Was often called on to provide wellness education and predischarge education and was recognized for my ability to explain medical care procedures clearly and simply.
  - Rotated charge nurse duties with other qualified members of the nursing team.
  - Served as a mentor and example for student nurses rotating through the hospital's precepting program. Was a member of the skin care committee.

**MEDICAL TECHNICIAN.** The Hospital for Sick Children, Montreal, Quebec, Canada (1991-95). Worked in a research facility.

| | |
|---|---|
| **PERSONAL** | Am an enthusiastic, energetic, and outgoing individual. Possess the ability to adapt quickly. |

Date

Administrator
Muncy Medical Center
P.O. Box 449
Muncy, IN 89053

In the first job on her
resume,
her skills are shown with
a functional emphasis.
Even though her
previous jobs were not
in the medical field, she
shows her work
experience without gaps.
Don't leave off
experience which you
feel is unrelated. The
employer is curious
about all of your work
experience. (The general
rule
is that you should go
back
at least ten years.)

Dear Sir or Madam:

I would appreciate an opportunity to talk with you soon about how I could contribute to your organization through my experience in the area of medical accounts management.

As you will see from my resume, I currently handle accounting and data entry for a company which has recently computerized its operations while experiencing a 20% growth in patient volume. I am skilled at accounts receivable/payable, billing/collections, insurance liaison, data entry, and customer service within a medical environment.

In previous jobs I excelled in a field dominated by fire and rescue professionals. I started out as a Fire Dispatch Operator for the City of Raleigh and was promoted to Telecommunications Supervisor of Wake County's Emergency Operation Center based on strong work performance and professional recommendations. A hard-working and highly motivated individual, I am always seeking to refine my skills and knowledge. I am certified as an Emergency Medical Technician and trained to provide CPR and other medical support.

You would find me to be a dedicated person who would pride myself on contributing to your goals and objectives. I can provide outstanding personal and professional references.

I hope you will call or write me soon to suggest a time convenient for us to meet and discuss your current and future needs and how I might best serve them. Thank you in advance for your time.

Sincerely yours,

Katie Eubanks

# KATIE EUBANKS

1110½ Hay Street, Fayetteville, NC 28305 • preppub@aol.com • (910) 483-6611

| | |
|---|---|
| **OBJECTIVE** | To contribute to an organization that can use a well-organized young professional who offers outstanding medical accounts management skills along with extensive data entry experience and expert understanding of medical terminology. |
| **EXPERIENCE** | **MEDICAL ACCOUNTS MANAGER.** U.S. Health Services, Raleigh, NC (2001-present). While balancing accounts totaling $190,000 monthly, mastered new computerized accounting procedures as the company expanded to a new automated accounting and billing system; continuously increased my efficiency as patient volume increased by 20%. |

- *Accounts receivable:* Receive and post payments to patients' accounts.
- *Accounts payable*: Prepare a wide range of bills for companies and individuals.
- *Billing/collections*: Bill more than 150 patients monthly; follow up on past due accounts.
- *Insurance billing*: Prepare paperwork for Medicare, Medicaid, and commercial companies for insurance billing purposes.
- *Data entry*: Perform data entry for hundreds of accounts which require numerous entries weekly.
- *Customer service/public relations*: Have earned a reputation as a hard-working professional with a cheerful disposition and a helpful attitude toward the public.

**TELECOMMUNICATIONS SUPERVISOR III.** Wake County Emergency Operation Center, Raleigh, NC (1995-01). Was promoted to this job because of my excellent performance in the job below; was commended for remaining calm in emergencies and for my ability to soothe people in stressful situations while supervising the Emergency Operation Center.

- At a time when the emergency dispatch field was dominated by fire and rescue professionals, became a respected supervisor because of my significant contributions to the city/county when they were enhancing their 911 system.
- Monitored electronic telecommunications equipment; maintained detailed dispatch records for all emergency response.

**FIRE DISPATCH OPERATOR.** City of Raleigh Fire Department, Raleigh, NC (1990-94). Learned to operate complex communications equipment and acquired transcriptionist skills while monitoring multichannel fire and rescue dispatch equipment.

- Made decisions about appropriate equipment to dispatch to emergencies.
- Received a Letter of Congratulation from the Chief of Police and was promoted.

**INSURANCE CLERK.** Mainline Insurance Company, Dallas, TX (1988-90). While operating a wide range of office equipment and learning internal operations of an insurance company, determined correct charges for patients' premiums, and distributed correct insurance policies to both companies and individuals.

| | |
|---|---|
| **EDUCATION** | Studied Computer Programming, Wake Technical College, Raleigh, NC, 1998-99. Completed Supervisory School, Wake Technical College, Raleigh, NC, 1986. Certified Emergency Medical Technician; completed Basic Life Support studies, 1990. |
| **SKILLS** | *Medical equipment*: Skilled in oxygen setup and knowledgeable of equipment used to record vital signs; operate traction equipment. *Medical skills*: Can provide basic life support, CPR, airway management, splinting, bandaging, hemorrhage control, and shock management. |
| **CERTIFICATIONS** | Certified as an EMT and in CPR, State of North Carolina, since 1990. |
| **PERSONAL** | Am a highly motivated person who strives to make a contribution in my job. |

Date

Exact Name of Person
Title or Position
Name of Company
Address (no., street)
Address (city, state, zip)

Dear Exact Name of Person: (or Dear Sir or Madam if answering a blind ad.)

In the back of her mind, this young professional has two main areas of interest. She enjoys medical office environments, and she also enjoys banking and financial services. Although the letter and resume are heavily weighted toward the medical community, she "comes across" as a doer and achiever, and the resume could appeal to many types of employers.

I would appreciate an opportunity to talk with you soon about how I could contribute to your organization through my versatile skills related to medical office operations and financial services as well as through my proven sales ability, initiative, and creativity oriented toward improving the "bottom line."

As you will see from my resume, most recently I played a key role in the start-up of a new orthopedics practice. While developing office systems and office procedures "from scratch," including designing all forms, I used and trained other employees to use UNIX software and made valuable suggestions which the UNIX vendor applied to refine and upgrade the system. Skilled in bookkeeping and insurance claims administration, I have filed insurance claims and performed ICD-9 and CPT-4 coding. I also handled accounts payable/receivable and payroll and acted as Credit Manager. In my previous job at Scotland Memorial Hospital, I was rapidly promoted to coordinate business office systems and supervised a large staff while acting as the "internal expert" on the computer system and software problems.

In earlier experience in the banking field, I was involved in loan administration, supervised teller transactions, and managed credit card accounts. I am skilled in dealing with the public.

I am confident you would find me in person to be a poised communicator and dynamic personality who enjoys solving technical and business problems. I have been told that I am a "natural" for sales, although I personally believe that the ability to sell a product has a lot to do with the salesperson's product knowledge. A fast learner with the ability to rapidly master new areas of knowledge, I am always eager to learn new things and accept new challenges.

I hope you will welcome my call soon to arrange a brief meeting at your convenience to discuss your current and future needs and how I might serve them. Thank you in advance for your time.

Sincerely yours,

Rosalind Rulnick

# ROSALIND RULNICK

1110½ Hay Street, Fayetteville, NC 28305 • preppub@aol.com • (910) 483-6611

---

**OBJECTIVE**

To add value to a company that can use a creative professional and dynamic communicator who offers proficiency with computer software, expertise in managing offices and developing business systems, as well as knowledge of the medical and financial fields.

**EXPERIENCE**

**OFFICE MANAGER**. Gravelley & Associates, Chapel Hill, NC (2000-present). Worked with UNIX software and made numerous suggestions which the UNIX vendor used to upgrade and refine the system; supervised six clerical employees in medical office operations and trained the entire staff in the operation of the computer system.
- *Business development*: Joined this practice during its initial setup and played a key role in helping it become a profitable operation; developed office systems and internal procedures "from scratch" including designing all forms.
- *Insurance claims administration*: Filed insurance claims and performed ICD-9 and CPT-4 coding.
- *Customer service*: Acted as Patient Accounts Representative and Receptionist.
- *Accounting/bookkeeping*: Handled accounts payable/receivable and payroll and acted as Credit Manager.
- *Written communication*: Composed reports, memos, and correspondence.

**BUSINESS OFFICE SYSTEM COORDINATOR**. Scotland Memorial Hospital, Scotland, NC (1996-00). Began with this hospital as a **Patient Account Representative** and was promoted to coordinate all systems in the business office; earned a reputation as a creative problem-solver who could develop efficient and simple new procedures and work flows.
- *Office systems coordination*: Supervised a large staff composed of insurance clerks, file room clerks, mail room personnel, cashiers, and switchboard operators; worked closely with the business manager to interview, hire, and train employees.
- *Customer service*: Supervised four people while overseeing the process of interviewing patients, determining sources of financial aid, collecting past due accounts, and filing insurance claims.
- *Computer consulting*: Acted as the internal expert/consultant on the operations of the computer system used to maintain patient information; performed keying and batching and continuously found innovative new ways of managing data.

**PERSONAL BANKER**. Cape Fear Bank & Trust Company, Raleigh, NC (1993-96). Began with this financial institution as a Sales Finance Secretary and earned rapid promotions in succession to Assistant to Installment Loan Manager; Senior Teller; and Personal Banker.
- *Loan administration*: Approved loan applications, conducted credit history investigations, sold and opened new accounts, and became skilled in solving banking problems.
- *Teller transactions*: Ordered currency and coin from the Federal Reserve, sold financial services, balanced vault and teller windows, trained tellers.
- *Credit card accounts*: Managed Ready Reserve and Master Charge Accounts and computed terms for payment.

**EDUCATION**

Completed two years of college coursework, Raleigh Community College, Raleigh, North Carolina, 1990-92; attended college at night while excelling in my full-time job.

**PERSONAL**

Outstanding personal and professional references on request. Am an adaptable team player who works well under pressure. Creative person who welcomes new learning opportunities. Single; will cheerfully relocate and travel as my employer's needs require.

Exact Name of Person
Exact Title
Exact Name of Company
Address
City, State, Zip

**MEDICAL OPERATIONS
MANAGER**

Dear Exact Name of Person (or Dear Sir or Madam if answering a blind ad):

I would appreciate an opportunity to talk with you soon about how I could contribute to your organization through my experience gained while serving in the U.S. Army where I have advanced ahead of my peers and excelled in roles usually reserved for higher ranking and more experienced personnel.

As you will see from my enclosed resume, I am a versatile and adaptable professional whose experience and training has for the most part been related to medical services as well as with providing security for human and material assets. Having completed more than 4,200 hours of training, I have also been the recipient of honors including the Meritorious Service, two Army Commendations, and five Army Achievement Medals as well as numerous honors for my contributions during the war in the Middle East.

Accomplishments of which I am especially proud include being recognized as "NCO of the Year" from among 1,320 candidates at the Frankfurt Regional Medical Center in Germany; serving as a Drill Sergeant which allowed me to act as a mentor and role model for young people in the early stages of their career; and being part of a team which developed a prototype medical program which was on the "cutting edge" of technology and resulted in reducing training costs for American military personnel.

I am very proud of the track record I have built while serving my country in the U.S. Army and am confident that the skills which have made me successful, productive, and effective are the skills other organizations are looking for. My ability to communicate with and motivate others, my adaptability, my decisiveness, and my coolness under the pressure of rapidly changing priorities and conditions are all qualities I am sure will allow me to continue to contribute in any industry or environment.

I hope you will contact me soon to suggest a time when we might meet to discuss your needs. I can assure you in advance that I could rapidly become an asset to your organization. Thank you in advance for your time.

Sincerely,

Nigel Steven Johnson

Alternate last paragraph:
I hope you will welcome my call soon to suggest a time for us to meet and discuss your current and future needs and how I might serve them. Thank you in advance for your time.

# NIGEL STEVEN JOHNSON

1110½ Hay Street, Fayetteville, NC 28305    •    preppub@aol.com    •    (910) 483-6611

**OBJECTIVE**

To offer my reputation as a quick learner who handles pressure and change with authority and sound judgment, along with my military experience with an emphasis on medical services and law enforcement, to an organization in need of a skilled leader and manager.

**EDUCATION & TRAINING**

Received certification as an **Emergency Medical Technician**, City Colleges of Kansas, 1993. Was an honor graduate of several courses while completing in excess of 4,200 hours of training including Ranger School, the military's "stress test" of mental and physical condition; an instructor training program; and basic and advanced middle management schools.

**SKILLS**

Possess knowledge in areas including **personnel protection, military medical operations, communications equipment, computers, security, urban combat, reconnaissance, surveillance,** and **close quarters combat.**
**Weapons skills:** M16A2, 9 mm, M60 machine gun, up to 50 caliber machine guns, and M203 grenade launcher; am familiar with small arms repair
**Computer knowledge:** MS Word, Excel, and PowerPoint; Windows 3.0 and Windows 95

**EXPERIENCE**

*Consistently selected for roles usually reserved for more experienced, higher-ranking personnel, am excelling in this track record of accomplishments, U.S. Army:*
**MEDICAL OPERATIONS MANAGER.** Ft. Louis, TX (2001-present). Supervise 28 people providing emergency medical care, laboratory, radiology, and patient care support for a 1,500-person task force based at the nation's largest military post worldwide.
- Developed plans which reduced training costs as well as authoring the Standard Operating Procedures for battlefield patient evacuation.
- Control a $2.3 million inventory of vehicles and medical equipment.

**TRAINING, SCHEDULING, AND OPERATIONS SUPERVISOR.** Ft. Winooski, WI (2000-01). Cited for "self-confidence, authority, and enthusiasm," ensured the smooth operation of the U.S. Army's Physician Assistant School including scheduling of 350 students annually and serving as Equal Opportunity Representative.
- Earned several awards and honors in recognition of my contributions during the creation of the Computer Assisted Response Expert for Medical Emergency Decisions (CAREMED) prototype project and was one of only two team members to act as presenters/demonstrators to members of Congress in December 2000.

**MEDICAL CLINIC SUPERVISOR.** Germany (1996-00). Supervised 13 employees in a medical clinic which served a 2,000-person community while acting as the advisor to senior administrators on daily clinic operations and maintaining a $230,000 annual budget.
- Oversaw areas including personnel, finance, physical security, training, counseling, and evaluation preparation in a job usually reserved for more experienced supervisor.
- Cited as creator of a "flawless" facility closure plan, oversaw the project to completion.
- Earned a Meritorious Service Medal and was chosen from 1,320 people as "NCO of the Year" for the Frankfurt Regional Medical Center.

**PATIENT CARE SPECIALIST.** Ft. Flynn, OR, and Saudi Arabia (1995-96). Acted as administrator of a 29-bed unit in a 241-bed medical center and was frequently called on to be Acting Ward Master in his absence.
- Earned numerous medals and awards for my contributions.

**PERSONAL**

Work well in supervisory jobs which require decisiveness and natural leadership skills as well as while contributing to team efforts toward reaching common goals. Secret clearance.

Date

Exact Name of Person
Exact Title
Exact Name of Company
Address
City, State, Zip

**MEDICAL SECRETARY**

Dear Exact Name of Person: (or Dear Sir or Madam if answering a blind ad)

With the enclosed resume, I would like to make you aware of my background as an articulate, self-motivated professional. I would also like to acquaint you with my experience in office management and administration, customer service, personnel management, and staff development as well as with the exceptional leadership, communication, and organizational skills that I could put to work for your company.

As you will see from my resume, I am currently excelling as a Medical Secretary and Transcriptionist at one of the nation's largest and most prestigious teaching hospitals. While building a reputation as a highly skilled and detail-oriented professional, I manage the operation of this busy office, coordinating meeting schedules, preparing all written correspondence, and providing administrative support. In this position as well as in an earlier job with an environmental services company, I have demonstrated my ability to analyze and interpret complex technical and medical information and effectively present this material in nontechnical terms while composing reports and correspondence.

Throughout my career in office management and administration, I have shown exceptional leadership qualities and strong customer service skills. In one position, I directed the work of up to three members of the secretarial staff, setting individual goals for each employee to ensure that all work is accomplished within tight deadlines. In another job, I began with the company as a Receptionist, and was rapidly promoted to oversee administrative and clerical support for the sales department before advancing to a position as the Secretary to the Director of Digital Data Products.

With an Associate's degree in Business Administration from Smithfield Technical Community College, I have a strong educational foundation to support my practical experience. Although I am held in the highest regard by my present employer and can provide excellent references at the appropriate time, I am interested in selectively exploring career opportunities where I can more fully utilize my strong supervisory and staff development skills.

If you can use an experienced and reliable professional whose abilities have been proven in a variety of challenging leadership, administrative, and customer service roles, I hope you will welcome my call soon when I try to arrange a brief meeting to discuss your goals and how my background might serve your needs. I can provide outstanding references at the appropriate time.

Sincerely,

Megan Russell

# MEGAN RUSSELL

1110½ Hay Street, Fayetteville, NC 28305   •   preppub@aol.com   •   (910) 483-6611

**OBJECTIVE**

To benefit an organization that can use a motivated, experienced professional with exceptional communication and organizational skills who offers a background of excellence in positions of responsibility in administrative, office management, and customer service.

**EDUCATION**

Associate's Degree in Business Administration, Smithfield Technical Community College, Smithfield, WI, 1989.

**COMPUTERS**

Familiar with many of the most popular computer operating systems and software, including Windows 3.1, 95, & 98; Microsoft Word and Excel; Lotus Notes; and others.

**EXPERIENCE**

**MEDICAL SECRETARY** and **TRANSCRIPTIONIST.** Wyndam University Medical Center, Smithfield, WI (2001-present). Provide administrative and clerical support at this busy teaching hospital; order prescriptions for patients.

- Built a reputation as an articulate communicator with a strong detail orientation and the ability to handle multiple simultaneous responsibilities while managing office operations.
- Conduct training and staff development for all new medical administrative personnel.
- Program meetings for staff members, coordinating schedules to avoid conflicts.
- Perform medical and administrative transcription from tapes recorded by physicians.
- Familiar with all office automation equipment, including computers, photocopiers, facsimile machines, multi-line telephone systems, etc.
- Proofread, edit, type, and prepare all outgoing correspondence for the office; analyze and interpret complex medical information in order to compile reports.

**ADMINISTRATIVE ASSISTANT.** C-E Environmental, Inc., Smithfield, WI (1995-00). Managed the work load for the office, assigning administrative and clerical duties to the appropriate employee as well as providing training to all new administrative and clerical personnel.

- Directed the work of three employees in the secretarial department, developing individual goals to ensure the office completed all assigned tasks within deadlines.
- Read, interpreted, and analyzed highly technical data while proofreading, editing, and preparing reports and documents related to business development as well as government and private contracts.

With Wandel & Goltermann, Inc., (Smithfield, WI) a high-tech firm selling electrical testing equipment, advanced in the following "track record" of increasing responsibilities:

*1995:* **EXECUTIVE SECRETARY** to the **DIRECTOR OF DIGITAL DATA PRODUCTS.** Provided administrative support to the Digital Data Products department; performed all word processing, secretarial, and receptionist duties as well as overseeing the Director's personal and professional appointment schedule.

*1990-94:* **SALES DEPARTMENT SECRETARY.** Handled written and verbal communications between the company and its customers while also overseeing all office management and administrative support to the sales department staff.

- Scheduled, coordinated, and made all necessary preparations and arrangements for meetings involving the sales force and sales management staff.

*Other experience:*    Excelled in a part-time customer service job with a major food chain.

**PERSONAL**

Excellent personal and professional references are available upon request.

Date

Exact Name of Person
Title or Position
Name of Company
Address (number and street)
Address (city, state, and zip)

Dear Exact Name of Person: (or Dear Sir or Madam if answering a blind ad.)

There are a couple of things you can learn from this resume. Notice that the address line on the resume has two addresses —the address where he currently resides, and the address to which he will be moving shortly. In the first paragraph of the cover letter, he alerts his reader to the fact that he is relocating because of his wife's job. This will reassure the prospective employer that he is not leaving his current position because of work-related problems.

With the enclosed resume, I would like to indicate my interest in your organization and my desire to explore employment opportunities. My wife and I have recently relocated to Atlanta because my wife has been promoted and relocated by her employer, Farmington Industries. We have bought a house and are hoping to make Atlanta our permanent home.

As you will see from my enclosed resume, I have excelled in a track record of outstanding results within the social services and human services field. I am a dedicated social worker who "found my field" after a distinguished "first career" serving in the Air Force in the recreational and transportation fields. As a manager in the Air Force, I thoroughly enjoyed the challenges involved in training and counseling young soldiers, and I was successful in helping many troubled young people turn their lives around and become positive, contributing, and well-adjusted members of society. After military service I earned my Bachelor of Science in Social Work (magna cum laude). As a Social Worker, I have discovered that I have a "gift" for comforting both the young and elderly, and I have been enriched by work experience in hospice, hospital, and mental health environments.

I hope you will welcome my call soon to arrange a brief meeting at your convenience to discuss your current and future needs and how I might serve them. I can provide excellent references. Thank you in advance for your time.

Sincerely yours.

Frederick Hallgarth

Alternate last paragraph:
I hope you will call or write me soon to suggest a time convenient for us to meet and discuss your current and future needs and how I might serve them. Thank you in advance for your time.

# FREDERICK HALLGARTH

*Until 12/15/01:* 1110½ Hay Street, Decatur, GA 28305       (910) 483-6611
*After 12/16/01:* 538 Pittsfield Avenue, Atlanta, GA 58401       (805) 483-6611

---

**OBJECTIVE**

I want to contribute to an organization that can use a dedicated social worker who is known for my caring manner and for my belief that the elderly as well as children deserve to be honored and given a helping hand by sincere, empathetic professionals.

**EDUCATION**

Earned a **Bachelor of Science in Social Work (B.S.W.) magna cum laude** with a 3.83 GPA, Georgia College, Decatur, GA, 1998.

**CERTIFICATIONS**

Certified in CPR and First Aid by the American Red Cross
Received Certification of Completion from a Personal Intervention Course (PIC)

**EXPERIENCE**

**MENTAL HEALTH PROGRAM MANAGER.** Decatur County Mental Health, Decatur, GA (2000-present). In a group home for nine male juvenile sex offenders aged 14-18, monitored and assisted children on a 24-hour-a-day basis.

- Administered prescription medicine for charts; was responsible for safety of my clients.
- Transported clients to appointments and to outings as deemed appropriate by Decatur County Mental Health.
- Became very knowledgeable of the special needs of this particular client population, and excelled in handling and diffusing hostile situations with clients.
- Learned how important it is to assure proper administration of prescription medicines to clients.

**HOSPICE INTERN.** Home Health Care of Decatur, Decatur, GA (1999). Derived enormous satisfaction from this four-month internship in a hospice environment.

- It gave me a great feeling of accomplishment to help someone through his last journey in life in a peaceful way; I also learned that the dying still have much to contribute to those around them, and I greatly enjoyed listening and providing a comforting presence to the little children and the elderly whom I saw die.
- Learned how gratifying it is for people to die in their own natural surroundings.

**SOCIAL WORKER TRAINEE/VOLUNTEER.** Veterans Administration Hospital, Decatur, GA (1996-98). While earning my B.S.W. degree, worked more than 3,000 hours with older people in the Intermediate Ward; became skilled in working with older people with AIDS, Hepatitis C, cancer, and with amputees.

- Functioned as the personal assistant to many elderly people, and took them to doctors' appointments, on outings, and to activities.
- Became a favorite assistant of the nursing staff; often assisted them in various activities.

**TRANSPORTATION SPECIALIST.** U.S. Air Force, various locations (1990-95). Worked in the purchasing, logistics, and transportation field training and managing up to six individuals; became skilled in purchasing items ranging from paper clips to heavy industrial equipment.

- Developed excellent supervisory and personnel administration skills.

**RECREATIONAL SPECIALIST.** U.S. Air Force, various locations (1980-89). Developed a recreational program which was voted "best" in the parent organization while advancing to top management positions in the recreational management field.

- Supervised up to eight recreational assistants while supervising athletic events, overseeing the maintenance of athletic fields, and overseeing a wide range of athletic events, competitions, tournaments, and activities.

**PERSONAL**

Can provide outstanding personal and professional references. Have a true love of geriatric patients and children and feel that they are often the "throwaway citizens" in society.

Date

Exact Name
Exact Title
Exact Name of Organization
Exact Address
City, State zip

Dear Exact Name of Person: (or Dear Sir or Madam if answering a blind ad)

If you want to compare
the resumes and cover
letters of two nursing
home administrators,
compare this resume
with the resume of Ms.
Reese on the following
page. Ms. Spears, unlike
Ms. Reese, has worked
for numerous
organizations.

With the enclosed resume and this cover letter, I would like to make you aware of my interest in being considered for the position of Long-Term Care State Facilitator. In addition to my expert knowledge of nursing center administration and long-term care, I offer a reputation as a highly effective communicator, creative problem solver, and skilled crisis manager.

As you will see from my resume, I am a Licensed Nursing Home Administrator (L.N.H.A.) and have excelled in administrative positions within the nursing care field. In most of my jobs, I have taken on a wide range of problems and have developed and implemented solutions that improved the census, boosted morale, improved staff skills, and resolved a wide range of problems which had resulted in deficiencies.

In my current position, I have decreased deficiencies from eight to one while increasing the census from 87% to 99%. In my previous position, I increased the census from 90% to 97% while decreasing deficiencies from 14 to five. I am skilled at planning, organizing, and directing administrative functions and monitoring conformance to regulatory guidelines. In one job, I took over the management of an organization which was experiencing a variety of staffing problems, and I restored confidence in the staff while improving public relations and profits.

I am well aware of the many significant contributions your organization makes to the long-term care industry. As an administrator, I have utilized the services you provide in inservice training as well as in mediation and problem solving. Based on my understanding of your role within the nursing home and long-term care industry, I feel I could make valuable contributions through my ability to establish and maintain outstanding relationships as well as through my highly professional approach to solving problems within our very unique industry.

I hope you will give me the opportunity to talk with you in person about my interest in this position. I can provide outstanding personal and professional references at the appropriate time, and I can assure you in advance that I am a loyal and hard-working professional who would be a valuable addition to your team. Thank you in advance for your time.

Yours sincerely,


Maureen Spears, L.N.H.A.

# MAUREEN SPEARS, L.N.H.A.

1110½ Hay Street, Fayetteville, NC 28305 • preppub@aol.com • (910) 483-6611

**OBJECTIVE**

To offer my exceptionally strong problem-solving, public relations, marketing, and communication skills to an organization that can use a skilled administrator with expert knowledge of nursing center administration and long-term care.

**EXPERIENCE**

**ADMINISTRATOR.** NC Nursing Center, Charlotte, NC (2000-present). Through my public relations, leadership, and strong administrative abilities, have accomplished numerous ambitious goals which included boosting patient and staff morale, improving staff training and effectiveness, strengthening community relations, and making facility improvements.
- Cut deficiencies from eight to one; increased census from 87% to 99%.

**ADMINISTRATOR.** Dunn Nursing Center, Dunn, NC (1995-00). Took over the management of this organization which experienced a suspension of admissions; was given a provisional license and four months later received a permanent license for the first time in its three-year history.
- Increased the census to 97% from 90%.

**ADMINISTRATOR.** Raleigh Nursing Center, Raleigh, NC (1993-94). Through my management and problem-solving skills, played a key role in "turning around" an 84-bed nursing facility experiencing numerous internal difficulties.
- Just 12 days after I was hired, the facility received its provisional license and, six months later, regained its licensure status; then I recruited, hired, and trained department heads.

**ADMINISTRATOR.** Primary Care of Raleigh, Raleigh, NC (1992-93). Led this 70-bed long-term care facility to show a profit for the first time in four years while also increasing the census from 90% to 95%; reduced aged receivables to 22% of total receivables.
- Planned, organized, and directed all administrative functions and monitored conformance to guidelines promulgated by regulatory agencies.
- Within one month, hired and trained four new department heads and worked with them to dramatically improve the quality of services provided.

**ADMINISTRATOR.** The North Carolina Diabetes Institute, Inc., Morganton, NC (1990-92). Took over the management of an organization that was experiencing a variety of staffing problems; stabilized and restored confidence in the staff while improving public relations, increasing the census, and boosting profits.
- Planned and directed administration for this 56-bed long-term facility.

**EDUCATION & TRAINING**

**A.S. degree, Banking and Finance,** Whetmore College, Reading, PA, 1989.
Completed 50-week **Administrator-in-Training and Medical Terminology Course.**
Licensed Nursing Home Administrator **(L.N.H.A.)** and **CPR** certified.
Completed courses in finance, customer service, word processing, and management.

**PERSONAL**

Outstanding references. Proven leader with strong human relations and communication skills.

Date

ATTN: Box 3151
c/o Oklahoma City Publishing Company
P.O. Box 902
Oklahoma City, OK 89723

## NURSING HOME DIRECTOR AND MEDICAL FACILITY DIRECTOR

No matter how experienced and refined a senior manager might get, a job hunt is still an intimidating exercise filled with anxiety. This nursing home administrator is "leaving home" professionally since she is leaving the only professional home she has ever known.

Dear Sir or Madam:

With the enclosed resume, I would like to make you aware of my interest in utilizing my considerable experience in health care management within your organization.

As you will see from my enclosed resume, I served Elder Village of Oklahoma City as its Licensed Nursing Home Administrator for the past 19 years. In 1999, I resigned from that position in order to seek new opportunities and new challenges. Currently I am working with an in-home care organization as a consultant on a special project which involves its marketing program as well as the correction of several deficiencies recently noted by the Division of Facility Services.

I excelled in every aspect of my job at Elder Village, from public relations, to budgeting, to Medicare and Medicaid insurance billing, to human resources and personnel administration. I am an expert in dealing with matters pertaining to regulation and compliance, and I am proud of the fact that the Division of Facility Services inspected Elder Village on all state and federal compliance and gave the facility a 100% deficiency-free inspection survey result—an almost unheard-of accomplishment.

As I look back over my accomplishments at Elder Village, I am especially proud of my achievements related to human resources administration and personnel management. It was my responsibility to manage a staff of up to 170 people, who included 35 licensed nurses as well as employees involved in dietary, housekeeping, social services, physical therapy, and other activities. I created the organization's human resources policies and procedures, oversaw the development of the organization's first employee manuals, and maintained constant vigilance over personnel files to assure employee compliance with all regulations pertaining to licenses, certifications, and other matters.

If you can use a hard-working professional with vast knowledge related to health care management, I hope you will contact me to suggest a time when we could meet. I can assure you in advance that I have a strong bottom-line orientation and am known for my highly creative approach to problem solving and decision making.

Sincerely,

Myrna Joan Reese

# MYRNA JOAN REESE

1110½ Hay Street, Fayetteville, NC 28305 • preppub@aol.com • (910) 483-6611

---

**OBJECTIVE**

To offer my management, public relations, and customer service skills to an organization that can use a respected manager with proven versatility in business administration.

**LICENSE & CERTIFICATIONS**

Licensed Nursing Home Administrator by the State of Oklahoma.
All areas of health care as it relates to long-term skilled care including certified in CPR, Fire Safety, Drug Management, and other areas.

**EDUCATION**

**Bachelor of Science degree,** Oklahoma State University.
Completed extensive ongoing professional education in all areas related to health care trends and management as well as business administration including budgeting and finance, human resources administration, other areas.

**EXPERIENCE**

*For 19 years, was the administrator of Elder Village of Oklahoma City, a nursing home and medical facility known for the highest quality standards; resigned from this position in order to pursue other opportunities. In May 2001, the Division of Facility Services inspected Elder Village on all state and federal regulations compliance; the facility was given a 100% deficiency-free inspection/survey result. With more than 600 regulations to comply with, this is considered an almost impossible task to accomplish, and my management skills were considered the key to this rare accomplishment.*

ADMINISTRATOR. Elder Village of Oklahoma City, Oklahoma City, OK (1982-01). Took over the management of this facility in 1980 and directed its growth over the next 19 years; Elder Village is a skilled nursing care and heavy rehabilitation facility which employs up to 170 people while providing nursing care and services for 159 patients.

- **State-of-the-art facility:** Provided oversight for numerous renovations and construction projects which resulted in a comfortable home for the 159 residents of this facility that provides services including round-the-clock nursing and physical therapy.
- **Human resources administration**: Developed all human resources policies and procedures; oversaw the development of the organization's first employee manuals. Take pride in the fact that many of the facility's current employees have worked at Elder Village for nearly 20 years.
- **Staff:** Hired and managed the 170-person staff which included 35 licensed nurses as well as employees in all functional areas.
- **Personnel Administration:** Maintained continuous vigilance over personnel files to assure up-to-date compliance of all personnel with regulations pertaining to their licenses, certifications, current CPR, health cards, TB testing, documentation of all time sheet discrepancies, vacation days, paid leave days, leaves of absence, family medical leave, inservice certification, drug testing, and any drug rehabilitation programs.
- **Medicare and Medicaid Insurance billing:** Provided stringent oversight for billing for this facility which was Medicare, Medicaid, and VA Certified.
- **Budgeting and Finance:** Managed budgeting related to $7 million in annual revenues; figured payroll calculations for every payroll period.
- **Quality Assurance:** Developed continuous Quality Improvement Programs for each department and was vigilant in maintaining quality assurance in all departments.
- **Outstanding Reputation in the community and with regulators:** Maintained excellent public relations with physicians, hospitals, health organizations, and patients' families and friends; was monitored by 52 licensing agencies, and handled numerous regulatory visits, announced and unannounced, from the Division of Facility Services, Department of Social Services, Department of Human Resources, Fire Marshal, Health Department, others.

**PERSONAL**

Hardworking. Creative. Honest. Detail Person. People Person. Superior communicator.
Am in excellent health and ready for a new challenge for my management abilities!

Exact Name of Person
Exact Title
Exact Name of Company
Address
City, State, Zip

**OFFICE MANAGER**

Dear Exact Name of Person: (or Dear Sir or Madam if answering a blind ad)

With the enclosed resume, I would like to make you aware of my outstanding track record in the areas of customer service, office administration, human resources, as well as accounting and collections. I would also like to express my interest in exploring employment opportunities within your organization.

As you will see from my resume, since 1999 I have worked as an office manager at a busy dental practice, where I handle a wide range of matters which include responsibility for resolving the most stubborn customer service and financial problems. On a daily basis I deal with insurance companies and patients as I file claims electronically and explain the complexities of insurance benefits to patients. I am also responsible for a wide variety of human resources matters as I coordinate all hiring, implement staff training and continuing education, lead staff meetings, and coordinate performance reviews.

Skilled at operating a computer with the Microsoft Office Suite and Windows, I daily utilize customized software used for scheduling, billing, ledger activities, insurance filing, and other functions.

I have a sunny disposition and am known for my ability to relate gracefully to customers from all backgrounds. I truly enjoy helping others, and I have been praised by my employers for my strong customer service, problem-solving, and decision-making skills. You will notice from my resume that I worked in responsible positions even during high school, when I became a valued employee of a chiropractic office.

I look forward to the opportunity to speak with you soon. Thank you in advance for your time and consideration.

Sincerely,

Jennifer Boose

# JENNIFER BOOSE

1110½ Hay Street, Fayetteville, NC 28305  •  preppub@aol.com  •  (910) 483-6611

**OBJECTIVE**

I want to contribute to an organization that can use a hard-working and congenial professional who is skilled in all aspects of office management and customer service as well as insurance payment processing and collections.

**EDUCATION**

Completing **Associate's degree in Business Management & Human Resources**; have completed the majority of coursework toward this degree at Leeward Community College, Pearl City, HI.

Completed **Medical/Dental Assistant Program**, International Correspondence School.

Have excelled in extensive continuing education as well as on-the-job training related to **customer service, office administration, accounting, collections, billing, and insurance payment processing.**

**EXPERIENCE**

**OFFICE MANAGER.** James D. Kirk, D.D.S., PA, Pearl City, HI (2000-present). Oversee the operation of this busy dental office; have made numerous valuable contributions that improved customer service and profitability for the practice.

**Management and Human Resources:** Supervise personnel while overseeing the smooth implementation of procedures and scheduling; known for my ability to deal tactfully with staff questions and concerns.

- Develop daily personal production goals for doctors and hygienists to ensure that the office consistently meets or exceeds monthly objectives.
- Maintain personnel records pertaining to attendance, performance evaluations, interviews, disciplinary actions, and other matters; coordinate vacation schedules.

**Employee Training:** Act as staff trainer and coordinator of staff training; oversee all office hiring and subsequent training of employees; schedule and arrange staff development and continuing education for each staff member.

- Coordinate, schedule, and lead staff meetings; manage performance planning/reviews.

**Accounting, Payments, and Collections:**

- File insurance daily, to include filing claims electronically; post insurance payments and close claims; post payments to the correct provider.
- Remain abreast of insurance payment changes and annual ADA codes.
- Skilled at deciphering insurance coverage and explaining insurance benefits to patients.
- Prepare monthly statements, make daily bank deposits, and run daysheets.

**Reports:** Monitor statistics for the practice, collecting data, tabulating information, and recording the proceedings of business meetings in order to prepare a variety of written reports including end-of-month reports.

**Marketing:** Assist in developing advertisements; coordinate marketing projects.

**Computers:** Coordinate computer maintenance as well as upgrade training on computers and the training of new personnel on computer operations.

- Researched office management and insurance billing applications and recommended more efficient software for the office; implemented the upgrade, installing the new program to a Local Area Network (LAN) comprised of a server and two workstations.
- Utilize **Microsoft Word** and customized software used for scheduling, ledger activities, reporting, insurance filing, and other matters on a daily basis; perform backup.

**PERSONAL**

Excellent personal and professional references are available upon request.

**PATIENT ACCOUNTS
REPRESENTATIVE**

Dear Exact Name of Person: (or Sir or Madam if answering a blind ad.)

With the enclosed resume, I would like to formally inquire about the possibility of joining your organization in some capacity which could utilize my strong leadership skills, highly motivated personal nature, and proven ability to boost profitability, maximize revenue, and develop solid working relationships.

As you will see from my resume, I completed a course at East Carolina University emphasizing leadership and decision-making skills. In my current position as a Patient Accounts Representative, I was responsible for patient accounts and was praised in a formal written evaluation for "doing an excellent job in keeping the DOS down in both 399 and 601." I was recognized for achieving the highest collection percentage for the month of June, 2001 in my region, which included WV, VA, and NC; I collected 177% of my dollar goal! I am known for my initiative, persistence, and accuracy as well as my organizational skills and cheerful disposition.

If you can use a dedicated, hard-working professional who can quickly become a valuable asset to your organization, I hope you will contact me to suggest a time when we might meet to discuss your needs. I can provide outstanding personal and professional references. Thank you in advance for your time.

Sincerely,


Virginia Franks

# VIRGINIA FRANKS

1110½ Hay Street, Fayetteville, NC 28305  •  preppub@aol.com  •  (910) 483-6611

---

**OBJECTIVE**

To contribute to an organization which could use my strong leadership skills and highly motivated personal nature along with my proven ability to boost profitability, maximize revenue, and develop solid working relationships.

**EDUCATION**

Pursuing Associate of Science degree, Weston Technical Community College, Weston, PA; have completed one year of course work towards an A.S. degree.

Graduated from Weston Senior High School, Weston, PA, 2000.
- During one summer, completed a course at East Carolina University emphasizing leadership and decision-making skills.
- Was elected President of the Beta Club.
- Was elected Captain of my cheerleading squad.
- Traveled to Paris and London in summer 1996, and became familiar with the customs and lifestyle of Europeans.

**EXPERIENCE**

**PATIENT ACCOUNTS REPRESENTATIVE.** Fresenius Medical Care, Weston, PA (2000-present). Have proved my ability to work accurately and cheerfully under the pressure of tight deadlines as Patient Accounts Representative.
- In 2001, was recognized for achieving the highest collection percentage for the month of June in my region, which included WV, VA, and NC; collected 177% of my dollar goal!
- Am responsible for Beckley 1399 and Richmond 1601 patient accounts; was praised in a formal written evaluation for "doing an excellent job in keeping the DOS down in both 399 and 601."
- Assure that transfers are received in a timely manner from billing groups.
- Collect money from insurance companies; have developed a network of contacts within insurance companies so that I now have a working relationship with key personnel.
- Have become known for my initiative and persistence in finding out what is required in order to get claims paid and then always sending out paperwork which is complete and accurate.
- Have been evaluated in writing as "a joy to have working in our office" due to my upbeat nature and cheerful disposition.
- Always produce my reports on time, and am frequently consulted by others in the office about technical matters related to billing procedures.
- Am extremely well organized, and believe in doing a job right the first time.

**SALES REPRESENTATIVE.** KSS School Supplies, Roanoke, VA (2000). In my first job after graduating from high school, acted in an advisory and consulting role to teachers seeking books and supplies used to teach children of all ages.

**SECRETARY.** Greenscape, Inc., Weston, PA (1998-99). In an after-school job during my junior year of high school, worked in a landscaping business answering phones, greeting the public, typing letters, opening mail, and handling nearly every type of office task.

**DATA PROCESSOR.** H&R Block, Weston, PA (1997 and 1998). During my junior and senior years of high school, worked after school for this tax preparation service.

**PERSONAL**

Known as a very hard worker. Am athletic; enjoy softball, volleyball, basketball,

Exact Name of Person
Exact Title
Exact Name of Company
Address
City, State, Zip

**PATIENT ADMINISTRATION SUPERVISOR**

Dear Exact Name of Person: (or Dear Sir or Madam if answering a blind ad)

With the enclosed resume, I would like to offer my experience in the medical record keeping and medical administration field as well as my reputation for sound judgment and ability to meet challenges "head on" and produce results.

As you will see from my resume, while serving my country in the U.S. Army, I earned respect for my accomplishments in supervising and training others to provide timely and accurate services. With strong computer skills and expert technical knowledge of medical records maintenance, patient accountability, insurance, and third-party collections, I have earned three U.S. Army Commendation Medals in recognition of my professionalism and dedication.

Having worked in medical records management in numerous locations worldwide, I have adapted to the varying operational pace at combat hospitals, major medical centers, medical evacuation environments, and support clinics. In each case, I quickly earned respect for my emphasis on customer satisfaction as well as for my positive leadership skills.

If you can use a skilled manager and medical records specialist with excellent computer skills and a reputation for producing results, I hope you will welcome my call soon when I try to arrange a brief meeting to discuss your goals and how my background might serve your needs. I can provide outstanding references at the appropriate time.

Sincerely,


Alex Gaines

Alternate Last Paragraph:
If you can use a skilled manager and medical records specialist with excellent computer skills and a reputation for producing results, I hope you will write or call me soon to suggest a time when we might meet to discuss your needs and goals and how my background might serve them. I can provide outstanding references at the appropriate time.

# ALEX GAINES

1110½ Hay Street, Fayetteville, NC 28305    •    preppub@aol.com    •    (910) 483-6611

---

**OBJECTIVE**

To offer a background of accomplishments and knowledge of medical administration with an emphasis on medical records maintenance, third-party collections, patient accountability, and customer service along with excellent training and supervisory skills.

**EDUCATION, TRAINING, & SPECIAL SKILLS**

Completed extensive training which included the **Patient Administration**, **Army Medical Management Information Systems**, and **Medical Terminology** courses as well as programs on computer software applications and professional leadership development. **Computers:** Studied Computer Programming, Highland Park Junior College, Lansing, MI. Experienced with TAMMIS (accounting and management system), DEERS (Defense Enrollment Eligibility System), CHCS (Composite Health Care System), and ACCESS (medical information system); Windows 98 and 95, Excel, and Word; Unix; Harvard Graphics

**EXPERIENCE**

**DISTRIBUTION SPECIALIST.**   Wal-Mart, Lansing, MI (2001-present). Work in traffic distribution at one of this retail giant's largest distribution centers.

Advanced in the following track record of accomplishment in the medical field while proudly serving my country in the U.S. Army:

**PATIENT ADMINISTRATION SUPERVISOR.**  Ft. Campbell, KY (2001).  Received my third U.S. Army Commendation Medal for "exceptionally meritorious service" as the supervisor of eight people in a combat support hospital.
- Earned praise for my attention to detail while screening more than 1,350 medical records and ensuring important data was contained in preparation for an inspection.
- Set up personnel administration centers in support of two major training exercises: was cited for providing excellent services despite manpower shortages and adverse weather.

**MEDICAL RECORDS MANAGER.**  Walter Reed Army Medical Center, Washington, DC (1997-01).  Maintained, retrieved, and released medical records for 80,000 patients.
- Cited for blending management skills with technical expertise, reduced a paperwork backlog 80% and ensured standards were exceeded despite severe staff shortages.
- Gained extensive experience and knowledge of collections procedures and in dealing with private insurers while supervising seven military and three civilian administrative personnel at the military's largest and most sophisticated medical center worldwide.
- Played a vital role in implementing a new Tricare Insurance System and in the development and implementation of an Outpatient Third-party Collection Program.

**MEDICAL RECORDS SPECIALIST.**   Korea (1996-97). Screened patients to determine their eligibility for medical care in the admissions and outpatient room of a medical evacuation hospital.
- Coordinated paperwork for personnel being airlifted for more extensive care.
- Earned my second U.S. Army Commendation Medal and was especially cited for my high level of technical expertise, positive attitude, and flexibility.

**MEDICAL RECORDS SPECIALIST.** Ft. Lee, VA (1991-96). Provided patient support services in the admissions and benefits/insurance areas while supervising five more-junior medical records specialists. Received a U.S. Army Commendation Medal in recognition of my dedication and professional accomplishments which included processing more than 200,000 inactive medical records during a one-month special project requiring extensive overtime.

**PERSONAL**

Have been cited on numerous occasions as a professional who can be counted on.

Date

Exact Name of Person
Exact Title
Exact Name of Company
Address
City, State, Zip

Dear Exact Name of Person: (or Dear Sir or Madam if answering a blind ad)

With the enclosed resume, I would like to take the opportunity to introduce you to my versatile background and track record of success based in large part on excellent verbal and written communication skills and the ability to sell ideas and concepts to others.

As you will see from my resume, while serving in the U.S. Army I have been highly productive and successful in two diverse career fields. With extensive training and experience in medical applications and a strong customer service orientation, I also consistently exceeded sales goals after being selected to participate in personnel recruiting and marketing activities.

With experience in patient records, accounts, and auditing administration, I have supervised the patient affairs office for a major medical center as well as the treasurer's office insurance support service activities at Walter Reed Army Medical Center. One accomplishment I am especially proud of was being handpicked from among 60 qualified candidates Army-wide as a Consultant at the office of the Army Surgeon General during an automation project. I also made vital contributions which resulted in two separate situations when the hospital in which I was working was in 100% compliance during a JCAHO (Joint Commission on Accreditation of Healthcare Organizations) visit.

I consistently exceeded sales goals and contributed to unit success and recognition as a sales, marketing, and personnel recruiting representative. During one period I achieved an impressive 289% of my goal and I was frequently sought out to share the knowledge which allowed me to effectively prospect throughout the Kenosha area for qualified young people and sell them on the merits of a military career. When I left the military, I received the highest award given for excellence in my field.

I hope you will welcome my call soon when I try to arrange a brief meeting to discuss your goals and how my background might serve your needs. I can provide outstanding references at the appropriate time.

Sincerely,

Rachel K. Williams

# RACHEL K. WILLIAMS

1110½ Hay Street, Fayetteville, NC 28305  •  preppub@aol.com  •  (910) 483-6611

**OBJECTIVE**

To offer a versatile background emphasizing medical records and patient services administration as well as sales and market analysis and to contribute to an organization in need of a mature professional with excellent verbal and written communication skills.

**EDUCATION & TRAINING**

Am pursuing a **degree in Health Information Systems**, Carthage College, Kenosha, WI.
**A.S., Medical Records Administration**, Carthage College, Kenosha, WI, 1987.
Excelled in extensive U.S. Army-sponsored training in patient administrative services and personnel recruiting as well as a leadership development course.

**TECHNICAL KNOWLEDGE**

Troubleshoot and repair medical records computers, software, and components.
Utilize a variety of PC systems with dBase, Microsoft NT, Access, and Enable.

**EXPERIENCE**

Earned several medals and honors for my accomplishments while serving in the U.S. Army:
**SUPERVISOR, PATIENT AFFAIRS OFFICE.** Ft. Kenosha, WI (2000-present). Served as the liaison between the hospital and Army Reserve, ROTC, and National Guard units in order to process personnel and ensure their medical status and suitability for service.
- Became highly knowledgeable of the policies and procedures which allowed diverse units to work together within strict guidelines.
- Played an important role in the facility receiving 100% compliance on its JCAHO (Joint Commission on Accreditation of Healthcare Organizations) inspection.
- Tactfully resolved patient complaints and handled the facility's birth and death statistics.

**PERSONNEL RECRUITING, SALES, AND MARKETING REPRESENTATIVE.** Ft. Kenosha, WI (1993-00). Earned the highest awards possible, consistently set records while prospecting for and "selling" young people on the advantages of a military career in a sales territory based in Kenosha.
- Represented the Army to high school, college, and community leaders while building a high-visibility profile and carrying out awareness and active recruiting activities.
- Achieved the lowest rate of losses for candidates who had agreed to delay their entry into the service until after they completed a school year.
- Cited for high sales levels, in one period I exceeded my goal by an impressive 289%.
- Made contributions which allowed the station as a group to exceed sales quotas on numerous occasions and receive a "Superior Unit Award."
- Was frequently sought out by my peers for my knowledge of recruiting and sales techniques and effective marketing skills.
- Volunteered to work with at-risk teenagers in a statewide assistance program.

**CONSULTANT – PATIENT ADMINISTRATION.** Washington, DC (1990-93). Was handpicked from among 60 qualified applicants to act as the Department of the Army's representative during the developmental testing phase of an automation project – the new Composite Health Care System (CHCS) – at the office of the Army Surgeon General.
- Tested new software, advised civilian developers, and assisted during implementation to ensure the $1.1 billion-dollar automation project was a success.

***Highlights of earlier experience:*** Advanced as a Patient Administration Specialist: played a vital role in an evacuation hospital's 100% compliance during a JCAHO inspection (Korea).

**PERSONAL**

Received several honors including U.S. Army Commendation and Achievement Medals and was a member of a staff which received a Navy Meritorious Unit Commendation.

Date

Exact Name of Person
Exact Title
Exact Name of Company
Address
City, State, Zip

**PATIENT CARE SPECIALIST**

Dear Exact Name of Person: (or Dear Sir or Madam if answering a blind ad)

I would appreciate an opportunity to talk with you soon about how I could contribute to your organization through my experience, education, and training in the medical field and knowledge of medical procedures.

As you will see from my enclosed resume, I have built a reputation as a skilled and talented young professional who is dedicated to the medical profession. While serving my country in the U.S. Army, I received extensive training as a medical specialist with an emphasis on orthopedic surgery and care. I received several medals and awards for my professionalism and for effectiveness while working in jobs as many as three skill levels above my assigned level. My adaptability and versatility have been displayed while providing patient care in a medical clinic and on frequent exercises and projects with a combat engineering unit with worldwide missions.

I am on the national registry of Emergency Medical Technicians and a Certified Nursing Assistant as well as being certified in Combat Lifesaving, First Aid, and CPR. I am also pursuing an Associate in Science degree at Tiffin Technical Community College.

If you can use an experienced medical technician who is adaptable, dedicated, and willing to work hard to achieve success, I hope you will contact me to suggest a time when we might meet to discuss your needs. I can assure you in advance that I could rapidly become an asset to your organization.

Sincerely,

Scott Cleaves

# SCOTT CLEAVES

1110½ Hay Street, Fayetteville, NC 28305    •    preppub@aol.com    •    (910) 483-6611

**OBJECTIVE**     To contribute through my medical skills and knowledge of medical procedures to an organization that can use a self-motivated young professional who is recognized as a dedicated and exceptionally skilled individual.

**EDUCATION**     Am pursuing an Associate in Science degree, Tiffin Technical Community College, Tiffin, OH. Attended the U.S. Army's General Medical Orientation, Medical Specialist, Orthopedic Specialist Phase I, and Orthopedic Specialist Phase II Courses.

Completed numerous correspondence courses through the U.S. Army Academy of Health Sciences, Ft. Sam Houston, TX, including: Operating Room Specialist Sustainment, Practical Nurse Preparatory, and Practical Nurse Sustainment Courses.

**TRAINING &**     Attended training programs leading to certification in these areas:
**CERTIFICATIONS**    Emergency Medical Technician — am on the National EMT Registry

Certified Nursing Assistant I

Combat Lifesaving

CPR and First Aid

Completed nonmedical training programs including airborne, bus driver training, hazardous materials handling and certification, and combat engineering courses as well as professional leadership development courses.

**EXPERIENCE**     *Have built a reputation as a talented young medical specialist, U.S. Army:*

**PATIENT CARE SPECIALIST** and **INSTRUCTOR.** Ft. Bragg, NC (2000-present). In a medical clinic setting, provided assistance for all phases of inpatient and outpatient care as well as simultaneously acting as an instructor in various medical subjects.

- Handled direct patient care which included conducting medical examinations, collecting and preparing specimens for lab analysis, and administering immunizations.
- Maintained accurate and up-to-date medical records on each patient.
- As an Instructor for personnel in an engineering organization, taught classes in subjects ranging from first aid and CPR; to inventory control including ordering supplies, equipment, and medications; to the proper procedures for supervising clinical and field medical facilities.
- Was awarded Armed Forces Expeditionary and Humanitarian Service Medals for my contributions to the success of operations in Honduras.
- Received the Army Commendation Medal for "meritorious achievements" while supervising supply operations during a large-scale training exercise, a job usually reserved for a professional three skill levels higher; developed sources for hard-to-find items and reduced duplications, thereby saving countless manhours and funds.
- Recognized with an Army Achievement Medal for efforts during an exercise in Georgia with an engineering unit, identified and treated two people for the early signs of heat injuries and saved them from potentially life-threatening conditions.
- Received an Achievement Medal for sustained performance during activities which included independent leadership of a cleanup crew following Hurricane Fran in North Carolina, establishment of two base camps in Haiti which are still in use, leading a construction team in Puerto Rico, and accident-free driving records in numerous projects.

**ORTHOPEDIC TECHNICIAN.** Lancaster, PA (1996-00). Worked in a field hospital environment where my responsibilities included assisting doctors during minor orthopedic surgical procedures and with patient care.

**PERSONAL**     Offer a reputation as a hard worker who can be counted on to work well with others.

**PATIENT REGISTRATION SPECIALIST**

Dear Sir or Madam:

With the enclosed resume, I would like to make you aware of my background in medical, insurance, customer service, and sales environments. I am interested in exploring employment opportunities with your organization and offer exceptional communication and organizational skills which I could put to work for you.

As you will see from my resume, I am currently excelling as a Patient Registration Specialist for the Emergency Room at Irwin-Klein Memorial Hospital. I tactfully deal with patients from diverse backgrounds in a fast-paced work environment in order to obtain vital information and provide outstanding customer service. Although I am highly regarded by my present employer and can provide excellent references at the appropriate time, I am interested in exploring career opportunities with other companies that can use a dedicated hard worker.

Throughout my experience in customer service and sales, I have built a reputation as an articulate communicator who is adept at handling difficult customer service situations. A persuasive and effective salesperson, I quickly develop a rapport by focusing on the customer's concerns and emphasizing my desire to see their needs met.

If you can use an enthusiastic young customer service professional with a background in challenging medical, insurance, and sales environments, then I hope you will contact me to suggest a time when we might meet to discuss your goals and how my background might serve your needs. Thank you in advance for your time.

Sincerely,

Alisa Maria Colvin

# ALISA MARIA COLVIN

1110½ Hay Street, Fayetteville, NC 28305   •   preppub@aol.com   •   (910) 483-6611

---

**OBJECTIVE**

To benefit an organization that can use an enthusiastic young professional with strong communication and organizational skills who offers a background of excellent performance in medical, insurance, customer service, and sales environments.

**EXPERIENCE**

**PATIENT REGISTRATION SPECIALIST.** Irwin-Klein Memorial Hospital, Tacoma, WA (2001-present). Provide exceptional customer service while interviewing patients in a fast-paced environment to obtain registration information.
- Determine the reason for the patient's visit in order to facilitate prioritizing cases according to the severity of each individual's condition.
- Admit patients into the hospital, entering patient information into the Meditech system and editing or updating information for follow-up or repeat visitors.
- Register orders for laboratory testing, perform complete breakdown of patient charts, and discharge patients from Emergency Room care.

**CUSTOMER SERVICE REPRESENTATIVE.** Northwest Insurance Company, Tacoma, WA (2000-01). Processed a heavy volume of inquiries from customers, medical offices, and other service providers concerning verification of benefits and resolution of claims.
- Verified benefits and coverage for hospitals and doctors' offices in order to ensure that customers were approved for treatment.
- Effectively responded to a variety of questions and complaints from customers who were calling to correct or determine the status of their medical claims.
- Processed medical claims for doctors and hospitals seeking reimbursement for service provided to our customers.

**SALES REPRESENTATIVE.** Dress Cove, Tacoma, WA (1999-00). Became known for my highly developed customer service skills while assisting store patrons in the selection and purchase of fine clothing, accessories, and related merchandise.
- Created effective, eye-catching displays; stocked, straightened, and merchandised my assigned area of the store.
- Operated a cash register and took credit card, check, and cash payments.

**SALES REPRESENTATIVE.** Memory Lane, Tacoma, WA (1999). Provided customer service, presented information on the cameras, videocassette recorders, and related merchandise that the store sold, and closed the sale.
- My strong product knowledge and natural sales ability allowed me to effectively persuade customers to purchase items; developed rapport with individuals.

Other experience:
- In my spare time, utilize my exceptional customer service and sales abilities as a highly effective **SALES REPRESENTATIVE** for the Avon line of cosmetics.
- While attending college, exercised my strong written communication skills as a **REPORTER**, authoring articles on student life, sports, and academic affairs for the school's newspaper, *"The Observer."*

**EDUCATION**

Completed nearly two years of college-level course work in Telecommunications and Medical Assistant programs, Central Washington State University and Ellensburg Regional Community Technical College, Tacoma, WA.

**COMPUTERS**

Familiar with Meditech patient registration system and word processing programs.

In this section, you will find resumes and cover letters of experienced nursing professionals. We have devoted a complete section to nurses because many feel that nursing professionals are the backbone of the medical profession.

**Junior nurses may have advantages over more experienced nurses.**
In a job hunt, junior nurses may often have an advantage over their more experienced counterparts. Prospective employers often view them as "more trainable" and "more coachable" than their seniors.

**Junior nurses may have disadvantages compared to their seniors.**
Almost by definition, the junior nurse is less tested and less experienced than senior or mid-level nursing professionals, so the resume and cover letter of the junior nurse may often have to "sell" his or her potential to do something he or she has never done before. Lack of experience can be a stumbling block to the junior nurse, but remember that many employers believe that someone who has excelled in one area of nursing can excel in other areas.

Junior nurses are often still experimenting in their careers, and they have more freedom than older job hunters to try new areas within the nursing field.

**Looking for a career change?**
A great resume to examine if you want to see a nurse in career change is the resume and cover letter of Carmen Santiago on pages 18 and 19. She is an experienced nursing professional who is seeking to apply for a newly created position within the medical center where she currently works. You will see how she focuses her cover letter on the credentials and experience which are most relevant to the job she wants.

**Some advice to junior nurses...**
If senior nurses could give junior managers a piece of advice about careers, here's what they would say: Manage your career and don't stumble from job to job in an incoherent pattern. Try to find a niche or niches within nursing that interest you, and then identify prosperous industries which need work performed of the type you want to do. Learn early in your working life that a great resume and cover letter can blow doors open for you and help you maximize your salary.

**A CURRICULUM VITAE**

Dear Dr. Smith:

With the enclosed curriculum vitae describing my credentials and experience, I would like to introduce myself and express my interest in exploring employment opportunities with you as a Family Nurse Practitioner.

As you will see from my CV, I am currently finishing a Master of Science in Nursing in the Family Nurse Practitioner Program at Duke University School of Nursing. I am excelling academically and maintaining a 3.5 GPA while working full-time as an Emergency Room Nurse. I previously earned a B.S.N. and A.D.N.

One of my distinctive areas of competence is my extensive background in critical care nursing. As a Registered Nurse in the Emergency Department at Womack Army Medical Center, I supervise Licensed Practical Nurses and Medics. I expertly oversee emergency nursing, clinical nursing, and triage nursing.

In previous experience as a Critical Care Nurse Specialist in Colorado, I provided post-operative care to surgical patients in these areas: general surgery; cardiovascular, vascular, and thoracic; neurology; urology; reconstructive plastic surgery; pediatric; acute trauma; acute head trauma; multisystem failure; and orthopedic. In prior positions, I worked as a Critical Care Registered Nurse in a Cardio-Thoracic Intensive Care Unit and other Intensive Care Units as well.

I am genuinely excited about the medical care I will be able to provide as a Family Nurse Practitioner, and I have a special interest in women's health. You would find me in person to be an exceptionally strong communicator who is well equipped for the challenges of teaching and educating patients about their illnesses and treatments. As you can see from the fact that I have embarked on the adventure of obtaining my master's degree, I am an extremely hard worker who is committed to refining my skills and abilities to the highest level. Quality care is always my focus, and I am seeking a position in a practice that will value an ambitious and dedicated professional who could enhance the image and patient care of the practice.

I hope we will have the opportunity to meet in person, and I would ask that you contact me to suggest a time and place for us to meet in person if my considerable skills and talents are of interest to you. Thank you in advance for your time.

Sincerely,

Margaret Smith

# MARGARET SMITH, B.S.N., R.N.

1110½ Hay Street, Fayetteville, NC 28305   •   preppub@aol.com   •   (910) 483-6611

---

## *Curriculum Vitae*

### Professional Credentials

**Licensed Registered Nurse**, North Carolina (Certificate #CYZ1230)
**Certified** as an **Advanced Cardiac Life Support (ACLS), Neo-natal Life Support (NALS), Pediatric Advanced Life Support (PALS),** and **Basic Cardiac Life Support (BCLS)**
Provider by the American Heart Association.
Passed AACN-approved critical care course, 1987.

### Professional Organizations

Inducted into Phi Theta Kappa National Honor Society
Member of the following professional organizations:
- American Association of Nurse Practitioners, 1991-present
- American Association of Critical Care Nurses, 1992-present
- Society of Critical Care Medicine, 1993-present

### Education

Finishing **Master of Science in Nursing, Family Nurse Practitioner Program**, Duke University Medical Center, Durham, NC; will graduate May 2003.
- Currently maintaining a 3.5 GPA in this rigorous program while working full-time as an Emergency Room nurse.

Completed Pre-Med prerequisite courses, Community College of Aurora, Aurora, Colorado, May 2000.
**Bachelor of Science in Nursing (B.S.N.) Degree** from Thomas Jefferson University, Philadelphia, PA, 1995.
**Associate of Science Degree in Nursing (A.D.N.)**, Harrisburg Area Community College, Harrisburg, PA, 1987.

### Residency

Dr. Demitri Anjelis, MD, Family Practice, Philadelphia, PA

### Clinical Rotations for Duke University
### Family Nurse Practitioner Program

- **Sexual and Reproductive Health** —three-month rotation with Drs. David Schuster and Guy Peters, Charlotte Obstetrics & Gynecology, Charlotte, NC (2001).
- **Child Health in Family Care** —three-month pediatric rotation with Dr. Masoud Caxton, Pediatrics & Adolescent Medicine, Chapel Hill, NC (2001).
- **Internal Medicine** —three-month rotation in internal medicine with Dr. Rudy Alfano, Internal Medicine & Acute Care Clinic, Burlington, NC (2000).
- **Acute and Chronic Health Problems** —three-month rotation with Drs. Robert Burton and Paul Dickson, Group Family Practice, Greensboro, NC (2000).

### Publications and Papers

Published a Focus on Critical Care article, *"Panic and Concerns of Our Health Care Colleagues,"* published in 1995.

Personally completed most of the research for and co-authored a research paper, *"AnimalCare as a Nursing Intervention to Decrease the Stress Response in the Critically Ill Patient."*

### Teaching Experience

Prepared and presented an instructional seminar on "Concepts of Celebrex Consumption."

### Experience

**REGISTERED NURSE, EMERGENCY DEPARTMENT.** Womack Army Medical Center, Fort Bragg, NC (2000-present). Supervise Licensed Practical Nurses and Medics at this major military medical center.
Performed the following types of nursing:
- Emergency nursing
- Clinical nursing
- Triage nursing

*Started with Fitzsimmons Army Medical Center in Aurora, Colorado as an* **INDIVIDUAL CONTRACT NURSE** *in the Surgical Intensive Care Unit* (1995-97; *when the contract ended, applied and was selected for a position as a* **NURSE SPECIALIST, GS-11.** (1997-2000).
- Provided post-operative care to surgical patients in the following areas:
  - General Surgery
  - Cardiovascular, vascular, and thoracic
  - Neurology
  - Urology
  - Reconstructive plastic surgery
  - Pediatric
  - Acute trauma
  - Acute head trauma
  - Multisystem failure
  - Orthopedic
- Utilized Marquette monitoring systems.
- Analyzed components of oxygen delivery and consumption in treating patients.
- Was nominated for the Nightingale Award in 1998.

**REGISTERED NURSE, CRITICAL CARE UNITS.** Swedish Medical Center, Englewood, CO (1995-1997).
- Provided pre-operative, post-operative, and operating room critical care nursing to the following classes of patients:
  - Post-operative open heart surgery
  - Post-operative general surgery
  - Acute spinal cord injury
  - Acute trauma
  - Acute head trauma
  - Acute MI
  - Multi-system failure
- Utilized Siemens monitoring systems and clini-comp computers for nursing.
- Served as a member of the open heart surgery team.

**REGISTERED NURSE, INTENSIVE CARE UNITS A & B.** Phily Medical Center, Philadelphia, PA (1987-1989 and 1990-1995). Provided immediate postoperative nursing care for open heart surgery patients and acute MI patients.
- Worked with both medical and surgical IABP-Therapy patients.
- Handled TPA-Therapy for acute MI patients.
- Rendered expert care to patients requiring Ventricular Assist Devices.
- Utilized state-of-the-art Hewlett-Packard monitoring and telemetry systems for patient care.

**CLINICAL COORDINATOR** and **REGISTERED NURSE.** Central Pennsylvania Cardiac, Thoracic, and Vascular Surgeons, Philadelphia, PA (1990). Performed preoperative and postoperative patient education for individuals recovering from cardiac, vascular, and thoracic surgical procedures.
- Provided counseling and support for patients and family members.

## Volunteer Experience

With Habitat for Humanity Project in Boston, MA, investigated issues associated with and assisted the hungry and homeless population of the Harrisburg community, to include working in several area soup kitchens.

*Excellent personal and professional references are available upon request.*

**CERTIFIED NURSE AIDE**

Dear Sir or Madam:

With the enclosed resume, I would like to make you aware of my background as a dedicated Certified Nurse Aide whose exceptional organizational and patient care skills have been proven in a challenging mental health/developmentally disabled, long term care, and home health environments.

As you will see from my resume, I completed the Certified Nurse Aide program through The Beagleton of Houndville, and received my licensure from the West Virginia Board of Nursing in 2000. In positions as a Certified Nurse Aide in long-term care and home health environments, I have demonstrated my ability to work independently while interacting with nursing staff and physicians to provide the highest possible levels of patient care.

Earlier as a Health Care Technician at a group home for clients with severe/profound mental and physical disabilities, I monitored and recorded behavioral changes to assist the physician in determining appropriate medication and course of treatment. I programmed individual and group activities designed to improve developmental skills and increase client independence, and worked closely with clients and their families to teach and refine socialization skills.

If you can used a skilled Certified Nurse Aide with experience in a variety of challenging clinical environments, I hope you will welcome my call soon when I try to arrange a brief meeting to discuss your goals and how my background might serve your needs. I can provide outstanding references at the appropriate time.

Sincerely,

Barkley M. Basset

# BARKLEY M. BASSET

1110½ Hay Street, Fayetteville, NC 28305 • preppub@aol.com • (910) 483-6611

| | |
|---|---|
| **OBJECTIVE** | To contribute to an organization that can use a versatile, hard-working young professional who offers a track record of accomplishments both as a Certified Nurse Aide in developmental and home health environments, as well as in distribution, warehousing, and supply. |
| **EDUCATION & TRAINING** | Completed the Certified Nurse Aide certification program through The Beagleton of Hieton, Houndville, WV, 2000. <br> Excelled in numerous training courses in leadership and management, supply and inventory control, personnel administration, and computer operation sponsored by the U.S. Army. |
| **CERTIFICATIONS** | Certified Nurse Aide, West Virginia Board of Nursing, Houndville, WV, 2000-present. Community CPR certification (adult, child, and infant), American Heart Association, expires 11/03. |
| **EXPERIENCE** | **CERTIFIED NURSE AIDE (PRIVATE DUTY).** Houndville, WV (2001-present). Provided exceptional in-home care to a bedridden patient; performed patient assessment, monitored vital signs, and ensured that the patient was responding appropriately to treatment. |

- Assisted with feeding and fed the patient when necessary, as well as helping the patient perform basic personal hygiene, bathing, grooming, and dressing.

**CERTIFIED NURSE AIDE.** Beagleton of Houndville, WV (2000). Completed re-certification as a Nurse Aide at Beagleton, then accepted this position, assisting the nursing staff and physicians in providing direct patient care services to elderly and bedridden individuals in this long-term care facility.

- Measured patient's vital signs and administered oxygen by nose feeder, mask, or tent.
- Assisted with catheterizations, set-up and monitored feeding pumps, and performed accuchecks to measure blood sugar levels of diabetic patients while also handling wound care, enemas, etc.
- Assisted clients with personal hygiene, dressing, bathing, grooming, and feeding; encouraged and prepared the patient to achieve greater independence in daily living.

**RESIDENT HEALTH CARE TECHNICIAN.** Stimplekins Associates, Houndville, WV (1999-00). In a group home for handicapped and disabled children, programmed developmental and educational activities for individual clients and for the group; provided supervision daily and during outings.

- Monitored patient behavior and reported any incidences to the appropriate staff member while providing care to patients with severe/profound mental and physical disabilities.
- Completed PIC training; developed skills in subduing violent patients.

**SUPERVISOR & INVENTORY MANAGEMENT SPECIALIST.** U.S. Army, Ft. Bark, WV (1994-99). Gained a varied and well-rounded base of experience in the supply field while providing support to several different types of companies; qualified to operate forklifts up to 12,000 lbs.

- Provided leadership to as many as 20 personnel involved in stock record keeping and inventory management; developed knowledge in different types of work environments.
- Controlled equipment listings and count cards for multimillion-dollar inventories.
- Provided support for high-ticket items as copiers and fax machines.

| | |
|---|---|
| **PERSONAL** | Am a fast learner who strongly believes in always giving 100%. Excellent references. |

Date

**CERTIFIED NURSE AIDE**

Dear Sir or Madam:

I would appreciate an opportunity to talk with you soon about how I could contribute through my skills and experience as a Certified Nurse Aide (CNA).

As you will see from my enclosed resume, I graduated from a 420-hour course in Anniston, AL, and was the top student in my class with a 98.1 GPA. Since earning this certification, I have also completed a Piedmont Technical Community College course and was certified in CPR.

Presently attending PTCC in the General Studies program, I offer experience as a CNA and have worked in both home health care and nursing home settings. When I worked for a home health care organization, I provided services which included taking vital signs and recording them as well as helping patients with range-of-motion exercises, bathing, dressing, feeding, and other aspects of personal care.

Earlier for two health care centers in Alabama, I learned to work on a team which joined together in providing the best possible care for residents. I received several Letters of Recommendation for my efforts in supporting the welfare of patients. I took vital signs and entered information on charts, monitored medication, and assisted patients with many aspects of personal care.

If you can use a caring and compassionate young professional with strong patient care skills, I hope you will contact me to suggest a time when we might meet to discuss your needs. I can assure you in advance that I could rapidly become an asset to your organization.

Sincerely,

Jessica Rodriguez

# JESSICA RODRIGUEZ

1110½ Hay Street, Fayetteville, NC 28305　•　preppub@aol.com　•　(910) 483-6611

---

**OBJECTIVE**　　To offer excellent nursing skills in an environment where superior communication and motivational abilities would be beneficial and the ability to work well independently and as a contributor to team success would be valued.

**EDUCATION**　　Pursuing an Associate's degree, Piedmont Technical Community College, LA.
Graduated from Piedmont High School, Piedmont, LA, 2000: displayed a high level of self-motivation and ability to handle my time effectively while working in a fast-food restaurant after school and on weekends and volunteering in the school library.

**TRAINING**　　Graduated from the 420-hour CNA course, Anniston Assessment Center, AL, 1997.
* Achieved the highest average in the class with a 98.1 GPA.

**CERTIFICATIONS**　　*Certified Nurse Aide (CNA),* Anniston, AL, 1997.
*CPR,* Piedmont, LA, 2001.

**SPECIAL SKILLS**　　*Patient care skills:* have operated a Hoyer lift and changed IV bags
* Take vital signs and keep accurate charts and patient records
* Assist patients with personal care – feeding, bathing, dressing, and moving around
* Monitor medications

*Other:* offer basic computer knowledge and can type

**EXPERIENCE**　　**CERTIFIED NURSE AIDE (CNA).** Southern Hospitality Home Health, Piedmont, LA (2001-present). Contributed to the care of home-bound patients in such areas of support as taking vital signs as well as helping bathe, feed, and dress patients.
* Provided patients with help doing range-of-motion exercises which would in turn allow them more freedom and in many cases lead to an eventual return to independence.
* Cooked and cleaned patients' homes and instructed them in hygiene and personal care.
* Assisted patients to the bathroom and helped them move around inside the home.
* Applied my communication skills working with patients with a variety of conditions and prognoses.
* Became known for my dependability and punctuality.

**CNA.** Manor Pines Nursing Center, Anniston, AL (2000-01). Learned to be part of a team working together to provide patients with the best possible care.
* Provided direct patient care which included taking vital signs and charting daily activities participated in by patients under my care.
* Assisted patients with dressing, feeding, bathing, and walking and encouraged them to take responsibility for whatever they could do on their own.

**CNA.** Piedmont Health Care Center, Piedmont, AL (1997-99). Received several Letters of Recommendation for my efforts on behalf of the patients and my professionalism while developing excellent nursing skills and a reputation for dedication.
* Took vital signs and entered information on the individual patient's chart.
* Monitored medications and helped give enemas.
* Charted intake and output.

**PERSONAL**　　Am a team player who works well independently. Have a reputation as a creative, dedicated hard worker. Skilled in handling multiple tasks and seeing each is done correctly. Excellent references are available.

Date

Exact Name of Person
Exact Title
Exact Name of Company
Address
City, State, Zip

**CERTIFIED NURSING
ASSISTANT**

Dear Exact Name of Person (or Dear Sir or Madam if answering a blind ad)

With the enclosed resume, I would like to make you aware of my background as an experienced and reliable professional with exceptional customer service skills who offers experience in medical, office administration, and other environments requiring attention to detail and strong people skills.

As you will see, I have recently completed the Certified Nursing Assistant I & II program from Langston Technical Community College and received my certification from the Michigan Board of Nursing. While completing this program, I completed internships at Langston Medical Center and Highland House of Langston, a local long-term care facility. I provided patient care in support of the nursing staff, taking vital signs, monitoring catheters and IVs, and changing IV bags. I performed wound care, cleaning wounds and replacing bandages, as well as feeding, cleaning, bathing, and turning patients. At Highland House of Langston, I was additionally responsible for the care of elderly and bedridden patients, including Alzheimer's patients. I feel that my strong combination of education, practical experience, and genuine compassion for my patients would make me a valuable addition to your operation.

If you can use a motivated, hard-working professional who is dedicated to providing quality patient care and offers a track record of success in customer-focused environments requiring attention to detail, then I look forward to hearing from you soon. I assure you in advance that I have an excellent reputation, and would quickly become an asset to your organization.

Sincerely,

Lisa Niles

# LISA NILES

1110½ Hay Street, Fayetteville, NC 28305　　•　　preppub@aol.com　　•　　(910) 483-6611

| | |
|---|---|
| **OBJECTIVE** | To benefit an organization that can use an experienced and dependable  professional with extensive experience working in medical and other environments where attention to detail and quality customer relations are emphasized. |
| **CERTIFICATIONS** | Certified Nurse Aide I & II, listing #026943, Michigan Board of Nursing, expires 2003.<br>Certified in Adult & Child CPR, American Heart Association, expires 2002. |
| **EDUCATION** | Completed the course of study for Certified Nursing Assistant I and II, Langston Technical Community College, Langston, MI, 2001.<br>• Was evaluated as a "delightful student who performs well with patients." |
| **EXPERIENCE** | **CERTIFIED NURSING ASSISTANT.** Langston Medical Center and Highland House of Langston, Langston, MI (2001). While completing a two-month internship, provided general patient care in support of the nursing staff at this large local long-term care facility.<br>• Took vital signs; monitored catheters and IVs; changed IV bags.<br>• Performed wound care, cleaning wounds and replacing bandages.<br>• Performed colostomies and conducted blood sugar tests.<br>• Fed, cleaned, bathed, and turned patients; changed bedding.<br>• At Highland House, was additionally responsible for care of elderly and bedridden patients, including Alzheimer's patients.<br><br>**SECRETARY.** Stanley Steemer, Langston, MI (1999-00). Performed administrative, clerical, and receptionist function for this busy location of the nationwide carpet cleaning company.<br>• Answered multi-line phone systems, directing calls, taking messages, and scheduling appointments for carpet cleaning service.<br>• Prepared all office correspondence, typing letters, memos, reports, and other documents; prepared monthly billing statements.<br>• Updated and maintained files, ensuring that all customer information was current.<br><br>**BEAUTICIAN.** Personal Creations, Langston, MI (1998-99). Effectively managed my time while assisting customers with a variety of hair care needs at this busy salon.<br>• Worked closely with customers, determining their needs and advising them.<br><br>**HOME HEALTH CARE PROVIDER.** (1997-98). Provided in-home health care to my husband during his illness.<br>• Became knowledgeable of transplants, aneurysms, heart attacks, strokes, and medical terminology related to cardiac care.<br>• In the aftermath of his death, learned to cope with grief and bereavement.<br><br>**OPTICAL SHOP SALESPERSON.** Valley Eye Clinic, Langston, MI (1992-96). Performed customer service, receptionist, and office administration duties for this busy optical shop; maintained inventory and ordered supplies.<br>• Worked closely with patients, assisting in the selection of eyeglass frames.<br>• Performed liaison between patients and optometrist. |
| **PERSONAL** | Outstanding personal and professional references are available upon request. |

Date

TO: Eric at Castleton

By fax to: 1-800-533-2814

Dear Eric:

    With the enclosed resume, I would like to begin the process of exploring employment opportunities within your organization. I am particularly interested in opportunities at Under the Sea Hospital. As you will recall, we spoke by telephone this morning and you asked me to fax a resume to you.

    As you will see from my enclosed resume, I am a Certified Nursing Assistant II and have excelled in jobs in various types of environments including nursing homes, home health services, state hospitals, and major medical centers. On numerous occasions I have been recognized for superior initiative and outstanding performance.

    I can provide excellent personal and professional references, and I would appreciate an opportunity to show you in person that my outstanding nursing skills and compassionate personality could become valuable assets to your organization.

    I hope you will contact me to suggest a time when we might meet to discuss your needs and how I might help you. Thank you in advance for your time.

        Sincerely,

        Ariel D. Mermaid

# ARIEL D. MERMAID

1110½ Hay Street, Fayetteville, NC 28305    •    preppub@aol.com    •    (910) 483-6611

| | |
|---|---|
| **OBJECTIVE** | To offer my experience as a Certified Nursing Assistant (CNA)  to an organization that can use my background as a nursing assistant as well as my outstanding qualities including initiative and a cheerful personality. |
| **EDUCATION** | **Certified Nursing Assistant II** training, Oceanville Technical Community College, Oceanville, HI, 2001.<br>**Certificate for Nursing Assistant,** Oceanville Technical Community College, Oceanville, HI, 1987. |
| **LICENSE** | **License for Nurse Aide II,** State of Hawaii, listing # XYA123; expires 06/2004.<br>**HI License as Nursing Assistant** #193333. |
| **EXPERIENCE** | **CERTIFIED NURSING ASSISTANT.** Flounder Hospital, Oceanville, HI (2000-present). Handle all the responsibilities of a nurse except for dispensing medicine, and have become widely respected because of my skill in delivering quality patient care with a cheerful and outgoing personality. |

- Handle tube feedings, monitor blood sugar, insert foleys and D/C foleys; set up IVs for nurses and D/C IVs; monitor vital signs as well as height and weight and record them in the computer.
- Handle tracheostomies and suctioning; change colostomy bags; have become skilled with telemetry.

**NURSING ASSISTANT**. Tritonton of Oceanville, Oceanville, HI (1997-00). Performed routine medical diagnostic functions for residents.  Ensured living areas were clean and in order. Assisted patients with bathing, eating, grooming when required.  Annotated patients' status on medical records.

**NURSING ASSISTANT.**  Scullyville State Hospital, Scullyville, HI (1992-97). In addition to regular nursing assistant duties, escorted ambulatory patients to doctor's appointments which were away from our facility. Supervised various group activities.  Reported to staff on patient changes in behavior or habits.  Performed "suicide watch" monitoring on unstable patients which required close observation of patient and detailed written reports of their actions in 15-minute intervals.

**NURSING ASSISTANT.** St. Sebastian Nursing Center, Scullyville, HI (1991). Provided and recorded routine diagnostic analysis for geriatric patients.  Documented patient records.

**NURSING ASSISTANT.**  Ursula Center Nursing Home, Ursula, HI (1988-90). Skillfully performed duties encompassing total geriatric patient care with compassion and sensitivity.

**NURSING ASSISTANT.**  Home Health Services of Mermenton County, Scullyville, HI (1987). Blended my nursing abilities with my domestic skills to provide exceptional care for patients in their homes.

| | |
|---|---|
| **AWARDS** | Have been recognized on many occasions for my outstanding performance. |

- Have been presented five **Service Awards** as a testimonial to dedication to patient care.
- Was the recipient of a **Certification of Appreciation.**

| | |
|---|---|
| **PERSONAL** | Interests include community affairs, family and improving my nursing skills. |

Date

Exact Name of Person
Title or Position
Name of Company
Address (number and street)
Address (city, state, and zip)

**CHARGE NURSE AND CLINICAL COORDINATOR**

Dear Exact Name of Person:  (or Sir or Madam if answering a blind ad.)

With the enclosed resume, I would like to express my interest in exploring employment opportunities with your organization.

As you will see, I offer nursing skills honed in medical clinic and coronary step-down unit environments. Presently working as the Charge Nurse and Clinical Coordinator for a busy local clinic, I supervise two Licensed Practical Nurses and a Phlebotomist while overseeing support activities ranging from controlling inventory, to providing triage for patients being admitted, to assisting in patient and family education efforts. My daily activities include assisting in minor procedures and administration of medications as well as in phlebotomy, PFTs, nebulizer treatments, oxygen therapy, vital signs, and EKGs. I also handle administrative functions such as scheduling, providing referrals to specialists, completing insurance authorizations, filing, and operating computer systems for record keeping.

In an earlier job as a Charge Nurse and Preceptor for a coronary step-down unit, I supervised 11 people providing total patient care in a 32-bed unit.  In this capacity, I personally provided and supervised others in providing the full range of pre- and post-operative care for coronary patients. I received cross -training in open-heart and medical-surgical step down, CCU, and nephrology care while also participating in educating patients and family members on all aspects of disease management including proper aftercare, dietary issues, and medication and possible drug interactions.

My education and training include an Associate Degree in Nursing and the completion of Basic and Advanced Cardiac Life Support (BCLS and ACLS) certification training.

If you can use an articulate and enthusiastic nursing professional with excellent organizational skills, I hope you will contact me to suggest a time when we might meet to discuss your needs. I can provide outstanding references at the appropriate time.

Sincerely,

Sherry Stevens

# SHERRY STEVENS

1110½ Hay Street, Fayetteville, NC 28305  •  preppub@aol.com  •  (910) 483-6611

**OBJECTIVE**  To benefit an organization that can use an enthusiastic professional with exceptional communication and organizational skills who offers nursing experience honed in medical clinic and coronary step-down environments, as well as experience in sales of insurance products.

**EDUCATION**  **Associate Degree in Nursing (ADN)**, Rapid City Technical Community College, Rapid City, WA, 1998.
Completed two years of college-level course work in General Studies, Rapid City Technical Community College, Rapid City, WA, 1989-1991.
Completed **Basic** and **Advanced Cardiac Life Support** certification training (**BCLS** and **ACLS**), Rapid City Valley Medical Center, Rapid City, WA, 2000 & 2001.

**EXPERIENCE**  **CHARGE NURSE** and **CLINICAL COORDINATOR.** Westside Medical Center of Rapid City Valley Health Systems, Rapid City, WA (2001-present). Supervised two Licensed Practical Nurses and a phlebotomist while overseeing operation of the nursing staff for this busy local clinic; trained new personnel for the clinic.
  • Entrusted with the responsibility of maintaining and monitoring inventory control and dispensing of all narcotics as well as medications from the sample closet.
  • Contribute patient and family education in situations requiring tact and diplomacy.
  • Perform phlebotomy, PFTs, nebulizer treatments, oxygen therapy, vital signs, and EKGs; administer medications and assist in minor procedures.
  • Provide triage for all patients being admitted to the clinic, arranging the patients so that the most serious cases receive the quickest attention from the doctor.
  • Schedule patients, provide referrals, complete insurance authorizations, and perform filing and basic computer operations.
  • Manage the accurate and timely ordering of all supplies needed by the clinic.

**CHARGE NURSE** and **PRECEPTOR, CORONARY STEP-DOWN.** Rapid City Valley Medical Center, Rapid City, WA (1998-2001). Supervised as many as 11 personnel, including eight registered nurses, two Certified Nurse Aides, and a monitor technician while providing total patient care for this 32-bed facility.
  • Started IVs and performed insertion of Foley catheters and NG tubes; administered medications orally, intravenously, and subcutaneously.
  • Provided pre- and post-operative care for cardiac catheterization, pacemaker insertion, PTCA, cardioversion, defibrillators & CABG, and other coronary patients.
  • Assisted in procedures which included stress testing, chest tube insertion, thoracentesis, lumbar punctures, and CVP lines.
  • Served as Preceptor on the Coronary Care Step-Down Unit for RNs and RN candidates.
  • Cross-trained in open-heart and medical-surgical step down, CCU, and nephrology.
  • Performed wound care, phlebotomy, telemetry monitoring and interpretation, suture and staple removals, and 12-lead EKGs.
  • Educated patient and family on proper aftercare, dietary issues, medication and possible drug interactions, and disease management.

**INTERN** and **STUDENT NURSE.** Various locations, Rapid City, WA (1995-1998). Performed clinical rotations in pediatrics, rehabilitation, Emergency Room, Orthopedics, Neurology, child abuse, and medical-surgical units while completing my student nurse practicum at medical facilities throughout Cumberland County.

**PERSONAL**  Known as an articulate communicator a with a passion for excellence.

Exact Name of Person
Exact Title
Exact Name of Company
Address
City, State, Zip

**CHARGE NURSE AND STAFF NURSE**

Dear Exact Name of Person (or Dear Sir or Madam if answering a blind ad)

With the enclosed resume, I would like to make you aware of my background as an articulate nursing professional with exceptional communication and organizational skills who offers a background of supervision and training as well as patient care and education in critical care and nephrology environments.

In my most recent position, I excelled as a Charge Nurse and Staff Nurse on the Nephrology Unit at a major regional medical center. I specialized in peritoneal dialysis, and I have more than 13 years experience in providing care to patients suffering from renal failure. Earlier I worked as an Intermediate Care (step-down) Nurse, providing patient care for trauma, ventilator, cardiac, tracheostomy, and other patients who were transferred out of the ICU, but were not stable enough to go to a regular floor. In previous experience as a Licensed Practical Nurse, I performed phlebotomy services at a local blood bank, strictly observing all precautions related to the handling of blood products and related biohazards.

As you will see from my enclosed resume, I completed the Associate's degree in Nursing program at Gumbo Technical Community College, and have supplemented my education with courses in American Sign Language, computers, and Basic Cardiac Life Support (BCLS). Certified as a BCLS Instructor, for more than 11 years I have served as a patient educator facilitator, and my skills in this are were recognized with first-place honors at the Gumbo Area Health Education Center (GAHEC) Spring Community Fair.

If you can use an accomplished, hard-working nursing professional who is known for loyalty to her employers as well as for exceptional patient care and education skills, I hope you will call or write me soon to suggest a time when we might meet to discuss your current and future needs and how I might serve them. I can provide outstanding references and would quickly become an asset to your organization.

Sincerely,

Jenny Brook Gump

Alternate last paragraph:
I hope you will welcome my call soon to arrange a brief meeting to discuss your current and future needs and how I might serve them

# JENNY BROOK GUMP

1110½ Hay Street, Fayetteville, NC 28305　·　preppub@aol.com　·　(910) 483-6611

**OBJECTIVE**　To benefit an organization that can use an experienced nursing professional with exceptional communication and organizational skills who offers a background in nursing supervision and training as well as patient care and education in critical care and nephrology environments.

**EDUCATION**　**Associate's** degree in **Nursing (ADN)**, Gumbo Technical Community College, Shrimp, AL, 1990.

Graduated from the **Licensed Practical Nurse** program, Gumbo Technical Community College, Shrimp, AL, 1984.

Completed a number of advanced training programs offered through Shrimp Gumbo Health Systems, including the Basic Cardiac Life Support (BCLS) Instructor course, a 16-week American Sign Language course, and more than 150 hours of ongoing education in computers.

**HONORS**　Selected as **Nurse of the Year** for Shrimp Gumbo Health Systems, 2000 and 1992.

**LICENSES & CERTIFICATIONS**　Licensed **Registered Nurse**, Alabama Board of Nursing Certificate #073573.
Certified as a Basic Cardiac Life Support (BCLS) Instructor, expires November, 2005.

**AFFILIATIONS**　Member, American Nurses Association, 1990-present.

**EXPERIENCE**　*With Shrimp Gumbo Health Systems, Shrimp, AL, have advanced in the following "track record" of increasing responsibilities at this major regional medical center:*
*2001-present:* **CHARGE NURSE** and **STAFF NURSE, NEPHROLOGY.** Supervised as many as 10 personnel on the nursing staff while serving as Charge Nurse in charge of training new employees; provide expert care to patients suffering from renal dysfunction and kidney-related disorders on this busy nephrology unit.

- Perform patient assessments in order to determine the patient's care needs and monitore treatment progress.
- Provide education on medications, diet, and other related matters to patients and their families to assist them in the transition to home care.
- Operate a variety of computerized medical equipment and computers; monitore patient's status using telemetry equipment.
- Update and maintain records of patient care to ensure that all documentation is current and accurate.
- Design and create new care plans for the Nephrology Unit; formerly served on a committee planning procedures for dealing with seclusion and patient restraint issues.
- Specialize in peritoneal dialysis and care for patients with renal failure.

*1991-00:* **CHARGE NURSE** and **STAFF NURSE, INTERMEDIATE CARE UNIT.**
Provided total patient care to medical-surgical, hospice, cardiac step-down, and other patients who were discharged from the Intensive Care Unit (ICU) but were not stable enough to receive care on the regular floors.

- Assisted physicians with procedures and performed telemetry monitoring, phlebotomy, wound care, and care and maintenance of patients with tracheostomy and NG tubes.
- Treated overflow and post-ICU patients from every specialty area in the hospital.

**LICENSED PRACTICAL NURSE.** John Elliott Blood Bank, Shrimp, AL (1984-1990). Performed phlebotomies, sterilizing the venipuncture site before drawing blood from the donor in order to augment the blood supply available for use by local hospitals and clinics.

**PERSONAL**　Excellent personal and professional references are available upon request.

Exact Name of Person
Title or Position
Name of Company
Address (number and street)
Address (city, state, and zip)

**CLINICAL ASSISTANT**   Dear Exact Name of Person:  (or Sir or Madam if answering a blind ad.)

With the enclosed resume, I would like to express my interest in exploring employment opportunities with your organization.

As you will see, I offer a blend of clinical and administrative abilities gained while excelling in a versatile work history in the medical field. I have completed extensive related training including a Medical Assistant Program and a Phlebotomy course as well as courses in Secretarial Science and Business.

Presently a Clinical Assistant for a family practice environment, I have become known for my compassionate and professional approach to dealing with patients, physicians, and other medical professionals. My duties range from preparing patients for exams, to performing medical procedures and assisting physicians, to performing diagnostic and screening tests. I also enter data into patient charts, refill prescriptions, and administer medications and vaccinations.

Earlier as a Phlebotomist and Medical Laboratory Aide in a Veterans Administration Hospital, I became skilled in utilizing universal blood and body fluid precautions while collecting samples and then doing all required tests on each sample. Prior to this job, I was one of three Medical Assistants in a women's clinic with five doctors and one nurse practitioner.  In this capacity, I handled all aspects of procedures from screening patients, to documenting medical histories, to assisting in physical examinations as well as minor surgeries.

If you can use an adaptable and compassionate medical professional who is knowledgeable of insurance billing, inventory control, and office operations and administration, I hope you will contact me to suggest a time when we might meet to discuss your needs. I can provide outstanding references at the appropriate time.

Sincerely,


Jodie Thomas Damon

# JODIE THOMAS DAMON

1110½ Hay Street, Fayetteville, NC 28305 • preppub@aol.com • (910) 483-6611

**OBJECTIVE**
To contribute to an organization that can use a skilled medical professional with excellent clinical/administrative abilities and a congenial attitude when dealing with patients and others.

**EDUCATION**
Graduated from the Medical Assistant Program, Mercer Career Institute, Chicago, IL.
Completed Phlebotomy course, Hunter Vocational School, Chicago, IL.
Completed Secretarial Sciences Studies, City College of Chicago, Campus in Germany.
Continuing my education in business at Clarksville Technical Community College, TN.

**EXPERIENCE**
**CLINICAL ASSISTANT.** Riverbend Family Practice, Clarkesville, TN (2000-present). Utilize phlebotomy skills in an LPN working position. Am known for my professional and compassionate attitude in my interactions with patients, physicians, and other staff members while expertly performing all aspects of the job of Clinical Assistant.
- Prepare the patient for exams; perform medical procedures, and assist physician during exams; perform diagnostic and screening tests.
- Chart pertinent data in patients' medical records while also scheduling patients for consultations and diagnostic tests, refilling prescriptions, and assisting office manager and physicians in other tasks; administer medications and vaccinations.

**MEDICAL LABORATORY AIDE.** Veterans Hospital, Clarkesville, TN (1998-00). Worked primarily as a Phlebotomist as well as a Lab Aide.
- Performed venipuncture on inpatients, outpatients, and employees throughout the hospital complex utilizing universal blood and body fluid precautions.
- Collected patient samples with sufficient volume and correctness to do all tests required; performed positive identification of patient and specimen through entire process of phlebotomy, accessioning, receiving, aliquoting, distributing, and storage.
- Acted as the first-line contact between the Clinical Laboratory and the patient.
- Became very knowledgeable of the VA procedures used to review patient data, answer telephones, and count or record numerical data on AMIS reports.
- Handled patient information in a confidential and professional manner.
- Skillfully applied my knowledge of inventory procedures used to classify chemical reagents, antibiotics, expendable supplies, data, and files while utilizing my ability to interpret commercial chemical nomenclature, calculate simple ratio equations, and safely mix chemical ingredients.

**MEDICAL ASSISTANT.** Women's Health Center of Radcliff, Radcliff, KY (1996-98). As one of three Medical Assistants for five doctors and one nurse practitioner, handled the screening of OB patients, obtaining vital signs, determining weight, and collecting urine specimens; documented medical histories; assisted doctors in physical examinations as well as minor surgeries/biopsies, colonoscopy, IUD insertions/removal, NORPLANT insertions/removals, Cone Leep biopsies; ensured OSHA regulations were followed.
- Set up procedure room; explained procedures and postoperative care to patients.
- Priced and ordered instruments needed for office operation or instrument repair.

**Other experience:**
**RED CROSS VOLUNTEER.** Radcliff, KY and Ft. Campbell, KY (1996-present). While working full-time, volunteered up to 30 hours per week at Blanchfield Army Hospital.

**PERSONAL**
Can provide outstanding references. Knowledgeable of insurance billing.

Exact Name of Person
Title or Position
Name of Company
Address (number and street)
Address (city, state, and zip)

**HEAD NURSE**  Dear Exact Name of Person: (or Dear Sir or Madam if answering a blind ad.)

With the enclosed resume, I would like to indicate my interest in your medical center and my desire to explore employment opportunities.

As you will see from my enclosed resume, I offer experience as a Head Nurse and am known for my compassionate style when dealing with patients and their families. I decided on a career in nursing after working in administrative support roles at two medical offices and discovering my strong desire to become more involved in patient care.

I hope you will welcome my call soon to arrange a brief meeting at your convenience to discuss your current and future needs and how I might serve them. Thank you in advance for your time.

Sincerely yours,

Belinda Warren

Alternate last paragraph:
I hope you will call or write me soon to suggest a time convenient for us to meet and discuss your current and future needs and how I might serve them. Thank you in advance for your time.

# BELINDA WARREN

1110½ Hay Street, Fayetteville, NC 28305 • preppub@aol.com • (910) 483-6611

---

**OBJECTIVE**  To contribute to an organization that can use a skilled nursing professional who offers effective communication skills along with a reputation as a hard-working and compassionate person.

**EDUCATION**  **Associate's degree in Nursing,** Towson Technical Community College (TTCC), MD, 2000.
Certificate in **Surgical Technology,** TTCC, 1984; completed extensive on-the-job training at Towson Medical Center.
Certified CPR Instructor.

**EXPERIENCE**  **HEAD NURSE.** Cliffdale Primary Care, Towson, MD (2000-present). In addition to supervising the clinic staff of nine LPNs, lab technicians, and phlebotomists, order supplies and equipment while overseeing and controlling the completion of numerous tests and procedures which include:

|                          |                            |
|--------------------------|----------------------------|
| pulmonary function testing | flex sigmoidoscopy      |
| stress testing           | visual acuity testing      |
| peak flow meter usage    | immunizations/vaccinations |
| monitoring EKGs          | sterilization of equipment |

- Act as liaison between pharmaceutical company representatives and physicians; accept samples and stock pharmaceutical supplies for clinic use.
- Assist during in-office surgical procedures.
- Make insurance referrals and authorizations along with referrals to other doctors.

**FULL-TIME NURSING STUDENT.** Towson Technical Community College, MD (1995-00). Placed on the President's List in recognition of my academic achievements.

**CLINICAL STAFF MEMBER** and **ADMINISTRATIVE ASSISTANT.** Medical Drive Obstetrics and Gynecology, Towson, MD (1987-93). Handled support activities ranging from taking patients' vital signs, to answering phones and routing messages, to setting up appointments and making referrals to other medical practices.

- Called in prescriptions; also conducted telephone triage by advising patients and helping determine how urgent their situation was.
- Developed mutually beneficial relations with pharmaceutical representatives, including acting as liaison between them, the physicians, and the nursing staff.

**SURGICAL ASSISTANT.** Dr. Dennis Michaels, Towson, MD (1984-87). Provided chairside assistance in periodontal surgeries as well as handling office support activities including making appointments, preparing surgical instruments, taking X-rays, and working with ultrasound equipment.

**Highlights of earlier experience:** Gained skills in sales, office operations, credit application processing, and letters/contract preparation.

**SPECIAL SKILLS**  Am proficient with various office machines including typewriters, copy machines, personal and office computers, and X-ray and ultrasound equipment.

**PERSONAL**  Offer exceptionally strong communication skills. Excellent references.

**LICENSED PRACTICAL
NURSE**

Dear Sir or Madam:

I would appreciate an opportunity to talk with you soon about how I could contribute to your organization through my nursing skills and outgoing personality.

Please call or write soon to suggest a convenient time for us to meet and discuss your needs and how I might serve them. I can provide outstanding personal and professional references. Thank you in advance for your time.

Yours sincerely,

Chris Chambers

# CHRIS CHAMBERS

1110½ Hay Street, Fayetteville, NC 28305     •     preppub@aol.com     •     (910) 483-6611

---

**OBJECTIVE**

Am applying for a position as a Licensed Practical Nurse. Offer a variety of indepth experience as an LPN in the past 18½ years. Am certain that, with my past experience and diversified knowledge, I would be of great assistance to both patients and doctors.

**EDUCATION**

Graduated from Central Washington Technical College, Seattle, WA, with a degree in Practical Nursing.

**EXPERIENCE**

**LICENSED PRACTICAL NURSE (LPN).** Highland House of Seattle, Seattle, WA (2001-present). Work with geriatrics patients on a skilled nursing floor; on occasion; am in charge of the 155-bed facility and staff.

**LICENSED PRACTICAL NURSE  (LPN).** Carrollton Nursing Home and Cumberland County Detoxification Unit, Mental Health Center, Seattle, WA (1998-01). Worked as a Contract Nurse (PRN) for the Carrollton Nursing Home at which I was employed full-time while also working for the Cumberland County Detoxification Unit from 1998-2001.

**LICENSED PRACTICAL NURSE.** Village Green Care Center, Seattle, WA (1997). Cared for 30 patients on a Medicare-skilled floor and gained extensive hands-on training in the areas of medication and administration, gastrostomy feeding, taking verbal and written orders, writing nursing summaries, demonstrating skills as a charge nurse, as well as providing treatments and assessments of the patient on admission and on a daily basis.

**LICENSED PRACTICAL NURSE.** Cumberland Hospital, Seattle, WA (1994-96). Cared for mentally disturbed adolescents in a long-term setting. Received additional training related to teaching adolescents basic behavioral skills in a group setting, administering medication, and preparing written documentation.

**LICENSED PRACTICAL NURSE.** Metroplex Home Health Agency, Killeen, TX (1992-93). Cared for patients in their private homes. Received hands-on training related to teaching patients proper diet techniques, giving insulin injections, and preparing changes and other documentation pertaining to care provided. Was known for my attention to detail in carefully following verbal and written orders.

**LICENSED PRACTICAL NURSE.** Cape Fear Valley Medical Center, Seattle, WA (1989-91). Over a one-year period, excelled in floating assignments that included extensive experience in medical/surgery, orthopedics, urology, and OB-GYN. Gained extensive hands-on experience in team leadership, treatment administration, giving PRN medications, taking verbal and written orders, conducting charting, and writing nursing care plans.

**LICENSED PRACTICAL NURSE.** Durham County General Hospital, Durham, NC (1984-89). Worked in a medical and surgical intensive care unit. Received additional training related to the care of patients on respirators, and completed a basic IV insertion course.

**LICENSED PRACTICAL NURSE.** Chapel Hill, NC (1980-84). Gained experience in cardiothoracic surgery and in kidney transplant operations. Completed an EKG course and received additional hands-on training in monitoring cardiac arrhythmias and patients on dialysis.

**PERSONAL**

Am a caring professional who understands patient needs for warmth and empathy.

**LICENSED PRACTICAL
NURSE**

Dear Sir or Madam:

With the enclosed resume, I would like to make you aware of my background as a Licensed Practical Nurse with exceptional organizational, communication, and patient relations skills who has excelled in a track record of accomplishment in obstetrics/gynecology and medical/surgical, and geriatric nursing in challenging environments worldwide.

As you will see, I have completed the Practical Nurse and Medical Specialist course from the Academy of Health Sciences at Fort Harbor, WA. I have supplemented these programs with numerous additional military training programs, including the Medical Proficiency Training Program, Algorithm-Directed Troop Medical Care Course, Deployable Medical Systems New Equipment Training, Medical Management of Chemical Casualties, and Hazard Communication Program.

Currently working as a Licensed Practical Nurse providing medical-surgical care on a 20-bed intermediate care ward at a busy 296-bed DEPMEDS-equipped Combat Support Hospital, I supervise and train 13 personnel at the Fort Harbor Medical Inprocessing Center, which handles more than 1,200 soldiers monthly. I also oversee the security and maintenance of more than $300,000 worth of medical equipment, immunization medicines, and expendable supplies. On my own initiative, I have organized and developed a Breast Health Awareness Program for females inprocessing to Fort Harbor, and I served as a phlebotomist for the Operation Life Gift Bone Marrow Drive.

My earlier nursing experience was focused in obstetrics and gynecology. In Korea, I served on a 42-bed mixed ward comprising a 17-bed newborn nursery, a six-bed labor and delivery unit, and a 19-bed obstetrics and gynecology unit. In that position, I supervised a staff of three, acted as Preceptor to newly assigned personnel, and took on additional responsibilities as Infection Control Officer for the Ward, Fire & Safety Officer, and Time Schedule Coordinator. At Fort Port, I served as a Licensed Practical Nurse in the 25-bed obstetrics and gynecology ward of a busy regional medical center.

If you can use an experienced nursing professional with a strong background in obstetrics and gynecology and exceptional patient relations skills, I hope you will contact me to suggest a time when we might meet.

Sincerely,

Irene Fisher

# IRENE FISHER

1110½ Hay Street, Fayetteville, NC 28305   •   preppub@aol.com   •   (910) 483-6611

---

**OBJECTIVE**

To benefit an organization that can use an experienced licensed practical nurse with exceptional organizational and patient relations skills who offers a background in obstetrics/gynecology and medical/surgical nursing in challenging environments worldwide.

**EDUCATION**

Completed the **Practical Nurse Course** and **Medical Specialist Course** at the Academy of Health Sciences, Fort Harbor, WA.
Supplemented my education with a large number of medical courses taken as part of my military training, including:
- Medical Proficiency Training Program, Fort Harbor, WA, 1998.
- Algorithm-Directed Troop Medical Care Course, Fort Harbor, WA, 1996.
- Deployable Medical Systems New Equipment Training, Fort Port, NY, 1996.
- Medical Management of Chemical Casualties, Fort Port, NY, 1996.
- Hazard Communication Program, Korea, 1994.

**LICENSES**

**Licensed Practical Nurse** for the state of Washington, certificate #054772, expires 12/31/03.
**Licensed Practical Nurse** for the state of New York #0024016, expires 1/31/03.

**EXPERIENCE**

*As a Licensed Practical Nurse with the United States Army, excelled in demanding positions while advancing in a track record of accomplishment:*
**LICENSED PRACTICAL NURSE.** U.S. Army, Fort Harbor, WA (2000-present). Serve as a Practical Nurse on this 20-bed Intermediate Care Ward which is part of a busy, 296-bed DEPMEDS-equipped Combat Support Hospital.
- Supervise and train 13 hospital personnel in proper operational procedures for the Medical Inprocessing Center, handling more than 1,200 soldiers per month.
- Oversee the security and maintenance of more than $300,000 worth of equipment, immunization medicines, and expendable supplies.
- Provide total nursing care for 20 medical-surgical patients during deployments.
- On my own initiative, organized and developed a Breast Health Awareness program for all females inprocessing to Fort Harbor.
- Served as a phlebotomist for the Operation Life Gift Bone Marrow Drive.

**LICENSED PRACTICAL NURSE.** U.S. Army, Korea (1996-00). Provided patient care services for a 42-bed mixed ward including a 17-bed newborn nursery unit, a six-bed labor and delivery unit, and a 19-bed obstetrics and gynecology unit.
- Supervised three personnel and served as Preceptor for newly assigned personnel.
- Assisted in the performance of Cesarean sections, administered medication both orally and intravenously, and obtained lab specimens.
- Admitted and discharged patients; provided patient education on infant care and post-circumcision care.
- Monitored high-risk laboring patients as well as patients with no complications.
- Served as Infection Control Officer for the ward, as well as Fire & Safety Officer and Time Schedule Coordinator.

**LICENSED PRACTICAL NURSE.** U.S. Army, Fort Port, NY (1992-1996). Performed nursing care on a 25-bed Obstetrics & Gynecology ward in a busy medical center.
- Performed patient admission orientation, and education; conducted 10 pre-operative training courses for more than 150 patients.
- Provided direct and indirect patient care, including but not limited to obtaining lab specimens, starting IVs, and administering medication both orally and intravenously.

Date

Exact Name of Person
Exact Title or Position
Company Name
Company Address (number and street)
Company Address (city, state, and ZIP)

**NURSE LIAISON**     Dear Exact Name of Person (or Dear Sir or Madam if answering a blind ad)

With the application and enclosed resume, I would like to formally express my interest in receiving consideration for a position with your organization at the Lyster Army Community Hospital. Your company has been recommended to me by an employee, Becky Walters, who is a Discharge Planner.

As you will see from my resume I received my B.S.N. degree from the Medical College of Alabama in Huntsville in 1987. Since then I have earned a reputation as a compassionate, well-organized, and articulate professional and have built a strong background of versatile experience in private and public health environments. I believe that my background and education would allow me to contribute in any number of positions in the new medical center, and I am especially interested in pursuing jobs in discharge planning and utilization review.

Although I am highly regarded by my present employer (a TownCenter-related company), I will be leaving this organization in October to pursue other opportunities in the healthcare field where my compassionate manner of working with patients and families, my excellent presentation and communication skills, and my organizational and administrative abilities will be of value. I am certain that my track record of excellent performance in jobs which have included Nurse Liaison, Hospice Coordinator, Case Manager, Clinical Nurse, and Community Health Nurse would allow me to bring important skills to the new facility as it begins to serve this large military community.

With experience which has ranged from public health, to home health, to hospice, to long-term care, to clinical nursing I offer the maturity and adaptability to move into a new facility and quickly become an asset. If you can use an energetic and compassionate professional who is known for possessing a high level of initiative, I hope you will call me soon to arrange a brief meeting to discuss your goals and how my background might serve your needs. I can provide outstanding references at the appropriate time.

Sincerely,

Patricia T. Stewart

# PATRICIA STEWART

1110½ Hay Street, Fayetteville, NC 28305  •  preppub@aol.com  •  (910) 483-6611

---

**OBJECTIVE**   To contribute a diverse background in all phases of patient care to include assisted living, long-term care, and hospice environments where the ability to ensure that the details of planning for and providing care and discharging patients were carried out with compassion.

**EDUCATION**   **B.S.N. degree**, Medical College of Alabama, Huntsville, AL, 1987.
Have completed continuing education and training programs emphasizing pain control and chemotherapy as well as BCLS/CPR and infection control.

**EXPERIENCE**   **NURSE LIAISON.** TownCenter-related companies, Huntsville, AL (2001-present).
Conduct assessments of patients based on referrals in order to determine the person's placement into long-term, assisted living, domiciliary, intermediate, or rest home-level care.
- Took over a newly created position and have been credited with increasing community awareness of the assisted living option while educating patients and their families.
- Work with discharge planners and case managers to form accurate assessments.
- Conduct outreach to local physicians and am in constant touch with 15 different offices.

**Earned advancement in public health care with the Huntsville Regional Home Health Hospice, Huntsville, AL (1996-01):**
**2000-01: HOSPICE COORDINATOR.** Was credited with "dramatically increasing referrals through networking" as coordinator of patient care services for the Hospice care portion of the hospital's programs.
- Supervised three registered nurses, three home health aides, and a chaplain.
- Made arrangements for and coordinated education and development activities for staff members and volunteer workers.
- Provided marketing support services for the program; developed a patient care guide distributed to patients and their family members; updated policy manuals.
- Participated in developing and ensuring compliance with the operating budget.
**1996-00: CASE MANAGER** and **CLINICAL NURSE.** Supervised nursing aides to ensure implementation of care plans while personally providing care to home health patients.

**HOME IV NURSE.** Missile City Home Therapeutics, Huntsville, AL (1995-96). Provided individualized, specialized IV infusion therapy in a variety of patient care situations.

**COMMUNITY HEALTH NURSE.** Lyster Army Community Hospital, Ft. Rucker, AL (1995). Implemented nursing care and provided educational services to individuals and families who had been exposed to or were suffering from infectious diseases or illnesses.
- Performed the hospital's HIV Hospital Admissions testing study.
- Applied knowledge and communication skills presenting a variety of formal lectures.
- Performed physical assessments and developed patient care plans for HIV and AIDS.

**CASE MANAGER.** Hospice Home Health Services of Montgomery County, Montgomery, AL (1990-95). Excelled in meeting the special needs of the terminally ill and their families while providing quality nursing care and assisting in the training of hospice workers.

**REGISTERED NURSE.** Community Health Clinic, Germany (1989). Performed a wide range of nursing duties for an outpatient clinic serving a large military community.

**PERSONAL**   Am highly organized and known for my ability to educate, train, and inform others.

Date

**NURSING SUPERVISOR**

Dear Sir or Madam:

With the enclosed resume, I would like to make you aware of my background as a Licensed Practical Nurse and also express my interest in exploring nursing opportunities with your organization. I am particularly interested in the Director of Resident Services position which you recently advertised.

As you will see from my resume, I am currently excelling as a Nursing Supervisor at The Rehabilitation and Health Care Center of Village Green. I supervise up to seven Licensed Practical Nurses while also supervising up to 14 CNAs.

In previous jobs as a Charge Nurse, I worked in settings which included an Alzheimer's Unit with 42 patients as well as a nursing home.

I can provide excellent references at the appropriate time, and I would enjoy an opportunity to talk with you in person about my ability to make valuable contributions to your organization.

Sincerely,

Dorothy Dix

# DOROTHY DIX

1110½ Hay Street, Fayetteville, NC 28305   •   preppub@aol.com   •   (910) 483-6611

---

**OBJECTIVE**
I want to contribute to an organization that can use an experienced Licensed Practical Nurse who offers extensive management skills and supervisory abilities.

**EDUCATION**
Lemuel Shattuck Hospital School of Practical Nursing, Jamaica Plain, MA, 1993-94.
Graduated from Dorchester High School, Dorchester, MA, 1980.

**LICENSE**
Licensed LPN, NC Certificate #045241; renewal date 12/31/03
Community CPR Certificate, AHA, 6/23/04

**EXPERIENCE**
**NURSING SUPERVISOR.** The Rehabilitation and Health Care Center of Village Green, Nashville, TN (2001-present). Supervise 4-7 Licensed Practical Nurses while also supervising 10-14 CNAs; monitor resident care rounds, monitor medication pass and treatments, and provide inservices to LPNs and CNAs.
- Assist nursing staff as needed with lab specimen collection and IV therapy.
- Notify MDs and family members as needed.
- Prepare end-of-shift supervisor's report.
- Monitor staff at Carolina Inn of Village Green, an assisted living facility.
- Assist with monthly summaries as well as with nightly and weekly chartings.

**CHARGE NURSE & LICENSED PRACTICAL NURSE.** Whispering Pines Nursing Home, Nashville, TN (2000-01). As Charge Nurse, was the supervisor of the 11-7 shift; supervised 3-5 nursing assistants while also administering medications and performing treatments.
- Was the Team Leader for the Eden Alternative Program.

**RECEPTIONIST.** H&R Block, Nashville, TN (1999-00). In this seasonal position, distributed tax return checks, filed completed tax returns, answered telephones, set up client appointments, and processed rapid refund returns.

**LICENSED PRACTICAL NURSE.** Village Green Care Center, Nashville, TN (1998-99). Was a Charge Nurse for skilled geriatric patients while supervising 3-5 Certified Nursing Assistants.

**RESEARCH ASSISTANT.** Beth Israel Hospital, Department of Pathology, Boston, MA (1997-98). Was involved in training laboratory personnel as well as in the histological preparation of research samples. Maintained laboratory equipment and supplies. Prepared Epon embedded 1 Micron samples.

**LICENSED PRACTICAL NURSE.** Sherril House, Inc., Boston, MA (1996-97). Was Charge Nurse of an Alzheimer's Unit with 42 patients; supervised six CNAs.

**LICENSED PRACTICAL NURSE.** Oak Haven Nursing Home, Roxbury, MA (1995-96). Was Charge Nurse for 34 patients; supervised three CNAs.

**PERSONAL**
Enjoy helping others. Have excellent people skills. Am a highly motivated self-starter and go-getter who enjoys making a difference in others' lives.

Date

Exact Name of Person
Exact Title
Exact Name of Company
Address
City, State, Zip

**OPERATING ROOM STAFF NURSE**

Dear Exact Name of Person: (or Dear Sir or Madam if answering a blind ad)

With the enclosed resume, I would like to make you aware of my interest in exploring opportunities where my versatile nursing background and reputation as a skilled nursing professional would be valued.

As you will see from my resume, I offer a broad base of experience and knowledge with an emphasis on operating room experience. I also am familiar with heart team procedures and ambulatory care settings. Since 2000 I have been an Operating Room Nurse for the Ambulatory Surgical Center in Atlanta, GA, where I work with doctors from Village Surgical Associates on general cases such as laparoscopic gall bladders, hernias, and other LS procedures as well as other practices such as orthopedic, ENT, GYN, plastics, and endo patients.

At Valley View Medical Center in Atlanta, I was an OR Staff Nurse/Relief Head Nurse and then was handpicked as a member of the center's "Heart Team." I attended a three-month program in Open Heart Surgery at Atlanta Metropolitan University and then acted as one of the four nurses on Dr. George Smith's team of specialists.

Although I am well respected and satisfied with my present position, I am in the process of relocating to your area because my husband has started a new job with the Sheriff's Department.

I hope you will contact me soon to arrange a brief meeting to discuss my background and how I might contribute to your organization. Thank you in advance for your time and consideration of my qualifications.

Sincerely,


Maria Luisa Cardenas

# MARIA LUISA CARDENAS

1110½ Hay Street, Fayetteville, NC 28305  •  preppub@aol.com  •  (910) 483-6611

**OBJECTIVE**
To contribute to a medical organization that can use a Registered Nurse who has acquired expert knowledge of operating room, heart surgery, and general medical cases while earning a reputation as a skilled nursing professional with superior time management skills.

**EDUCATION & TRAINING**
R.N., Waynesville Technical Community College, GA, 1996.
Completed a three-month training program in Open Heart Surgery, Atlanta Metropolitan University, GA, 1997.
**L.P.N.,** Columbus Community College, Columbus, GA, 1987.
Attended the American Medical Association 30-day Supervisory Course, 1992.
Completed Medical Corpsman (L.P.N.) training, U.S. Army, 1979.

**LICENSES & CERTIFICATION**
**Registered Nurse,** Georgia License #229883, expires December 2005.
Have current Advanced Cardiac Lifesaving Certification (ACLS).
Am certified in CPR and First Aid.

**EXPERIENCE**
**OPERATING ROOM STAFF NURSE/RELIEF HEAD NURSE.** Ambulatory Surgical Center, Atlanta, GA (2000-present).  Manage 30 nurses and scrub technicians while working with physicians from Village Surgical Associates and other practices on a block schedule.
- Specialize in general cases which included laparoscopic gall bladders, hernias, and surgical patients as well as regular general cases.
- During surgical procedures, manage two scrub nurses while scrubbing and circulating as an assistant to doctors.
- Was a major contributor to decisions on upgrades for laparoscopic equipment.

**OR NURSE** and **RELIEF HEAD NURSE.**  Valley View Medical Center, Atlanta, GA (1998-00). Managed a staff of approximately 30 nurses and scrub technicians and was handpicked as part of the medical center's newly formed "Heart Team."

**HEART TEAM CIRCULATING AND SCRUB NURSE.** Valley View Medical Center, Atlanta, GA (1997-98). Received advanced training in open heart surgical procedures in a three-month program at Atlanta Metropolitan University; participated in nearly 1,000 heart surgeries.
- As a member of the team of specialists handpicked for the "Heart Team" headed by Dr. George Smith, was one of four nurses selected to assist in this specialized area.

**FULL-TIME STUDENT.**  Waynesville Technical Community College, GA, and Quincy State Junior College, IL (1993-96). Completed course work leading to licensing as an R.N.

**SUPERVISORY L.P.N.**  Equifax, Atlanta, GA (1991-93). Coordinated schedules and supervised 30 RNs who performed insurance physicals.

**OPERATING ROOM NURSE** and **PRIMARY CARE NURSE.**  Hendersonville Memorial Hospital, Hendersonville, GA (1989-91).  Simultaneously with the job with Equifax, also worked in the neurological ward for nine months and in the operating room for one year.

Highlights of other experience:
Was an **Operating Room Nurse,** Columbia Hospital, Columbia, GA.

**PERSONAL**
Am a flexible and creative professional with sound decision-making skills.

**REGISTERED NURSE**

Dear Ms. Smith:

With the enclosed resume, I would like to make you aware of my background as an accomplished nursing professional who offers experience in pediatrics, medical-surgical, orthopedic, and geriatric care in home health, hospital, and long-term care environments.

As you will see, I have recently completed my Associate's degree program in Nursing from Simmons Community College in Sampson, WV. I had previously completed the Licensed Practical Nurse program at Simmons Community College and have practiced as an LPN since 1996.

In my present job with Pediatric Services of America, I provide private duty pediatric home health care to critically ill children, most of whom are referred to PSA by the University of West Virginia and Kentucky Medical Centers. To enhance my abilities in this area, I attended a ventilator care seminar through PSA, as many of my patients require respirators or ventilators. I implement occupational, physical, and speech therapy programs as prescribed, and educate patients and family members on care-related issues.

While completing my Associate's degree in Nursing, I worked in a number of units at a long-term care facility. Prior to that, I served as a Licensed Practical Nurse on a 32-bed orthopedic and adolescent unit at Children's Hospital, a 175-bed pediatric teaching hospital in West Virginia. In this challenging environment, I gained valuable knowledge related to the care and treatment of orthopedic disorders resulting from birth injuries or genetic diseases.

In an earlier position at Wynhoven Nursing Center, I further developed my time management skills while supervising four nursing aides providing total patient care for 60 chronically ill patients in this long-term care facility.

If you can use a motivated, experienced nursing professional whose abilities have been tested in a wide range of challenging environments, then I look forward to hearing from you soon, to suggest a time when we might meet to discuss your needs. I can assure you in advance that I have an outstanding reputation and would rapidly become a valuable asset to your organization.

Sincerely,

Allison Hedgpeth

# ALLISON HEDGPETH

1110½ Hay Street, Fayetteville, NC 28305   •   preppub@aol.com   •   (910) 483-6611

**OBJECTIVE**  To benefit an organization that can use an experienced nursing professional with exceptional communication and time management skills who offers a background in pediatric, medical-surgical, orthopedic, and geriatric nursing in home health, hospital, and long-term care environments.

**EDUCATION**  **Associate's Degree** in **Nursing**, Simmons Community College, Sampson, WV, 2000. Graduated from the **Licensed Practical Nursing** program, Simmons Community College, Sampson, WV, 1996. Have supplemented my degree programs with courses to enhance my nursing skills, including a course in ventilator care offered by Pediatric Services of America.

**LICENSES**  West Virginia **Registered Nurse**, certificate #158876, expires December 2003. **Licensed Practical Nurse** for the state of West Virginia, expires 2003.

**EXPERIENCE**  **REGISTERED NURSE** and **LICENSED PRACTICAL NURSE.**  Pediatric Services of America, Sampson, WV (2000-present).  Provide private duty pediatric home health care to children who were critically ill, medically fragile, injured, or suffering from rare genetic diseases; more than 95% of my patients are referred through the University of West Virginia and Kentucky Medical Centers.
- Coordinate with doctors, nurses, families, case managers, and therapists to ensure optimum care for each patient.
- Provide ventilator and tracheostomy care and maintenance.
- Implement prescribed occupational, physical, and speech therapies; administered medication, both orally, intravenously, and by gastrointestinal tube.
- Perform family and patient education on issues related to the special care needed by critically ill or medically fragile children.
- Was recognized at a pediatric conference for my outstanding service to children with HIV and their families.

**LICENSED PRACTICAL NURSE.**  Mary Gran Nursing Center, Sampson, WV (1998-00). Worked as an LPN, delivering quality care to elderly patients in this long-term care facility while completing my Associate's degree program in Nursing.
- Managed a work load of 33 patients, performing assessments and administering medications and treatments.
- Worked in a number of different units on alternating weekends, honing my skills in various types of nursing.

**LICENSED PRACTICAL NURSE.**  Children's Hospital, Sampson, WV (1997-1998). Provided quality patient care for a 32-bed orthopedic and adolescent unit in a 175-bed pediatric teaching hospital associated with West Virginia State and Tulane Universities.
- Increased my knowledge related to the care and treatment of orthopedic disorders resulting from birth injuries or genetic diseases.

**LICENSED PRACTICAL NURSE.**  Wynhoven Nursing Center, Blackridge, WV (1996-1997).  Supervised and worked with four nursing aides, providing total nursing care for 60 chronically ill elderly patients  on a skilled nursing unit in this long-term care facility.
- Organized and prioritized patient care according to need, in order to appropriately direct the work of nursing aides under my supervision.

**PERSONAL**  Excellent personal and professional references are available upon request.

**REGISTERED NURSE, ORTHO/NEUROLOGICAL SURGICAL UNIT**

Dear Ms. Smith:

With the enclosed resume, I would like to make you aware of my background as a dedicated young nursing professional with strong communication and organizational skills who offers exceptional patient care skills honed in challenging environments on the Orthopedic/Neurological Surgical Unit at a major regional medical center. I am in the process of relocating to the Myrtle Beach area where my husband has accepted a new position.

As you will see, I completed my Associate Degree in Nursing (ADN) at Sandhills Community College, where I excelled in clinical rotations in ICU/CCU, Neurological/Surgical, Psychiatric, Pediatric, Obstetrics/Labor & Delivery, and Medical/Surgical nursing. I am a Licensed Registered Nurse for the state of Pennsylvania.

Since earning my RN license, I have worked on the Orthopedic/Neurological Surgical Unit at Pittsburgh Medical Center, performing skilled nursing care, patient assessment, and monitoring for pre and postoperative patients in these specialties as well as for Medical/Surgical patients. I work with a Physical Therapy team in my current position and am involved in providing a wide range of postoperative care. I am skilled in wound care and am also skilled in working with chest tubes and blood transfusions. My organizational and planning skills have served me well in my work with the peer review committee and with the organization and implementation of the hospital's United Way Fundraising campaign, which generated 18% more than the projected amount.

If you can use a nursing professional with experience in orthopedic/neurological as well as medical/surgical environments  along with a genuine commitment to providing the highest possible levels of patient care, then I hope you will contact me soon to suggest a time when we might meet to discuss your needs. I can assure you in advance that I have an excellent reputation and would quickly become a valuable asset to your organization.

Sincerely,

Natalie Crudup

# NATALIE CRUDUP

1110½ Hay Street, Fayetteville, NC 28305  •  preppub@aol.com  •  (910) 483-6611

---

**OBJECTIVE**  To benefit an organization that can use a motivated young nursing professional whose exceptional communication, organizational, and patient care skills have been proven in orthopedic and neurological surgical and intensive care/critical care environments.

**CERTIFICATIONS**  Licensed Registered Nurse, Pennsylvania Board of Nursing, 2002-05.
Certified in Community CPR (infant, children, and adult).

**EDUCATION**  **Associate Degree in Nursing (ADN)**, Sandhills Community College, Pittsburgh, PA, 2000. Received the Pennsylvania Nurse's Scholarship (2001) and Pinehurst Surgical Group Scholarship (2000) for academic excellence.
Completed a seminar, "Building People Relation Skills," 2001.
Completed a Neurosurgical Internship (16 hours).

**EXPERIENCE**  **REGISTERED NURSE, ORTHO/NEURO SURGICAL UNIT.** Pittsburgh Medical Center, Pittsburgh, PA (2000-present). Provide skilled nursing care to pre- and post-operative patients in the orthopedic and neurological surgical units as well as to medical-surgical patients at this large regional medical center.
- Perform regular patient assessments and monitoring; am skilled at handling chest tubes and blood transfusions.
- Work closely with physicians as part of an interdisciplinary team to promote excellence in patient care; played a key role on the Peer Review Committee.
- Work closely with a Physical Therapy Team to provide postoperative care.
- Perform wound care on surgical patients, cleaning incision sites, checking for infection, and changing dressings.
- Develop money-saving proposals to reduce supply expenditures; organized and implemented the United Way Fundraising campaign for 2002; exceeded program objectives by 18%.

**NURSING INTERN & NURSING STUDENT.** Pittsburgh Community College, Pittsburgh, PA (1998-00). Excelled academically and in clinical rotations throughout the state; received several scholarships based on my academic performance, and represented the Association of Nursing Students in a number of fund-raising and volunteer activities.
***Clinical Rotations:*** Received exceptional evaluations for my performance while completing these clinical rotations:
- **Neurological/Surgical:** Valley Medical Center, Pittsburgh, PA. Developed exceptional skills in performing patient assessment and skilled care of neurosurgical patients.
- **Medical/Surgical:** Moore Regional Hospital, Pittsburgh, PA. Refined my patient care skills and administered medication orally, intravenously, and subcutaneously.
- **Psychiatric:** Dorothea Dix and Cumberland Psychiatric Clinic, Raleigh and Pittsburgh, PA. Developed skill in the care and treatment of psychiatric patients.
- **Intensive Care Unit/Critical Care Unit (ICU/CCU):** Moore Regional Hospital, Pittsburgh, PA. Increased my abilities related to skilled nursing in challenging environments where patients required constant observation and stabilization.
- **Obstetrics/Labor & Delivery:** Valley Medical Center, Pittsburgh, PA. Served in the Newborn Nursery, NICU, Postpartem, Labor & Delivery, and Antenatal Testing units.
- **Pediatrics:** Valley Medical Center. Increased my knowledge while working with infant, juvenile, and adolescent patients.

**PERSONAL**  Excellent personal and professional references are available upon request.

**REGISTERED NURSE, PEDIATRIC SPECIAL CARE UNIT**

Dear Sir or Madam:

I am writing to express my strong interest in exploring the possibility of becoming a Clinical Coordinator with your organization. With the enclosed resume, I would like to acquaint you with the extensive experience in emergency room, transplant center, and cardiovascular, surgical, and pediatric intensive care units which I could bring to your organization.

Through my experience in surgical intensive care and in the transplant center, I have had the unique experience of seeing both sides of organ donation, from the courage of donors that chose to give of themselves to save the lives of others, to the miracles that transplantation can bring into the lives of the recipients. I would like to become an active part of this process, and I feel that I could make a strong contribution to your operation.

In only four years as a Registered Nurse, I have excelled in nearly every critical and intensive care environment, and I have worked with a wide variety of patient populations. From Level I Trauma and surgical intensive care to organ transplantation in a major regional teaching hospital, where I gained experience with various "bridge to transplant" devices, I have constantly sought out formidable challenges in my career.

If you can use a talented nursing professional with exceptional patient care skills and technical knowledge that have been proven in a variety of difficult environments, then I look forward to hearing from you soon. I assure you in advance that I would quickly become an asset to your organization, and I thank you for your time and consideration.

Yours sincerely,

Gina Sanders

# GINA SANDERS

1110½ Hay Street, Fayetteville, NC 28305  •  preppub@aol.com  •  (910) 483-6611

**OBJECTIVE**  To benefit an organization that can use a dedicated nursing professional who thrives on challenge and offers extensive patient care experience in emergency room, transplant center, and cardiovascular, surgical, and pediatric intensive care environments .

**EDUCATION**  **Bachelor of Science in Nursing**, State University of New York at Buffalo, Buffalo, NY, 1994; graduated **magna cum laude**.

**CERTIFICATIONS**  Advanced Cardiac Life Support (ACLS) certification, scheduled for renewal 3/31/03. Basic Cardiac Life Support (BCLS) certification, expires 8/31/04.

**AFFILIATIONS**  Member, **American Association of Critical Care Nurses**, 1994-present.
- **C.C.R.N.** since August, 2000.

Member, **Sigma Theta Tau International** (National Nursing Honor Society), Gamma Kappa Chapter, State University of New York at Buffalo, College of Nursing, 1999.

**EXPERIENCE**  **REGISTERED NURSE, PEDIATRIC SPECIAL CARE UNIT.** Travel Nurse for Clinical One at Buffalo Valley Medical Center, Buffalo, NY (2000-present). Provide patient care for newborn, juvenile, and adolescent patients with a variety of serious medical illnesses that require skilled nursing in a pediatric intensive care environment.
- Contribute patient and family education in stressful situations requiring tact and diplomacy.
- Support and stabilization of pediatric population in various medical emergencies or impending crises.

**REGISTERED NURSE.** Northwest Texas Regional Medical Center, Amarillo, TX (1998-00). Provided patient care to post-operative cardiac, general surgery, and multi-organ trauma patients in the **Surgical Intensive Care Unit** and **Emergency Department** of this busy regional medical center which supports a Level I Trauma Unit.
- Demonstrated my versatility and adaptability while working two different departments; dealt with families and patients faced with life-changing illnesses and accidents which involved multi-organ trauma as well as severe head and spinal cord injuries.

*With University Medical Center in Tucson, Arizona, advanced to positions of increasing responsibility at this major regional teaching hospital:*
*1996-98:* **REGISTERED NURSE, CARDIOVASCULAR INTENSIVE CARE UNIT.** Excelled as a key member on a dedicated team of nurses in this challenging position with a fast-paced, aggressive University transplant center.
- Provided patient care to postoperative cardiac and vascular, heart and lung transplant, and other patients suffering from cardiac, pulmonary, and multisystem diseases.
- Gained valuable experience with "bridge to transplant" devices, including Cardio-West Artificial Heart and Ventricular Assist devices such as NOVOCOR, Thoratec, and IntraAortic Balloon Pump.
- Served as Clinical Preceptor for new RNs and RN candidates in the Cardiovascular Intensive Care Unit.

*1994-96:* **REGISTERED NURSE, CARDIAC INTERMEDIATE CARE UNIT.** Provided care for patients awaiting transplants as well as patient/family education on subjects related to lifestyle, diet, and medications after transplants; worked with a variety of patients requiring cardiac monitoring.

**PERSONAL**  Known as a dedicated, hard-working professional with a passion for excellence.

**RESPIRATORY CARE NURSE**   Dear Sir or Madam:

With the enclosed resume, I would like to make you aware of an experienced licensed practical nurse with exceptional time management and communication skills and a background in obstetrics and gynecology, respiratory care of ventilator patients, and general patient care.

In my most recent position with the Veteran's Administration Medical Center, I specialized in providing nursing care to respiratory patients, many of whom were totally dependent on ventilators and other life support equipment. I closely monitored the operation of this equipment to ensure that it was functioning properly. I also provided care to a number of physically challenged patients in addition to those that I cared for in my area of specialty.

At Servantes Medical Center, I served as an Obstetrics and Gynecology Nurse, where my primary responsibilities were caring for new and expectant mothers, transporting patients in labor to the delivery room, and providing nursing care in the obstetrics recovery room and newborn nursery.

I earned a certificate from the Licensed Practical Nursing Program at Sanderson Technical Community College and am licensed in the state of Oklahoma. I have supplemented my degree program with numerous continuing education courses designed to keep my medical skills up to date. My education and experience could be a valuable addition to your organization.

If you can use a motivated, caring Licensed Practical Nurse, I hope you will contact me to suggest a time when we might meet to discuss your needs. I can assure you in advance that I have an excellent reputation and would quickly become a valuable asset to your company.

Sincerely,

Megan Long

# MEGAN LONG

1110½ Hay Street, Fayetteville, NC 28305   •   preppub@aol.com   •   (910) 483-6611

**OBJECTIVE**    To benefit an organization that can use an experienced licensed practical nurse with exceptional organizational skills and a background in respiratory care of ventilator patients, obstetrics and gynecology, and general patient care.

**EDUCATION**    Graduated from the **Licensed Practical Nursing program**, Sanderson Technical Community College, Sanderson, OK, 1990.
Completed two years of additional nursing studies at the Medical Center School of Nursing in Columbus, GA.
Have attended numerous courses to supplement and update my medical knowledge, including the following:
- Communicable diseases, 60 hours, 2001.
- Orthopedics and AIDS – new methods of treatment, 60 hours, 2001.
- Ventilator care, 60 hours, 2001.
- Respiratory care, 8 hours, 2000.

**LICENSES**    Oklahoma Licensed Practical Nurse #009190, expires 12/31/05.

**AFFILIATIONS**    Secretary, Oklahoma Licensed Practical Nurses Association, 2001.

**EXPERIENCE**    *With the Veteran's Administration Medical Center, advanced in the following "track record" of increasing responsibilities:*
**RESPIRATORY CARE NURSE.** Sanderson, OK (2000-02). Served as a Licensed Practical Nurse, specializing in medical-surgical patients who were dependent on ventilators.
- Closely monitored the operation of respirators and other life support equipment to ensure that it was functioning properly.
- Administered medications to patients as directed by physicians.
- Performed emergency respiratory treatments, such as oxygen administration and IPPB treatments.
- Checked patient's vital signs and changed IV bags.
- Provided nursing care to other physically challenged patients in addition to my patients in the respirator ward.

**LICENSED PRACTICAL NURSE.** Sanderson, OK (1995-00). Provided continuous patient care in this busy medical center.
- Monitored, measured and recorded patient's vital signs; updated charts.
- Administered medication as directed by physicians.
- Transported patients between departments.
- Bathed patients and changed dressings.
- Assisted in other procedures under the supervision and direction of registered nurses and doctors.
- Mastered time management while providing nursing care to a large number of patients within a limited amount of time.

Other experience: **OBSTETRICS and GYNECOLOGY NURSE.** Servantes Medical Center, Sanderson, OK (1990-94). Provided care as a Licensed Practical Nurse to obstetrics, gynecology, maternal, and newborn patients in this large medical center.
- Transported patients to labor room.
- Provided nursing care in obstetrics recovery room and newborn nursery.

**PERSONAL**    Excellent personal and professional references are available upon request.

Exact Name of Person
Exact Title
Exact Name of Company
Address
City, State, Zip

**STAFF NURSE**

Dear Exact Name of Person: (or Dear Sir or Madam if answering a blind ad)

With the enclosed resume, I would like to make you aware of my interest in a pharmaceutical sales position with your company.

Although I am excelling in my current position as a Trauma/Surgical Intensive Care Unit Nurse at Columbus University Medical Center, I have decided that I wish to embark on a career in medical marketing and sales. My naturally outgoing personality and ability to establish strong relationships would be well-suited to pharmaceutical sales. For example, I was recently honored by being nominated by patients' families for a prestigious award given by Columbus for "outstanding care of family members." Respected for my gracious and personable style of interacting with others, I am intimately familiar with the organizational culture of hospitals and clinics and have a nurse's understanding of a wide range of pharmaceutical treatments.

Prior to graduating with a B.S. in Nursing from the University of Georgia at Atlanta in 1998, I gained clinical experience in orthopedic, pediatric, OB/GYN, community health, and surgical/ICU environments. One summer I worked with a pharmaceutical company aiding a pediatric hematologist/oncologist in research related to neutropenia.

With a reputation as an articulate and persuasive communicator, I gained valuable sales skills in summer jobs as a bank teller, a sales representative in the UGA Alumni Annual Fund office, and in Columbus University's athletic office.

I assure you that my decision to leave the clinical medical environment for pharmaceutical sales is a well-thought-out decision. I have been very deliberate about my career. Although I entered college as a Political Science major at Columbus University and excelled academically for two years, I decided to embark on a nursing career and transferred to the University of Atlanta where I maintained a 3.7 GPA in my major while earning my B.S. in Nursing. Now I wish to transfer my clinical experience and knowledge into pharmaceutical sales, and I am confident that I will be successful in contributing to a company's bottom line.

I hope you will welcome my call soon when I try to arrange a brief meeting to discuss your goals and how my background might serve your needs. I can provide outstanding references at the appropriate time.

Sincerely,

Anita Michelle Carlton

# ANITA MICHELLE CARLTON

1110½ Hay Street, Fayetteville, NC 28305    •    preppub@aol.com    •    (910) 483-6611

**OBJECTIVE**    To contribute my skills as an articulate and outgoing young medical professional to an organization that can use a Pharmaceutical Sales Representative who offers a track record of excellence as a nurse, outstanding communication skills, and previous sales experience.

**HONOR**    Have been nominated by patients' families to receive a respected award for outstanding care of their family members.

**CERTIFICATIONS**    Licensed **Registered Nurse,** Georgia Board of Nursing.
Certified as an Advanced Cardiac Life Support (ACLS), 1999, and Basic Cardiac Life Support (BCLS) provider, 1997, by the American Heart Association.

**EDUCATION**    **Bachelor of Science** in **Nursing**, University of Georgia at Atlanta, GA, May 1998.
•    UNC Nursing GPA 3.5; maintained 3.7 GPA for both semesters in 1997.
**B.A.** in **Political Science**, University of Georgia at Atlanta, GA, 1996; **3.2 GPA**.
Completed two years of studies in Political Science, Columbus University, Columbus, GA, 1992-94. Columbus GPA 3.2; transferred to UGA in 1994 in order to pursue nursing career.
•    Awarded **First Union Merit Scholarship,** 1993-94, for leadership and scholarship.
Completed training programs and workshops in CPR, BCLS, and ACLS.

**EXPERIENCE**    **STAFF NURSE (Trauma/Surgical ICU).** Columbus University Medical Center, Columbus, GA (1998-present). Provide total nursing care to postoperative and trauma patients at this prestigious regional medical center and teaching hospital.
•    Perform patient assessment and telemetry monitoring, communicating information on the patient's response to treatment to the surgical resident or attending physician.
•    Administer medications, fluids, and blood products; set up and monitor IVs.
•    Provide education and support to patients and their families, performing liaison between the patient's families and doctors.

**NURSE AIDE II (Surgical ICU).** Columbus University Medical Center, Columbus, GA (June 1997-1998). Was offered a job on Surgical ICU after excelling in my summer externship.
•    Assisted nurses in providing care to SICU patients. Administered enteral feedings, performed dressing changes, baths, linen changes, and equipment quality control checks.

**NURSE EXTERN (Surgical ICU).** Columbus University Medical Center, Columbus, GA (August 1997). Was specially selected for this externship from a large pool of applicants, and excelled in every aspect of my first clinical care experience in one of the nation's top medical centers.
•    At the end of this 10-week program in which I worked 36 hours per week providing care to critically ill surgical patients, performed RN responsibility under preceptor's supervision.

**Other clinical experience:** Completed three seven-week clinical rotations at UG Hospitals: one at Chris Johnson Hospital, one at Brookstone Clinic, and one at Columbus Medical Center.

**Research experience:** For two semesters at UGA in 1995, worked with a pediatric hematologist/oncologist in setting up a database of patients with neutropenia for Amgen, Inc.
•    Once the registry was set up, the patients received a very expensive treatment, G-CSF, at no cost while the pharmaceutical company Amgen, Inc., gathered data on neutropenia.

**PERSONAL**    Have a thorough knowledge of the organizational culture of hospitals and clinics.

Date

Mrs. Smith
Administrative Director, Radiology Department
Cape Fear Valley Medical Center

**STAFF REGISTERED NURSE, EMERGENCY DEPARTMENT**

Dear Mrs. Smith:

With the enclosed resume, I would like to make you aware of my qualifications for the position of Radiology Staff Nurse, specifically my background as a radiology nurse with more than nine years of service to Anderson Medical Center, and the extensive list of certifications and credentials with which I have supplemented that experience.

I am currently excelling as a Staff Registered Nurse in the Emergency Department, where my primary duty is to serve as Triage Nurse. I interview presenting patients, assigning a triage category and prioritizing the placement of patients into the appropriate treatment areas based on the nature and severity of the patient's condition. I monitor the condition of patients in the waiting area, and upgrade or downgrade their assigned triage categories based on changes in patient condition.

Although I am highly regarded within the Emergency Department, and can provide excellent references at the appropriate time, it is my desire to return to Radiology, where I previously served with distinction. As you will see, I hold certifications in ACLS, BCLS, and PALS, in addition to credentials which qualify me to administer a wide range of medications specific to radiology procedures, including nuclear medicines and special procedures.

My knowledge, my skills, and above all, my personal loyalty made me a strong asset to the Radiology Department in the past, and would continue to do so in the future. I was proud to be a part of the growth and development of the radiology team during the nine years I served, and I would relish the opportunity to rejoin that team. I have a deep respect for the expertise and reputation of the radiology team headed by Dr. Quantas, and it is my strong desire to be of service to him and the team.

Sincerely,


Larry French

# LARRY FRENCH

1110½ Hay Street, Fayetteville, NC 28305　　•　　preppub@aol.com　　•　　(910) 483-6611

**OBJECTIVE**　　To benefit an organization that can use an educated and experienced radiology nurse with exceptional communication and organizational skills in addition to extensive certifications and credentials specific to radiological medicine.

**EDUCATION**　　**Advanced Trauma Life Support Program**, Pitt Memorial Medical Center, Greenville, SC, 1990.
**Critical Care Core Curriculum,** North Carolina Memorial Hospital, Chapel Hill, NC, 1988.
**Associate's degree in Nursing**, Sandhills Community College, Southern Pines, NC, 1986.
Completed one year of college course work at Campbell University, Buies Creek, NC, 1983.

**CERTIFICATIONS**　　Licensed **Registered Nurse** certificate #079912, North Carolina Board of Nursing, expires December 2005.
Pediatric Advanced Life Support (PALS) Certified, expires September 2004.
Advanced Cardiac Life Support (ACLS) Certified, expires November 2002.
Basic Cardiac Life Support (BCLS) Certified, expires March 2004.

**EXPERIENCE**　　**STAFF REGISTERED NURSE.** Emergency Department, Anderson Medical Center, Chapel Hill, NC (2000-present). Provide patient triage and nursing care in the Emergency Department of this busy regional medical center.
- Conduct patient assessment and initiate diagnostic procedures for appropriate presenting patients.
- Assign each patient to the appropriate triage category based on the nature and severity of the patient's condition.
- Place patients into the appropriate treatment area according to triage category and prioritize order of treatment.
- Observe and monitor all patients in the waiting room of the Emergency Department, upgrading or downgrading assigned triage categories according to patient condition.
- Demonstrate communication skills while conducting triage interviews and communicating patient needs related to condition to the supervisor or charge nurse.

**STAFF REGISTERED NURSE.** Radiology Department, Anderson Medical Center, Chapel Hill, NC (1993-2000). Performed patient assessment, patient and staff education, and implemented treatment plans and crisis intervention for radiology patients.
- Administered medication both orally and intravenously, to include conscious sedation, pain management, anti-coagulants, and coronary-specific medications.
- Observed cardiopulmonary measuring devices, monitoring the patient's condition and providing crisis intervention.
- Assisted in the development and implementation of policies and procedures for nursing practice standards in the Radiology Department.
- Conducted contrast injection I.V.P. studies to aid in patient diagnosis.
- Earned radiology-specific credentials in the following procedures: nitroglycerin I.A. infusion, urokinase infusion, contrast injection I.V.P. studies, persantine infusion study, adenosine infusion study, and dobutamine infusion study.

**STAFF REGISTERED NURSE.** Emergency Room, Anderson Medical Center, Greensboro, NC (1989-1993). Performed patient assessment and assignment of triage categories, trauma nursing, crisis intervention, and acute care of adults and children (infants through adolescents).

**PERSONAL**　　Excellent personal and professional references are available upon request.

# SECTION IV.
## OTHER MEDICAL PROFESSIONALS

In this section, you will find resumes and cover letters of other medical professionals. Perhaps you will find an example in this section that will help you find a suitable model to use in creating your own resume and cover letter.

In this section you will find the resumes and cover letters of professionals such as a cytotechnologist, dental assistant, licensed massage therapist, medical administrative assistant, medical equipment maintenance services supervisor, a medical doctor, physician, medical logistics manager, medical supply supervisor, nuclear medicine technologist, nutritionist, pharmaceutical sales consultant, pharmacy technician, and physician assistant.

It is worth noting that the editor of this book feels strongly that a cover letter should always accompany a resume. That is why nearly every resume in this book is accompanied by a cover letter.

**CYTOTECHNOLOGIST**     Dear Sir or Madam:

With the enclosed resume, I would like to make you aware of my interest in the position of Cytotechnologist which you advertised recently in the Atlanta Observer.

As you will see, I am ASCP Certified, and I completed a post-baccalaureate Certificate in Cytotechnology at the University of Georgia at Atlanta after earning my B.S. degree in Biology from Atlanta University.

In my current job with Atlanta Regional Hospital in Atlanta, I screen Gyn and Non-Gyn slides. In my previous job which I held for three years at Atlanta Medical Center, I worked as a Cytotechnologist in a sophisticated, state-of-the-art medical center. At Atlanta Medical Center, I became experienced with thin prep Gyn Cytology, thin prep Non-Gyn Cytology, and with the collection and preparation of fine needle aspirations. I resigned my position at Atlanta Medical Center in order to take the position at Atlanta Regional Hospital because Atlanta Regional Hospital was closer to my home, thereby reducing my commute. As you will notice from my resume, my husband and I reside in Atlanta, and I would greatly enjoy the opportunity to work at Columbus Medical Center. I was born in Atlanta and graduated from Atlanta High School, and my husband and I are permanent residents of this community.

I can provide excellent personal and professional references, and I hope you will give me an opportunity to show you in person that I am the individual you are seeking.

Sincerely,

Yolanda M. Zion

# YOLANDA M. ZION

1110½ Hay Street, Fayetteville, NC 28305    •    preppub@aol.com    •    (910) 483-6611

---

**OBJECTIVE**

I want to contribute to a medical organization that can use an outstanding young cytotechnologist who offers a proven ability to establish and maintain cordial and professional relationships with people at all levels.

**CERTIFICATION**    ASCP Certified

**EDUCATION**

Post-Baccalaureate **Certificate in Cytotechnology**, University of Georgia at Atlanta, August 1996.
- Was a member of a very select, handpicked four-person class.

Earned **Bachelor of Science in Biology**, Georgia University, Atlanta, GA, May 1995.
- Received the Scott Ellis Scholarship for four years.

Graduated from Atlanta High School, Atlanta, GA, 1992.

**EXPERIENCE**

**CYTOTECHNOLOGIST.** Atlanta Regional Hospital, Atlanta, GA (2000-present).
Screen Gyn and Non-Gyn slides.

**CYTOTECHNOLOGIST.** Atlanta Medical Center, Atlanta, GA (1996-00).
At this sophisticated medical center, became experienced with the following:
- thin prep Gyn Cytology
- thin prep Non-Gyn Cytology
- collection and preparation of fine-needle aspirations.

**CYTOTECHNOLOGIST INTERN.** Atlanta Army Medical Center, Atlanta, GA (June-July 1996). Excelled in a two-month internship at this military medical center.
- Assisted with the preparation of Gyn and Non-Gyn specimens.
- Accompanied medical professionals on rotations to collect fine-needle aspiration specimens.
- Screened Gyn and Non-Gyn slides.

**CYTOTECHNOLOGIST CLINICAL ROTATION.** University of Georgia Medical Center, Atlanta, GA (1996).
Performed with distinction in a year-long clinical rotation while I was still in graduate school.
- Assisted with preparation of Gyn and Non-Gyn specimens.
- Screened Gyn and Non-Gyn slides.
- Accompanied medical professionals on rotations to collect fine-needle aspiration specimens.

**CYTOTECHNOLOGIST CLINICAL ROTATION.** State Laboratory, Atlanta, GA (1995).
Excelled in a year-long clinical rotation while I was still in graduate school.
- Screened Gyn slides and assisted in preparing Gyn specimens.

**PERSONAL**

Outstanding personal and professional references upon request. Highly motivated self starter with strong people skills and technical knowledge.

Exact Name of Person
Exact Title
Exact Name of Company
Address
City, State, Zip

**DENTAL ASSISTANT**

Dear Exact Name of Person: (or Dear Sir or Madam if answering a blind ad)

With the enclosed resume, I would like to make you aware of my background as a highly skilled dental assistant who has excelled in challenging clinical and mobile dental unit environments. I have extensive experience in general and pediatric dentistry, oral surgery, periodontics, endodontics, and prosthodontics.

As you will see from my resume, I have recently excelled as a Dental Assistant II for a community health center. In this position, I worked in a clinic environment for most of the year, and utilized my language skills in addition to my dental expertise while working as a key member of a mobile dental unit servicing a population of migrant farm workers during the summer months. In the clinic, I performed four- and six-hand chairside assisting, exposed and developed the full range of dental radiographs, and oversaw the ordering of materials and supplies for the practice.

In addition to completing the Red Cross Dental Assisting course, I graduated from the Dental Assistant II course offered by the University of Vermont's School of Dentistry, and am currently preparing to take the Certified Dental Assistant examination for state board licensure. I also hold a Bachelor's degree in International Relations and am fully fluent in both Spanish and English.

Although I was highly regarded by my previous employer and can provide excellent personal and professional references at the appropriate time, I am interested in pursuing other career opportunities with dental practices closer to my home. If you can use a self-motivated, reliable professional who offers extensive experience in all aspects of general and pediatric dentistry, then I hope you will welcome my call soon when I try to arrange a brief meeting to discuss your goals and how my background might serve your needs. I can provide outstanding references at the appropriate time.

Sincerely,

Heidi W. Schwartz

Alternate Last Paragraph:
I hope you will write or call me soon to suggest a time when we might meet to discuss your needs and goals and how my background might serve them. I can provide outstanding references at the appropriate time.

# HEIDI W. SCHWARTZ

1110½ Hay Street, Fayetteville, NC 28305    •    preppub@aol.com    •    (910) 483-6611

| | |
|---|---|
| **OBJECTIVE** | To contribute to a practice that can use a skilled dental assistant who offers a background of excellence in general and pediatric dentistry, oral surgery, periodontics, endodontics, and prosthodontics in mobile unit and clinic environments. |
| **CERTIFICATIONS** | Currently preparing to take the Certified Dental Assistant examination for state board licensure.<br>Certified in Community CPR (adult, infant, and child), American Heart Association.<br>Hold a current X-ray certification. |
| **EDUCATION** | **Bachelor's degree in International Relations,** University of Toledo, OH, 1995.<br>Completed the **Dental Assistant II** Preparatory Course, School of Dentistry, University of Vermont, Burlington, VT.<br>Finished Red Cross **Dental Assisting** Course, Pope Air Force Base, NC.<br>Graduated from the **X-ray Certification** course, Burlington Technical Community College, Burlington, VT.<br>Completed numerous continuing education courses at local Area Health Education Centers, including:<br>• Dental Management of the Stroke/Seizure Patient, Burlington Area Health Education Foundation, Inc.<br>• Nitrous Oxide Sedation for Dental Auxiliaries, Northeast Regional Area Health Education Center.<br>• Providing Dental Care for Uncooperative Dental Patients, Burlington Area Health Education Foundation, Inc.<br>• Hazardous Communication Training (OSHA)<br>• Infection Control and Blood Borne Pathogens (OSHA guidelines) |
| **EXPERIENCE** | **DENTAL ASSISTANT II.** Dr. Eric McLaughtin, Tri-County Community Health Center, Burlington, VT (2001-02). Played a key role in the success of this busy dental practice; worked in a clinic environment nine months of the year and in a mobile unit servicing a population of migrant farm workers during the summer months.<br>• Instructed new assistants in dental treatment room operations and procedures, to include oral surgery using IV sedation.<br>• Oversaw ordering of all needed office and dental supplies; scheduling service for equipment.<br>• Performed chairside assisting, including the use of four- and six-hand dentistry to pass and retrieve materials and instruments needed for the procedure to and from the dentist.<br>• Provided expert assistance in the operating room for oral surgery and other surgical procedures, skilled in administering intravenous sedation.<br>• Gained experience working with endodontics and application of sealants.<br>• Exposed and developed dental radiographs.<br>• Assisted with crown and bridgework as well as other restorative and cosmetic dentistry.<br><br>**DENTAL ASSISTANT.** Burlington County Medical Center, Burlington, VT (1997-00). In this part-time job simultaneous with the one above, was a vital member of the mobile unit, providing general dentistry and oral surgery under challenging field conditions.<br>• Assisted in all phases of general dentistry including surgical removal of impacted teeth, pediatric dentistry, and amalgam and composite fillings; maintained patient charts. |
| **LANGUAGES** | Fully fluent in both Spanish and English. |
| **PERSONAL** | Excellent personal and professional references are available upon request. |

Exact Name of Person
Title or Position
Name of Company
Address (number and street)
Address (city, state, and zip)

**LICENSED MASSAGE THERAPIST**

Dear Exact Name of Person:  (or Sir or Madam if answering a blind ad.)

With the enclosed resume, I would like to express my interest in exploring employment opportunities with your organization.

As you will see, I am a nationally certified massage therapist who offers experience in working with sports and trauma injuries.  I hold certification as a  Therapeutic Massage  and Bodywork Practitioner (NCTMB) from the American Massage Therapy Association and am licensed by the state and the city to practice therapeutic massage. A graduate of a 525-hour program, I completed core course work in anatomy and physiology, communications and somatics, Swedish massage, sports massage, and deep muscle massage with supportive curriculum in areas including business practices.

As founder and owner of my own business, I handle business functions in support of professional massage services which integrate with the different modalities depending on client needs. I provide massage for clients who are recovering from accidents, some with chronic muscular problems, and others who want massage therapy for relaxation and stress relief.

My services are provided through various area organizations and companies which include a minor league baseball team, a chiropractic center, a hair and nail salon, and a spa. I usually work with the baseball players before their home games and with the staff of the chiropractic clinic as needed to provide extra assistance for accident victims and patients with chronic muscular aches and pains. This has allowed me the opportunity to work with patients with insurance coverage for massage therapy and to assist the staff of the chiropractic clinic in writing some of the narrative materials for the insurance companies.

If you can use a highly reliable young professional who works well with medial professionals at all levels while contributing to the care of sports and trauma injuries, I hope you will contact me to suggest a time when we might meet to discuss your needs. I can provide outstanding references at the appropriate time.

Sincerely,

Lana Marie Markleson

# LANA MARIE MARKLESON, N.C.T.M.B.

1110½ Hay Street, Fayetteville, NC 28305   •   preppub@aol.com   •   (910) 483-6611

---

**OBJECTIVE**   I want to contribute to an organization that can use a respected young massage therapist who offers experience in working with sports and trauma injuries.

**CERTIFICATIONS**   Nationally certified Therapeutic Massage and Bodywork Practitioner (NCTMB) Member, American Massage Therapy Association.
Licensed by the State of Virginia and by the city of Roanoke to engage in the practice of therapeutic massage under the required business name "Christian Care."
Completed Parent Effectiveness Training (PET); certified in CPR by American Red Cross.

**EDUCATION**   Graduated from the 525-hour massage therapy program, Virginia School of Massage Therapy, Roanoke, VA, 2000; was cited for professionalism and high personal standards and ethics.
•   Completed course work which included these areas of emphasis:
**Core curriculum:** Anatomy and Physiology, Communications and Somatics, Swedish Massage, Sports Massage, and Deep Muscle Massage
**Secondary modalities:** Joint Movement, Polarity, Lymphatic Drainager, and Introduction to Oriental bodywork
**Supportive curriculum:** Business practices, case studies, hydrotherapy, introduction to touch, observation and analysis, pathology, and sensory/motor development

**AFFILIATION**   Board Member (Treasurer), Roanoke Area Massage Therapy Association (ROAMTA)

**EXPERIENCE**   **LICENSED MASSAGE THERAPIST.** Christian Care, Roanoke, VA (2000-present). As the owner and founder of this business, handle all business functions in addition to providing professional massage services integrated with the different modalities depending on muscle needs. Provide massage to clients in various situations—some recovering from an accident, some with chronic muscular problems, and some who just want relaxation and stress relief.
•   Have worked with various organizations and companies in these areas:
**Sports massage clientele:** For the Roanoke Baseball Team, am in my second season of providing professional massage therapist services; work with the players before home games and occasionally in between the games.
**Chiropractic clientele:** For the Caison Chiropractic Center, have worked as needed on accident victims and patients with chronic muscular problems experiencing aches and pains; have gained experience in working with patients who have insurance coverage for massage treatment. Provided massage therapy for insurance patients who were accident victims, and assisted the chiropractor in writing some of the narratives.
**Salon clientele:** For a prominent hair and nail salon, provided massage for relaxation purposes.
**Spa clientele:** Provided massages, facials, hot herbal bodywraps, and body polishing while also creating flyers and brochures describing the spa's services.

**SUBSTITUTE TEACHER & TEACHER'S ASSISTANT.** Kelsey Christian Academy, Roanoke, VA (1994-00). Displayed initiative while assisting teachers and filling in for absent teachers in grades from kindergarten through high school age.

**ADVISOR & GROUP LEADER.** Community organizations, Germany (1992-94). Held positions including library assistant, school bus monitor, treasurer, newsletter editor, and clerical assistant while living in Germany as the spouse of a military professional.

**Other experience:** Excelled in jobs as a Receptionist and Retail Assistant Manager.

**PERSONAL**   Highly reliable individual who works well with medical professionals at all levels.

Real-Resumes Series edited by Anne McKinney  151

Date

Exact Name of Person
Title or Position
Name of Company
Address (number and street)
Address (city, state, and zip)

Dear Exact Name of Person:  (or Sir or Madam if answering a blind ad.)

With the enclosed resume, I would like to express my interest in exploring employment opportunities with your organization.

As you will see, I offer a versatile background in medical administration gained while earning rapid advancement with the Veteran's Administration in the Iowa VA health care system.  My background includes high levels of knowledge in the fields of inventory control and supply, automated systems operation, and supervision. Originally hired as a File Clerk, I quickly displayed a level of knowledge and expertise which led to my rapid advancement to assignments as a Medical Clerk, then as a Patient Services Assistant, to my current job as Medical Administrative Assistant where I frequently am called on to act as the ranking administrative services officer.

In this capacity, I have earned respect for my expertise in areas which include administrative and operations management, the interpretation and application of regulations, and for my outstanding verbal and written communications skills.

Earlier I advanced to hold managerial roles in logistics, mail processing, and supply with the U.S. Army.  During my military career I was cited for my skill as a mentor and trainer who inspired "confidence and respect" from others while managing multimillion-dollar inventories and supervising as many as three junior managers and 12 employees.

If you can use a results-oriented professional who offers versatile experience in medical administration as well as strong knowledge in inventory control, automated systems, and supervision. I hope you will contact me to suggest a time when we might meet to discuss your needs. I can provide outstanding references at the appropriate time.

Sincerely,

Elizabeth Wenters

# ELIZABETH WENTERS

1110½ Hay Street, Fayetteville, NC 28305   •   preppub@aol.com   •   (910) 483-6611

---

**OBJECTIVE**

To offer versatile experience in medical administration to an organization that can use a results-oriented professional with a reputation for high levels of knowledge in the inventory control and supply, automated systems operations, and supervisory fields.

**EDUCATION & TRAINING**

Associate of Arts degree, San Bernardino Valley College, CA.

Attended U.S. Army leadership development schools as well as a 320-hour program for subsistence supply specialists; completed correspondence courses emphasizing logistics, maintenance, defense acquisition contracting, and physical inventory management.

**EXPERIENCE**

*Am advancing in the following track record of accomplishments, Veteran's Administration Central Iowa Health Care System, Des Moines, IA (1998-present).*

**MEDICAL ADMINISTRATIVE ASSISTANT.** (2001-present). Have been cited for expertise in administrative and operations management, interpreting and applying regulations, and outstanding verbal and written communication skills displayed as ranking administrative officer in the absence of the chief of Medical Administrative Services.

**PATIENT SERVICES ASSISTANT.** (1999-01). Became familiar with the activities of this department and polished skills which led to my promotion.
- Worked closely with the nursing coordinator while receiving and processing patients and counseling them on benefits; collected, verified, input, and assembled data on the gains and losses sheet; maintained activity logs.

**MEDICAL CLERK.** (1999). Gained a strong base of knowledge in the operation of a medical clinic while scheduling, greeting, and prioritizing patients according to the severity of their condition; processed patient records and documentation.
- Ensured consults were processed and non-VA documentation completed.

**FILE CLERK.** (1998). Was assigned to the Health Information Management Section, providing timely and accurate retrieval of medical records which often required conducting searches through various departments to locate records which had not been returned. Operated a switchboard with 510 main stations as a Telephone Operator.

Advanced to managerial roles in logistics, mail processing, and supply, U.S. Army:
**AUTOMATED LOGISTICS SUPERVISOR.** Ft. Hood, TX (1997-98). Described as a skilled mentor and trainer who "inspires confidence and respect;" managed controlled and reserve stock while interpreting supply documents in an automated environment.

**CONSOLIDATED MAILROOM SUPERVISOR.** Germany (1996-97). After approximately one year (1996-97) as a Unit Mail Clerk was promoted to supervise 11 clerks and train personnel processing mail for an 1,872-person community.

**SUBSISTENCE SUPPLY SUPERVISOR.** Ft. Campbell, KY (1995-96) and Korea (1995). Supervised as many as three junior managers and 12 employees in consecutive positions: most recently while overseeing receipt, storage, distribution, and accountability for subsistence rations and earlier as manager of the largest cold-storage plant in Korea.

*Highlights of earlier Army experience:* Promoted to increasingly higher supervisory levels.

**PERSONAL**

Am a versatile and adaptable professional who can handle pressure, stress, and deadlines.

Exact Name of Person
Exact Title
Exact Name of Company
Address
City, State, Zip

**MEDICAL EQUIPMENT
MAINTENANCE SERVICES
SUPERVISOR**

Dear Exact Name of Person (or Dear Sir or Madam if answering a blind ad)

I would appreciate an opportunity to talk with you soon about how I could contribute to your organization through my experience and skills in the specialized field of biomedical equipment maintenance and repair as well as through my outstanding planning, organizational, and supervisory skills.

As you will see from my enclosed resume, I am a Medical Equipment Maintenance Services Supervisor and have been recognized with several medals and awards for my accomplishments and professionalism. I received extensive training which included the U.S. Army's year-long Biomedical Equipment Repair Course as well as additional training in information systems and PC maintenance and repair.

Presently overseeing maintenance for an inventory of more than 500 pieces of equipment, I was selected for this position and have been credited with exceeding expectations in all areas of operations. I have transformed an inefficient operation into one which is known for being customer friendly, productive, and efficient. I took the initiative to locate sources of free parts and equipment and obtained more than $20,000 worth of equipment at no cost to the organization. I have achieved additional success in several overseas assignments with task forces in Bosnia and Haiti where I have often been the only biomedical equipment technician servicing multiple locations and developing outstanding services.

If you can use an experienced professional with technical and mechanical skills along with well-developed managerial and leadership abilities, I hope you will contact me to suggest a time when we might meet to discuss your needs. I can assure you in advance that I could rapidly become an asset to your organization.

Sincerely,

Ward McCally

# WARD MCCALLY

1110½ Hay Street, Fayetteville, NC 28305    •    preppub@aol.com    •    (910) 483-6611

---

**OBJECTIVE**

To contribute to an organization that can benefit from my experience and knowledge in the specialized area of biomedical equipment technology along with my excellent technical trouble-shooting skills and my ability to motivate and lead others to achieve results.

**EDUCATION & TRAINING**

Excelled in extensive training which has included the Army's year-long Biomedical Equipment Repair Course as well as the following programs and courses:
- automated maintenance management information systems for equipment
- troubleshooting, maintaining, and upgrading PCs
- radiation protection
- digital film system/ teleradiology and video teleconferencing driver training
- professional leadership development programs

**TECHNICAL SKILLS**

Troubleshoot to the component level, medical equipment including (but not limited to) defibrillators, anesthesia, X-ray, ventilators, monitors, suction apparatus, and lab equipment.

**EXPERIENCE**

*Have earned a reputation for my initiative and dedication to excellence as well as for my leadership, technical, and mechanical skills while serving in the U.S. Army:*
**MEDICAL EQUIPMENT MAINTENANCE SERVICES SUPERVISOR.** Ft. Benning, GA (2000-present). Recognized with several medals and awards for my expertise and versatility; independently handle the details of developing and overseeing all aspects of maintenance support for more than 500 pieces of equipment; supervise one technician.
- Was credited with transforming an inefficient and unproductive section into one which is recognized as being customer service oriented and highly productive.
- On my own initiative, located sources and obtained more than $200,000 worth of parts and test equipment at no cost to the organization.
- Prepare annual evaluation reports for one junior manager as well as monthly counseling statements for all employees under my command.
- Schedule and perform preventive maintenance, electrical safety tests, and calibration.
- Oversee and personally maintain automated records of equipment inventories.
- Control over 300 types of repair parts to include inventorying, ordering, and stocking.
- Earned Army Commendation and Achievement Medals for my accomplishments supporting the quality of health care for personnel providing humanitarian assistance in Haiti: trained local personnel in electrical wiring and in equipment maintenance and helped establish a maintenance program in a new dental clinic.
- Received my fourth Army Commendation Medal and a NATO Medal for serving in Bosnia as the lone medical maintenance support specialist for several facilities: participated in multinational support efforts and developed effective training and a calibration schedule which increased levels of support and service provided by a medial task force.

**BIOMEDICAL EQUIPMENT MAINTENANCE SUPERVISOR.** Ft. Bragg, NC (1997-00). Supervised four people while providing outstanding support maintenance for an 80,000-member organization with its worldwide fast-response mission.
- Recognized as a subject matter expert, was called on to train other technicians.
- Trained and set up the first forward contact team in preparation for a major project in Africa.
- Designed and built a shelving system for repair parts which significantly improved storage.

**BIOMEDICAL EQUIPMENT TECHNICIAN.** Ft. Bragg, NC (1995-96). Learned depot-level repair procedures and earned an Army Commendation Medal.

**PERSONAL**

Studied college-level English and History at the college level.

# JEFF JACOBS, M.D.

Date

**MEDICAL DOCTOR**

Dear Dr. Bridges:

I am responding to the advertisement in the June issue of *The Annals of Internal Medicine* for an Internist to join your organization. My experience in working with a group similar to yours is delineated in my attached resume.

Our medical group employs three physicians in a variety of medical specialties. For the past two and a half years, I have:

- worked closely with other specialists in the community who sought help in the diagnosis and treatment of adult diseases.
- collaborated with other specialists to ascertain the best approach to treating patients.
- gained experience working with a number of individuals of various ages and socioeconomic backgrounds.

All of these activities require not only up-to-date knowledge of medical treatment routines, but also a tactful understanding and nonthreatening approach to working with other physicians. You would find me to be a dedicated professional who offers the experience and knowledge needed to help achieve the realization of your organizational objectives.

I hope this brief letter conveys my enthusiasm for the position advertised. I am available for an interview at your convenience and look forward to meeting with you soon. I will contact you next week to discuss the opening with you.

Sincerely yours,

Jeff Jacobs, M.D.

Enclosure: Resume

# JEFF JACOBS, M.D.

1110½ Hay Street, Fayetteville, NC 28305   •   preppub@aol.com   •   (910) 483-6611

---

**EXPERIENCE**   **INTERNIST** (2000-present)
Pinkerton Primary Care Center
Cloville, OR
- Established a cardiac stress testing program in our clinic.
- Counsel other family practice physicians in our group on internal medicine problems.
- Care for a panel of adult patients five days per week.
- Conduct problem-solving meetings, work with ancillary staff on interpersonal dynamics.

**EDUCATION**   Hospital of Saint Patrick, Major Affiliate of Yale University
New Haven, CT
**Internal Medicine Residency,** 1998-2000

Saint George's University
Saint George's, Grenada
**Medical Doctor,** 1997
Maintained a 3.40 GPA

Hospital of Saint Patrick
New Haven, CT
**Internal Medicine Internship,** 1993-1994

Fairleigh Dickinson University
Rutherford, NJ
**Master of Science in Medical Laboratory,** 1992
Maintained a 3.96 GPA

American University of Beirut
Beirut, Lebanon
**Bachelor of Science in Medical Laboratory,** 1989

**CERTIFICATIONS**   American Board of Internal Medicine, 2002.
Advanced Cardiac Life Support Provider, 1997-present.

**LICENSES**   North Carolina, #XYZ-123, 2000-present.

**PROFESSIONAL**   American Medical Association (Member)

**SOCIETIES**   American College of Physicians
North Carolina Medical Society

**COMMITTEES**   Diabetes Practice Group
Mayo Medical Center, 1997-present.

**PERSONAL**   Avid outdoor enthusiast. Particularly interested in soccer.
**INTERESTS**   Hospital of Richardson Tennis Singles Champion, 1995.
Volunteer as a soccer coach on weekends.

Date

Exact Name of Person
Title or Position
Name of Company
Address (number and street)
Address (city, state, and zip)

**MEDICAL DOCTOR**

Dear Exact Name of Person:  (or Sir or Madam if answering a blind ad.)

With the enclosed resume, I would like to express my interest in exploring employment opportunities with your organization.

As you will see, I am a practicing Pediatrician providing outpatient and inpatient care to include after-hour coverage for a group of eight physicians and as a consultant in pediatric cases to the emergency room of a medical center. My activities also include overseeing the care of newborns in the medical center nursery as well as supervising and teaching senior residents and interns making rounds and when they are assigned on call.

I received my Medical Degree from Cornell Medical College in New York after earning a B.S. in Bacteriology and Public Health with a minor in Chemistry. I have completed the General Pediatrics Certifying Examination and am Board Eligible; have passed Part Three of the National Board of Medical Examiners test; and am licensed to practice medicine.

Simultaneously with my current position, I have also worked at two hospital-based satellite clinics. I played an instrumental role in organizing and setting up the delivery of one of these clinics where I worked closely with an internal medicine practitioner to provide care for children in a rural setting. At the other clinic, I worked with two other pediatricians proving primary care in a group practice setting.

If you can use an experienced specialist in pediatric medical care, I hope you will contact me to suggest a time when we might meet to discuss your needs. I can provide outstanding references at the appropriate time.

Sincerely,

Doris McAlister, M.D.

# DORIS MCALISTER, M.D.

1110½ Hay Street, Fayetteville, NC 28305    •    preppub@aol.com    •    (910) 483-6611

| | |
|---|---|
| **EXPERIENCE** | **House Staff Physician**, Duluth Medical Center, Duluth, MN (2000-present). Outpatient and inpatient pediatrics. Provide after-hours coverage for a call group of eight physicians, also provide coverage and consultation for the emergency room. Provide newborn care for nursery. Supervise and teach interns and senior residents on rounds and during on-call assignments. |
| | *Worked at the following hospital-based satellite clinics:* <br> Marietta Medical Care, Marietta, LA (1996-99). <br> Was instrumental in the organization and set up of the delivery of this practice; provide care to pediatric patients in a rural setting along with an internal medicine practitioner. |
| | Melrose Pediatric Care, New Orleans, LA (1994-95). <br> Provided primary care to pediatric patients in a group practice setting with two other pediatricians. |
| ***Residency & Internships*** | Pediatrics, Interfaith Medical Center, Brooklyn, NY (1992-94). <br> Pediatrics, Interfaith Medical Center, Brooklyn, NY (1991-92). <br> Pediatrics, Case Western Reserve University, Program B, Metro Health Medical Center, Cleveland, OH (1990-91). |
| **EDUCATION** | **Medical Degree**, Cornell Medical College, Cornell, NY, 1990. <br> **B.S., Bacteriology** and **Public Health**, with a minor in **Chemistry**, Washington State University, Pullman, WA, 1983. |
| **RESEARCH EXPERIENCE** | *Worked as a research assistant on the following:* <br> *Department of Chemistry, Tennessee State University*, Nashville, TN (1986-87). Performed enzyme and protein assays, purification of enzymes and protein fragments (high-pressure liquid chromatography) and protein modification techniques. Laboratory maintenance. |
| | *Department of Microbiology/Immunology, Meharry Medical College,* Nashville, TN (1985-86). Performed hemolytic plaque assays to measure mouse spleen antibody response to sheep red blood cells injected into live mice. Animal care. |
| | *Tulane University Medical School,* New Orleans, LA (1982). <br> Isolated, cultured, and identified bacteria collected from clinical isolates using conventional laboratory media. Used immunofluorescent antibody technique to identify a certain component of the bacteria cell wall. |
| **LICENSURES/ EXAMINATIONS** | General Pediatrics Certifying Examination, Board Eligible <br> North Carolina Medical License, 1994-present. <br> National Board of Medical Examiners, 1992 (Part Three - Passed) |
| **ORGANIZATION** | *Committee of Interns and Residents (CIR), 1992-94* <br> As the Department Representative, addressed patient care concerns, issues regarding residency education, and training; negotiated contracts with administrative staff at Interfaith Medical Center. |
| **MEMBERSHIPS** | American Academy of Pediatrics, Candidate Fellow <br> Louisiana Medical Society |

Exact Name of Person
Exact Title
Exact Name of Company
Address
City, State, Zip

**MEDICAL LOGISTICS MANAGER**

Dear Exact Name of Person: (or Dear Sir or Madam if answering a blind ad):

With the enclosed resume, I would like to introduce you to my background as an experienced nursing professional whose exceptional supervisory, organizational, and patient care skills have been proven in challenging medical environments worldwide.

As you will see from my resume, I completed the U.S. Army's Academy of Health Sciences program where I was the Honor Graduate of my class, and I am certified as a Licensed Practical Nurse. I addition to numerous military leadership and technical courses, I have also earned certification as a Basic Cardiac Life Support (BCLS) Instructor and Provider.

Recently with the U.S. Army, I served as the Project Manager for a forward surgical hospital, managed a family practice clinic, and oversaw a Medical Logistics operation, supervising inventory control and budgetary requirements. In these positions and as the Manager of a Surgical Intensive Care Unit, I have become accustomed to high levels of responsibility, controlling multimillion dollar budgets as well as interviewing, hiring, supervising, and training personnel.

My patient care skills are highly developed, and have been honed in earlier positions as a Coronary Care Recovery Nurse and Patient Care Specialist, as well as in the above positions.

If you can use a talented nursing professional with strong leadership abilities, I hope you will welcome my call soon when I try to arrange a brief meeting to discuss your goals and how my background might serve your needs. I can provide outstanding references at the appropriate time.

Sincerely,

Harold Bullard

# HAROLD BULLARD

1110½ Hay Street, Fayetteville, NC 28305    •    preppub@aol.com    •    (910) 483-6611

**OBJECTIVE**

To offer experience as a practical nurse to a medical facility that can use a mature professional with a reputation for persistence, initiative, and the ability to build teams and carry projects and assignments from concepts to completion.

**EDUCATION, TRAINING, & SPECIAL SKILLS**

Completed the U.S. Army's Academy of Health Sciences program leading to certification as a **Licensed Practical Nurse**, Ft. Campbell KY, 1989; was Honor Graduate of my class.
Earned Diploma in Forestry, Professional Career Development Institute, Lexington, KY, 2002.
Completed additional military training as a Combat Engineer and in leadership development as well as numerous medical specialty courses: IV Therapy, interpreting arterial blood gases, cardiac rehabilitation, dealing with the terminally ill, EKG interpretation, wardmaster duties, quality management, computer applications, and winter survival and emergencies.
Offer **computer knowledge** of MS Word and Excel, Windows 98, and the Internet.
Am licensed by the American Health Association as a **BCLS Instructor and Provider**.

**EXPERIENCE**

*Was widely recognized as a professional who could be counted on for time- and money-saving solutions which improved the quality of medical services, U.S. Army:*
**MEDICAL LOGISTICS MANAGER.** Ft. Campbell, KY (2000-present). Managed $1 million worth of medical supplies while analyzing budget requirements, identifying shortages and overstocks, acting as contracting officer for external support, and supervising four logistics specialists.

**PROJECT MANAGER.** Ft. Campbell, KY (1999-00). Provided overall management and direction for a functional reorganization during which a forward surgical hospital was designed, equipment obtained, 96 people hired, and staff trained.

**FAMILY PRACTICE CLINIC MANAGER.** Germany (1996-99). Provided clinical and administrative support for a five-doctor staff in a clinic treating 2,200 patients each month.
- Developed and administered quality assurance polices and procedures which guaranteed high standards of patient care.
- Evaluated job performance and wrote periodic performance appraisals as well as updating and formalizing job descriptions for more than 20 health care professionals.
- Implemented and managed a TRICARE Health Management Organizational Program, achieved 100% automation of all clinic records using the Composite Health Care Computer System, and provided TRICARE services for retirees.
- Served as chairman of the Patient Rights and Organizational Ethics Committee and was a key factor in earning Joint Commission on Accreditation of Healthcare Organizations (JCAHO) accreditation.

**MANAGER, SURGICAL INTENSIVE CARE UNIT.** Ft. Polk, LA (1994-96). Earned respect for my medical and administrative skills and attention to detail while reorganizing, modernizing, and fielding four intensive care units at an estimated cost saving of $1.2 million; trained and supported 40 nursing and ten administrative personnel.

**CORONARY CARE RECOVERY NURSE.** Honolulu, HI (1989-93). Served as leader of a team of patient care specialists with duties such as assessing patient care, hemodynamic monitoring, managing invasive care lines, and assisting during surgical procedures.

**PERSONAL**

Was awarded honors including two prestigious Army Meritorious Service Medals and one Commendation Medal in recognition of my accomplishments and professionalism.

Date

Exact Name of Person
Exact Title
Exact Name of Company
Address
City, State, Zip

**MEDICAL SUPPLY SUPERVISOR, U.S. ARMY EXPERIENCE**

Dear Exact Name of Person (or Dear Sir or Madam if answering a blind ad)

I would appreciate an opportunity to talk with you soon about how I could contribute to your organization through a combination of experience, knowledge, and skills which blends logistics and inventory management with the medical field.

As you will see from my enclosed resume, I am a versatile professional with an associate's degree in General Studies with a concentration in EMS Management and am a licensed EMT with a strong background in logistics and inventory control operations. During my career in the U.S. Army as a medical supply supervisor and laboratory specialist, I earned numerous honors and medals in recognition of my initiative, leadership, and professionalism and was handpicked for vital roles requiring expertise in the supply field. I have managed property accounts worth in excess of $20.7 million and supervised as many as 47 people while earning a reputation as an individual who can be counted on to get the job done, no matter how challenging or difficult.

I began my military service as a Medical Laboratory Specialist and rapidly gained a reputation as a skilled and proficient technician in settings which included a clinical chemistry branch, a histology laboratory, and a toxicology laboratory.

Since retiring from the U.S. Army, I have been successfully applying my sales and communication as well as my organizational abilities as a Sales Representative. While selling an average of four manufactured homes a month, I dealt with a wide range of people including customers, real estate agents, land owners, and contractors.

I am confident that through my military and more recent sales experience, I have built a reputation that would make me a valuable asset to any organization seeking mature, reliable professionals who can offer the ability to adapt to rapid change, pressure, and tight deadlines. If you can use a person of my skills and experience, I hope you will contact me to suggest a time when we might meet to discuss your needs.

Sincerely,


Jonathon DeCarlo

# JONATHAN DECARLO

1110½ Hay Street, Fayetteville, NC 28305   •   preppub@aol.com   •   (910) 483-6611

**OBJECTIVE**
To contribute an extensive logistics and inventory management background to an organization that can use a mature and dedicated hard worker who offers a blend of computer, sales and communication, and motivational skills as well as medical experience.

**EDUCATION, TRAINING, & LICENSES**
**Associate's degree with concentration in EMS Management**, Sanderson Technical Community College, Sanderson, NC, 1998.
Excelled in training including Operating Room, Medical Laboratory, and Medical Supply Specialist Courses as well as programs for medical logistics supervisors, a Primary Leadership Development Program, and hazardous material handling.
Licensed as an Emergency Medical Technician; current CPR certification expires April, 2004.
Licensed in Hazardous Material Handling; operation of forklifts (up to 10,000 lbs.) and buses (up to 90-passenger); Manufactured Housing Sales; and am a Registered Housing Specialist.

**EXPERIENCE**
**SALES REPRESENTATIVE.**  Paradise Housing, Sanderson, NC (2001-present). Apply communication, sales, and organizational skills while selling an average of four manufactured homes a month to include assisting customers in making selections, figuring payments, inventorying stock on hand, and scheduling employees.
- Work closely with people ranging from customers, to real estate agents, to land owners.

**Excelled in the following track record of advancement as a skilled and knowledgeable professional, U.S. Army:**
**MEDICAL SUPPLY SUPERVISOR.** Ft. Campbell, KY (2000-01). Received "commendable" ratings during major inspections as supervisor of 47 people ordering, receiving, issuing, and inventorying supplies and equipment for a medical supply company.
- Was cited for my sound supply economy practices which resulted in cost-effective operations while controlling a $60,000 operating budget.

**MEDICAL LOGISTICS SECTION SUPERVISOR.**  Ft. Campbell, KY (1999). Cited as a professional who could be counted on to get the job done, supervised 12 people while accounting for and overseeing maintenance on more than $385,000 worth of equipment and an additional $470,000 worth of contingency medical resupply kits.
- Provided instruction which produced skilled automated system users.

**SUPERVISOR, PROPERTY MANAGEMENT SECTION.** Ft. Ord, CA (1998). Handpicked to supervise eight people, advise a senior official on supply and personnel issues and act as assistant systems administrator for a task force accounting for property and equipment during base closures and unit functional reorganization projects.
- Designed and implemented a database used to track equipment transfers and turn-ins.

**MATERIAL BRANCH SUPERVISOR.** Ft. Ord, CA (1996-98). Credited with reducing medical excesses 75% while accounting for $49,000 worth of property and equipment, supervised 22 people operating automated systems; conducted training.

**PROPERTY MANAGEMENT BRANCH SUPERVISOR.** Germany (1993-96). Managed assets of $20.7 million for a 150-bed hospital, eight dental clinics, and seven clinics.

**PERSONAL**
Earned numerous honors including three Meritorious Service, one Army Commendation, and four Army Achievement Medals in recognition of my initiative and leadership.

**NUCLEAR MEDICINE TECHNOLOGIST**

Dear Sir or Madam:

I am writing to express my strong interest in a position as Staff Nuclear Medicine Technologist at Union Regional Medical Center. With the enclosed resume, I would like to make you aware of my experience as a Nuclear Medicine Technologist as well as my desire to utilize my experience for the benefit of your organization. Although I am excelling in my current job and can provide outstanding references at the appropriate time, I am relocating back to the Charlotte/Statesville area where I am from and where my family still lives.

As you will see from my resume, I excelled academically while earning my A.A.S. degree in Nuclear Medicine and have subsequently completed advanced professional training sponsored by the North Carolina NMT Society of Nuclear Medicine and the Society of Nuclear Medicine. I am certified by The Nuclear Medicine Technology Certification Board and by The American Registry of Radiological Technologists.

In only my second week of my two-month internship at Lenoir Medical Center, I was offered full-time employment. I am now considered the hospital's "resident expert" in lymphoscintigraphy, and I am responsible for training and supervising other technologists in this examination.

In addition to my technical expertise, I would like to make you aware that I am an outgoing individual who prides myself on my patient relations skills. Since we are the first people cancer patients see after their diagnosis, I do everything I can to comfort and reassure patients and to explain the procedures and techniques we use. I have become very respected by doctors for my analytical and diagnostic skills. I can expertly use all types of equipment and computers used in nuclear medicine.

If you can use a hard-working young healthcare professional known for reliability and intelligence, I hope you will contact me to suggest a time when we might meet to discuss your needs and how I might serve them. Thank you in advance for your time.

Yours sincerely,

Megan Locklear

# MEGAN LOCKLEAR

1110½ Hay Street, Fayetteville, NC 28305   •   preppub@aol.com   •   (910) 483-6611

---

**OBJECTIVE**
I want to contribute to an organization that can use an experienced young healthcare professional who offers expertise as a Nuclear Medicine Technologist.

**EDUCATION**
**Associate of Science (A.A.S.) degree in Nuclear Medicine**, Caldwell Community College and Technical Institute, Lenoir, KY, 2001.
Excelled academically, graduating with a 3.95 cumulative GPA; was a Dean's List student.

**AFFILIATIONS**
Member, North Carolina NMT Society of Nuclear Medicine and the Society of Nuclear Medicine.

**CERTIFICATIONS**
Certified Nuclear Medicine Technologist by The Nuclear Medicine Technology Certification Board, NMTCB Certificate # 020708.
Certified member, The American Registry of Radiologic Technologists, ID # 326893.

**EXPERIENCE**
**NUCLEAR MEDICINE TECHNOLOGIST.** Lenoir Medical Center, Lenoir, KY (2001-present). Am considered the hospital's "resident expert" in lymphoscintigraphy, and am excelling in all aspects of my job at a time when the hospital is experiencing a 200% increase and we are handling 100 cases a day in the Nuclear Medicine Department.

- **Quality assurance**: Am known for my emphasis on quality assurance while preparing radiopharmaceutical kits, checking in drugs, calculating and administering doses, and ensuring radiation safety.
- **Patient relations:** Order patient examinations, record all patient information and record keeping, explain procedures to patients, perform exams, start IVs, and give injections; give and prepare nonradioactive drugs such as stress-imaging agents.
- **Imaging and dark room functions:** Perform imaging and computer analysis; handle all aspects of darkroom filming; have become skilled in performing cardiac spect imaging and processing as well as therapeutic and diagnostic imaging.
- **Expertise in lymphoscintigraphy:** Rapidly mastered the techniques involved in this examination, and now teach/supervise all technologists in my department in this exam.
- **Versatility:** Have learned to perform all nuclear medicine scans, both old and new.

**NURSING ASSISTANT.** Summit Retirement Home, Lenoir, KY (1996-01). Became skilled in serving the needs of a geriatric population in a long-term care facility, and derived much enjoyment from working with this special and knowledgeable group of people known as the elderly.

Highlights of CLINICAL ROTATIONS, Nuclear Medicine Departments:
**Paduca Medical Center (two months).** Was offered full-time employment.
**Kernersville Memorial Hospital (two months).** Gained expertise in operating equipment.
**Memorial Mission Hospital (four months).** Earned confidence in my abilities and was entrusted with running my own camera while still an intern; took call for technologists. Offered full-time employment.
**Veterans of America Hospital (two months).** Refined my skills in operating the camera.

**EQUIPMENT**
Proficiently work with computers and equipment including the following:
**Computers:** Siemen computer, Max file, Starcam computer, Camstar 4000, Unix (Sun) Trionix, Toshiba UI, and Sparc 20
**Equipment:** Siemen Whole Body, Siemen Spect, Cap-n-Tec Dose Calibrator, Trionix Biad, Trionix Triad, GE-Starcam, GE-XRT Camstar, Pulmonex Xe System, Trionix ECG Gating Devices, Atomic Automatic Gamma Wall System, Mediphysics Generator, DuPont Generator, and Genysis Single Head.

Exact Name of Person
Title or Position
Name of Company
Address (no., street)
Address (city, state, zip)

**NUTRITIONIST AND
MARKETING MANAGER**

Dear Exact Name of Person: (or Dear Sir or Madam if answering a blind ad.)

I would appreciate an opportunity to talk with you soon about how I could contribute to your organization through my extensive experience in medical sales and marketing, medical billing, and nutritional consulting.

Fluent in English and Spanish, I hold an undergraduate degree in Nutrition and Dietetics **cum laude**, and I have worked as a full-time Nutritionist and Marketing Consultant for both the Beech-Nut and Quaker Oats Companies. In those jobs, I visited hospitals, doctors, health centers, and supermarkets to promote products and conduct special marketing events. I am a skilled public speaker and have coordinated numerous conferences and publicity activities.

I have also excelled in sales and sales management positions with a major pharmaceutical company. I began with the company as a Medical Marketing Representative and progressed rapidly into sales management responsibilities which involved training up to eight medical sales professionals. With my naturally outgoing personality and extensive background in the sciences and nutrition, I became one of the company's most valuable employees and most visible spokespersons.

You will see from my resume that I am a hard worker. While excelling in my full-time positions mentioned above, I worked part-time during the evenings and on the weekends for nearly ten years handling all medical billing for a six-doctor medical practice. I had a fully equipped office in my home, and I am very experienced in utilizing WordPerfect and medical billing software including Medifast.

You would find me to be a personable and well-educated individual who relates well to people and who adapts easily to new organizational environments. I can provide excellent personal and professional references.

I hope you will call me soon to suggest a time when we might meet to discuss your current and future needs and how I might serve them. Thank you for your time.

Sincerely yours,

Soraya Zahran, LDN

# SORAYA ZAHRAN, LDN

1110½ Hay Street, Fayetteville, NC 28305  •  preppub@aol.com  •  (910) 483-6611

**OBJECTIVE**

To contribute to an organization that can use an experienced young professional who offers an education as a dietitian along with experience in medical marketing and administration.

**EDUCATION**

Bachelor of Science in Nutrition and Dietetics, **cum laude**, University of Puerto Rico, 1984. Completed graduate-level internship in Dietetics, 1984-85.

**EXPERIENCE**

**NUTRITIONIST & MARKETING MANAGER.** Quaker Oats Company, Puerto Rico (2000-01). As the company's internal nutritionist, coordinated visits to hospitals and health centers in order to present lectures on nutrition, dietetics, and other subjects; explained the benefits of Quaker products in the outpatient setting.
- Trained sales professionals and suppliers regarding product knowledge.
- Marketed Quaker products through visits to doctors' and nutritionists' offices.
- Coordinated and participated in conventions in order to promote products.
- Trained and supervised outside publicists in developing marketing materials.

**MEDICAL MARKETING MANAGER.** Sterling Products, Intl., Puerto Rico (1995-00). For a major pharmaceutical company, marketed medical and pharmaceutical products to public and private hospitals; began with the company as a Medical Sales Representative and then progressed into sales management; supervised eight sales representatives.
- Became one of the company's most productive sales professionals as well as a highly visible and trusted spokesperson respected for my extensive expertise related to over-the-counter drugs.
- Developed special events at medical conventions to promote the company's products; coordinated all special publicity and promotional activities.
- Trained company as well as customer personnel on new products.
- Visited prospective new clients to present products; was known as a skillful negotiator with the ability to close the sale.
- Visited doctors, hospitals, and pharmacies to promote the company's products.

**NUTRITIONIST & MARKETING MANAGER.** Beech-Nut Nutrition Corporation, Puerto Rico (1990-94). As a Nutritionist, visited hospitals, health centers, doctors' offices, and supermarkets in order to explain the advantages of Beech-Nut products.
- Promoted products for babies and infants and expectant mothers; designed special promotions with supermarkets and stores which generated extensive sales.
- Marketed products and trained sales/marketing sales professionals for the company in both Puerto Rico and the Dominican Republic.

**CHIEF OF DIETETIC SERVICES.** Hospital Gubern, Puerto Rico (1985-89). Supervised a department with 12 employees; oversaw the training and scheduling of all employees.
- Performed nutritional assessments of hospital patients; provided dietary instructions to patients being discharged.
- Purchased nutritional products and food; integrated products into the hospital menu.

**COMPUTERS, LANGUAGES**

Extremely computer literate; skilled in using WordPerfect and Medifast for medical billing. Fluent in both English and Spanish.

**PERSONAL**

Have a U.S. Social Security Number. Extremely self-motivated individual. Adapt easily.

Exact Name of Person
Title or Position
Name of Company
Address (no., street)
Address (city, state, zip)

**Nutrition Products and
Services Manager**

Dear Exact Name of Person: (or Dear Sir or Madam if answering a blind ad.)

This letter is directed to an employment agency which has placed an advertisement in the newspaper. Since Ms. Wagner is relocating from the east coast to the west coast, she will utilize all available methods of contacting prospective employers.

I am writing in response to your ad in the *Los Angeles Times.* I am planning to relocate to the Los Angeles area and am sending you a copy of my resume so that you can assist me in my search for a challenging and rewarding position in this area.

As you will see from my resume, since early in 1997 I have been successful in a management position with the nationally known Nutrition for Life organization. Despite the fact that this corporation has declared bankruptcy and more than 800 locations have had to close, I have been able to not only keep my Raleigh, NC, locations open but have increased sales. In 2001, I edged out some tough competition to earn the respected "Manager of the Year Award" from among approximately 1,600 other professionals.

My degree is in Psychology and Sociology and I offer additional experience as a Social Worker. After demonstrating that I could handle a case load of 120-150 clients and consistently complete my cases ahead of schedule, I was promoted to Eligibility Specialist in the Department of Social Services.

I have managed a staff of up to 25 and all aspects of operations in a facility which reached the $900,000 level in annual sales and serviced as many as 300 clients a week.

I am an enthusiastic, energetic, and well-organized professional. I offer a talent for getting the most from employees and finding effective ways to keep things running smoothly and productively—even under very unsettled circumstances.

I hope you will welcome my call soon to discuss how you might be able to help me in my job search in your area. Thank you in advance for your time.

Sincerely yours,

Veronica Wagner

# VERONICA WAGNER

1110½ Hay Street, Fayetteville, NC 28305 • preppub@aol.com • (910) 483-6611

**OBJECTIVE**  To offer my superior communication and motivational skills to an organization that can use an experienced management professional who has demonstrated a bottom-line orientation and a talent for selling concepts and services through an enthusiastic and energetic style.

**EXPERIENCE**  **GENERAL MANAGER** and **CUSTOMER SERVICE MANAGER**. The Matthews Group (Nutrition for Life), Raleigh and Goldsboro, NC (1997-present). Continue to set sales records and steadily increase the customer base despite the fact that the parent corporation declared bankruptcy and more than 800 locations nationwide were forced to close.
- Singled out as **"Manager of the Year for 2001"** from among 1,600 qualified professionals nationwide, displayed knowledge of every aspect of Nutrition for Life operations.
- Increased sales by more than 50% during reorganization following a corporate takeover.
- Handled a wide range of functional activities ranging from setting sales and service goals, to developing business plans, to recruiting/training/supervising employees.
- Oversaw daily operational areas including financial management, inventory control, and customer follow up procedures.
- Handpicked for my effectiveness in running the Raleigh site, was selected to open the Goldsboro location and hold the position of interim area manager.
- During a two-month period prior to opening the Goldsboro center, hired and trained personnel and set up their operation.
- Applied my knowledge of marketing techniques while developing campaigns which used successful clients in radio ads and placed "lead boxes" throughout the city.
- Supervised up to 25 employees in a facility which saw from 250 to 300 clients a week and made $900,000 in its peak years before corporate reorganization.
- Maintained a $500,000 to $600,000 level with approximately 140 clients a week and about 12 employees in 1999.
- Through personal attention and rapport with clients, built a strong customer base which continues to generate about four new clients a week.

**ELIGIBILITY SPECIALIST**. Department of Social Services, Raleigh, NC (1990-97). Through my ability to communicate effectively with others and quickly establish rapport, was effective in working closely with agency clients to assess their needs and using established guidelines to determine their eligibility for various types of aid.
- Was promoted after managing a case load of from 120 to 150 clients and displaying my ability to organize and deal with a heavy schedule by always completing my cases on schedule and pitching in to help other social workers with theirs.
- Investigated approximately 60 cases a month through a combination of office and home visits to obtain information to determine eligibility for aid.

**EDUCATION**  **B.S., Psychology and Sociology**, University of Wisconsin, River Falls, WI, 1990.
- Earned recognition in "Who's Who Among American College Students" on the recommendation of Sociology Department faculty members.
- Maintained a 3.8 GPA and was one of the top two students in my graduating class.
- Received "Special Honors" and "Highest Academic Honors" upon my graduation.
- Founded and then served as president of the university's Sociology Club; planned and coordinated a wide range of campus activities for the Student Activities Committee.
- Completed independent study in Europe on the use of alternative medicines.

**COMPUTERS**  Experienced with all Microsoft products including Word, Excel, and Access.

**PERSONAL**  Am an energetic and enthusiastic individual with a flair for handling human, material, and fiscal resources. Contribute to my community in assisting the homeless and disadvantaged.

John LaMacchia
Pharmaceutical Industry Specialist
Performance Recruiters, Inc.

**PHARMACEUTICAL SALES
CONSULTANT**

Dear Mr. LaMacchia:

With the enclosed resume, I would like to make you aware of my interest in contributing to your organization through my experience as a Pharmaceutical Sales Consultant along with my extensive network of relationships and contacts within the medical community.

You will see from my resume that I am currently promoting cardiovascular and pulmonary products, and I have excelled in establishing relationships with doctors who normally do not see pharmaceutical sales representatives. My background as an Operating Room Technician and Urology Technician has helped me greatly in rapidly becoming successful in the pharmaceutical sales field. I also hold a B .A. in Chemistry.

If you can use a knowledgeable and tested medical sales professional, I hope you will contact me to suggest a time when we could meet. Although I can provide excellent personal and professional references at the appropriate time, I would appreciate your not contacting my current employer until after we have a chance to meet. Thank you in advance for your time.

Sincerely,


Ashley Johnson

# ASHLEY JOHNSON

1110½ Hay Street, Fayetteville, NC 28305　　•　　preppub@aol.com　　•　　(910) 483-6611

---

**OBJECTIVE**　　To contribute to an organization that can use a persuasive communicator and pro-active professional who combines outstanding sales and marketing abilities, including pharmaceutical sales experience, along with professional experience as a member of an Operating Room surgical team.

**EDUCATION**　　**Bachelor of Arts in Chemistry**, University of Colorado at Colorado Springs, Colorado Springs, CO.
- Emphasis in Organic Chemistry. Coursework relied heavily upon knowledge of Qbasic, Mathcad, Microsoft Office, Microsoft Excel, Microsoft Access, and Microsoft Word.

Completed 24 semester hours of study in the **Russian Basic Course**, Defense Language Institute, Monterey, CA, 1993-95.
- Developed conversational proficiency in the Russian Language.

Completed **United States Army Operating Room Specialist Course**, Ft. Sam Houston, TX, and Ft. Leavenworth, KS, 1991-92.
- Coursework included Anatomy and Physiology as well as Operating Room Procedures and Preparation.

**EXPERIENCE**　　**PHARMACEUTICAL SALES CONSULTANT.** Snyder HealthCare Sales (Zeneca Pharmaceuticals). Colorado Springs, CO (2001-present). Have consistently achieved personal and corporate sales objectives while promoting cardiovascular and pulmonary products.
- **Cardiovascular** products: Promote Zestoretic, Sular, and Zestril, which is the #1 Ace inhibitor.
- **Pulmonary** products: Promote Accolate, and through aggressive promotion experienced no sales decrease despite the recent release of a much-publicized similar drug.
- Have been able to schedule appointments with doctors who normally refuse to see pharmaceutical representatives.

**MATHEMATICS TEACHER.** Harnett County Schools, Colorado Springs, CO (2000). Taught and evaluated four 30-student, seventh-grade classes in Geometry and Algebra; prepared instruction materials, supervised classroom and maintained discipline while also conferring with school administration officials, teaching staff, and parents.

**FAMILY SUPPORT GROUP COORDINATOR**. 3rd Battalion, 10th Special Forces Group (Airborne), Ft. Carson, CO (1998-00). Directed a volunteer organization with the mission of supporting deployed soldiers and their families.
- Forecasted, planned, and organized both routine activities and special events in support of the organization and its members.
- Provided liaison between Family Support Group members and Fort Carson agencies.
- Supervised and trained Family Support Group staff (six personnel) and representatives (four personnel).

**OPERATING ROOM and UROLOGY TECHNICIAN.** U.S. Army MEDDAC, Fort Ord, CA (1995-97). Served as a member of Operating Room surgical team performing scrub and other support services for simple to highly complex procedures.
- Became skilled at expertly setting up instruments and equipment, transporting and preparing patients, as well as sterilizing instruments, labeling, and recordkeeping.

**PERSONAL**　　Interests include playing basketball, volleyball, and softball; travel; and family.

Exact Name of Person
Title or Position
Name of Company
Address (number and street)
Address (city, state, and zip)

**PHARMACEUTICAL SALES**
**REPRESENTATIVE**

Dear Exact Name of Person:  (or  Sir or Madam if answering a blind ad.)

I would appreciate an opportunity to talk with you soon about how I could contribute to your organization through my proven sales skills as well as my ability to train and develop other sales professionals.

As you will see from my resume, I have excelled in a track record of accomplishment based on my results-oriented communication skills, including my ability to negotiate deals, resolve critical issues in business situations, create innovate marketing campaigns, and close high-ticket sales. In my current position as a Pharmaceutical Sales Representative with Pfizer Pharmaceutical Division, I have been recognized for achieving the highest dollar volume of sales in the Raleigh Division and have been chosen to be the computer trainer because of my superior computer knowledge.

In my previous job as an Account Executive with IBM, I consistently set new sales records while serving up to 700 commercial and government accounts in cities in North Carolina. I was named Top Sales Executive for three months, a distinction I am proud of because I had a great respect for my outstanding sales colleagues.

Although I am excelling in my current position and can provide outstanding references at the appropriate time, I have decided to approach your company because I feel you could benefit from my considerable strengths in sales and sales management. I would appreciate your keeping my interest in your company confidential at this time.

If you can use a proven performer with a strong bottom-line orientation along with the ability to relate effectively to people at all levels, I hope you will contact me to suggest a time when we might meet to discuss your needs and how I might serve them. Thank you in advance for your time.

Sincerely,

Bobby Smith

# BOBBY SMITH

1110½ Hay Street, Fayetteville, NC 28305  •  preppub@aol.com  •  (910) 483-6611

**OBJECTIVE**

To benefit an organization that can use a persuasive, articulate professional who excels in motivating others, developing productive teams, planning sales campaigns, and managing projects.

**EDUCATION**

**M.P.A.**, South Carolina Central University, Damons, SC, degree expected in 2003.
**B.S., Business Administration,** South Carolina Central University, Damons, SC, 1996.
- Courses included statistics, accounting, economics, marketing, and organizational development.

Associate's degree in Logistics, Community College of the Air Force, 1994.

**AFFILIATIONS**

Member, Toastmasters International; have a reputation as a powerful motivational speaker. Donate time to Boy Scouts of America; enjoy helping youth build character and self-esteem.

**EXPERIENCE**

**PHARMACEUTICAL SALES REPRESENTATIVE.** Pfizer Pharmaceutical Division, Durham, Cary, Chapel Hill, and Burlington (2000-present). Have been recognized for achieving the highest dollar volume of sales in the Raleigh Division and have been chosen to be the computer trainer in that division because of my superior computer knowledge.
- Travel extensively while informing physicians about the features and benefits of Pfizer products.
- Discuss clinical studies and pharmacokinetic parameters related to the Pfizer product line and the competition's products.
- Every six months, travel to premier hospitals to reauthorize contracts for discount purposes.
- Excelled in the Pfizer Corporation Sales Training Program for Professional Pharmaceutical Representatives; am qualified to represent Pharmaceutical Division to health care professionals.
- Believe that integrity is of utmost importance for success in the sales field.

**ACCOUNT EXECUTIVE.** IBM, Raleigh, NC (1998-00). Consistently set new sales records while servicing up to 700 commercial and government accounts in cities including Durham, Raleigh, and Wake Forest; was **Top Sales Executive** for May and Jan 2000 and Aug 1999.
- Earned membership in the company's highly prestigious Leadership Club, an honor reserved for the most productive and talented sales managers.
- Developed and utilized creative and effective methods of closing sales.
- Prepared innovative mass mailings which resulted in contacts leading to sales.
- Prospected for and made cold calls on possible customers and handled accounts through all phases of sales presentations and closing of the sale.
- Became skilled in the effective methods of making sales to government accounts.
- Was known for creativity and strong negotiating skills in closing deals for high-ticket sales.
- Was commended for "natural" management skills and groomed for promotion to sales leadership.
- Completed training in advanced and intermediate sales and Total Quality Management (TQM).

**RETAIL SALES ASSOCIATE.** Sears Roebuck, Durham, NC (1989-97). Recognized as the **Top Sales Associate** for two consecutive years, assisted customers in the selection of personal computers and associated equipment.
- Sold double the store's 3% rate for maintenance agreements; maintained a 7% rate.

**PERSONAL**

Well-developed abilities as a motivational speaker. Enjoy developing ideas and teams.

Mr. Mike Smith
Pacific Coast Management
321 Mountain Blvd, Suite 92
Seattle, WA 90909

**PHARMACEUTICAL SALES**
**REPRESENTATIVE**

Dear Mr. Smith:

Thank you for your recent expression of interest in my background, and I am faxing with this cover letter an updated resume which describes my current job as a Pharmaceutical Sales Representative. In my current job servicing chain drug stores and doctors' offices in 30 cities, I am consistently ranked among the company's top producers in my efforts to increase market share, develop new accounts, and boost sales of Vanceril and Proventil H.F.A. I believe my rapid success as a Pharmaceutical Sales Representative has been due in large part to my background as an R.N., and I have come to be regarded by all the doctors and pharmacists with whom I work as a trusted advisor and Marketing Consultant.

As you will see, I have lived in the San Francisco area all my life, except for a few years after high school when I worked as a model for the Legends Agency in New York. After my stint in modeling, I earned my Bachelor's degree in Business Administration in 1992 and then graduated from nursing school as an R.N. in 1998. In a job with Interim Care prior to my current position, I traveled to surrounding counties handling a patient case load and training new nurses. In a previous job, I worked for Seattle Medical Center, where I advanced to increasing responsibilities as a Staff Nurse in the Medical Intensive Care Unit, Emergency Department, and Coronary Care Unit.

With a reputation as a doer and achiever, I have worked since I was 16 years old. As a high school junior and senior, I assisted in managing a skating rink and handled sales, concessions, special events, as well as opening and closing the business. I have also excelled as a Sales Representative with a local 50-year-old business which operates all over the east coast handling mostly commercial and industrial accounts. I have negotiated contracts, prospected for customers, and resolved problems in fair and diplomatic ways.

Although I am excelling in my current job and am highly regarded by the company, I would enjoy learning how your company could make use of my considerable marketing and sales abilities. I am sure my extensive contacts and outstanding reputation within the medical community could be of value to you. You would find me in person to be a congenial individual who interacts with others with poise and professionalism. I hope you will contact me soon to suggest a time when we could meet to discuss your needs and how I might be of service to you.

Yours sincerely,


Rebecca Skenteris

# REBECCA ADKINS SKENTERIS

1110½ Hay Street, Fayetteville, NC 28305  •  preppub@aol.com  •  (910) 483-6611

**OBJECTIVE**

To contribute to an organization that can use a persuasive communicator and proactive professional who combines outstanding sales and marketing abilities, including pharmaceutical sales experience along with professional nursing experience and a degree in Business Administration.

**EDUCATION**

Pursuing Master of Clinical Psychology studies, Golden Gate University, San Francisco, CA, 2001-present.

**Associate of Applied Science in Nursing degree**, Golden Gate Technical Community College, San Francisco, CA, 1998; excelled in extracurricular and academic activities:

- Earned **Dean's List** distinction, 1995-98.
- Was honored by selection as Marshal, Class of 1997.
- Received a faculty appointment to the Curriculum Committee and Steering Committee.
- Was named Class Historian, 1996-98.

**Bachelor of Business Administration degree, cum laude**, minor in Accounting and Economics, Golden Gate University, San Francisco, CA, 1992.

**EXPERIENCE**

**PHARMACEUTICAL SALES REPRESENTATIVE.** Simms-Price Pharmaceuticals, San Francisco, CA (2001-present). Manage a 30-city territory while servicing existing clients and developing new accounts.

- Because of my background as an R.N. with extensive medical knowledge and a thorough knowledge of medical terminology, quickly earned the respect of my clients; have become a respected Marketing Consultant and trusted advisor to pharmacists and doctors.
- Represent Vanceril (DS), Claritin, and Proventil H.F.A. to chain drug stores and doctors' offices.
- **Sales accomplishments**: Am ranked second in the district in total sales of Proventil H.F.A and second in percentage of growth in sales; am ranked 3rd in total sales of Vanceril Double Strength.

**CASE MANAGER.** Interim HealthCare, Berkeley, CA (2000-01). Traveled to surrounding counties while handling a 25-patient caseload; involved in training new nurses.

- Became skilled in time management while providing quality patient care and coordinating the efforts of physicians, ancillary medical personnel, and necessary community resources.

**Excelled in the following track record of progression to increasing responsibilities, Seattle Regional Medical Center of San Francisco, CA:**

**2000: STAFF NURSE, CORONARY CARE UNIT.** Handled patient care to include assessment, implementation of orders, treatment, and continuous monitoring of acutely ill.

**1999-00: STAFF NURSE, EMERGENCY DEPARTMENT.** Handled all aspects of patient care in a critical care setting while implementing triage protocol, assessing conditions and assisting with treatment, and continuously monitoring various conditions of medical, pre-surgical, and trauma-crash patients including MVAs, burns, ODs, gunshot wounds.

**1998-99: STAFF NURSE, MEDICAL INTENSIVE CARE UNIT.** Operated as a Float Nurse for Surgical Intensive Care Unit, the Coronary Care Unit, and Cardiac Intensive Care.

**MODEL.** Legends Agency, New York, NY (1986-90). After graduating from high school, worked as a model in New York in commercials which emphasized my face and eyes.

**COMPUTERS**

Proficient with Windows, Microsoft, Quicken, and WordPerfect. Outstanding references available.

**PHARMACY TECHNICIAN**

Dear Sir or Madam:

With the enclosed resume, I would like to make you aware of my versatile background as an articulate professional with exceptional communication and organizational skills who offers experience as a hotel auditor, pharmacy technician, budget assistant, and administrative clerk.

In my most recent position as a Pharmacy Technician with the Veterans Administration Hospital, I fill prescriptions for inpatient, outpatient, and physician orders. My attention to detail and strong organizational skills were demonstrated on a daily basis while preparing prescriptions in an environment that allowed no room for error.

In an earlier position in the hospitality industry, I served as Night Auditor and Desk Clerk for Barclay Towers in Virginia Beach. I essentially served as "manager on duty," supervising up to five desk clerks while overseeing customer service, guest registration, and reservations activity as well as training new personnel in all operational areas. I audited all daily transactions for the hotel and restaurant, ensuring that actual funds matched receipts in addition to updating and maintaining weekly and monthly accounting logs.

Previously as Budget Assistant for Information Services Command at Fort Bragg, NC, I managed a budget of nearly $1 million, providing fund control, purchasing approval, and monitoring of all telecommunications purchases. In my first position with the Civil Service, I worked as an Administrative Clerk for the Aviation Safety Office, providing security and maintenance of sensitive documents which included Aircraft Mishap Reports, Occupational Hazard Reports, and accident/crash reports.

As you will see, I have earned an Associate of Applied Science degree in Business Administration from Tulsa Technical Community College, which I have supplemented with a Pharmacy Technician diploma and a certificate in Accounting. I feel that my education and proven ability to succeed in versatile work environments would make me a valuable addition to your company.

If you can use an accounting professional with experience in the hospitality industry as well as highly developed analytical, communication, and organizational abilities, I hope you will contact me to suggest a time when we might meet.

Sincerely,

Jerri Blank

# JERRI BLANK

1110½ Hay Street, Fayetteville, NC 28305   •   preppub@aol.com   •   (910) 483-6611

**OBJECTIVE**   To benefit an organization that can use an articulate and experienced accounting professional with exceptional communication, analytical, and organizational skills who offers a versatile background as a hotel auditor, pharmacy technician, and budget assistant.

**EDUCATION**   Completed the **Pharmacy Technician diploma program,** Mansfield School of Business, Virginia Beach, VA, 1994.
Earned **Associate of Applied Science** degree in **Business Administration**, Tulsa Technical Community College, Tulsa, OK, 1991.
Received a **Certificate in Accounting for Military Comptrollers** from the Army Institute for Professional Development.

**EXPERIENCE**   **PHARMACY TECHNICIAN.** Veteran's Administration Medical Center, Tulsa, OK (2000-present). Prepare and dispense a wide range of medications while assisting the pharmacist at this busy regional medical center.
- Fill prescriptions for inpatient, outpatient, and physician orders; generate prescription labels for medication vials.
- Prepare inpatient medication drawers, stat & now doses, and IV bags; stock wards with medications and supplies

**NIGHT AUDITOR** and **DESK CLERK.** Barclay Towers, Virginia Beach, VA (1995-00). Served as "manager on duty" while also providing exceptional customer service and performing various accounting functions for this busy resort hotel.
- Audited all daily transactions for the hotel and restaurant, ensuring that actual funds matched receipts; updated and maintained weekly and monthly accounting logs.
- Supervised up to five desk clerks on the night shift; placed and confirmed reservations, registered guests and assigned rooms.
- Trained of new personnel in all operational areas, including guest relations, reservation system, switchboard operation, etc.
- Handled a large volume of cash and credit payments; maintained complete and accurate records of all financial transactions.

**BUDGET ASSISTANT.** Department of the Army, Ft. Bragg, NC (1990-95). Oversaw accounting functions for all telecommunications purchases at Informations Systems Command as well as performing various human resources and clerical duties.
- Supervised and trained three budget clerks.
- Managed a budget of nearly $1 million, overseeing fund control and approval in addition to monitoring utilization of funds for all telecommunications transactions.
- Received, analyzed and reviewed, reconciled, and recorded accounting information on telecommunications purchases for XVIII Airborne Corps and Fort Bragg.
- Prepared reports, ledgers and logs, memos, letters, and other written correspondence.

**ADMINISTRATIVE CLERK.** Department of the Army, Ft. Bragg, NC (1985-90). In my first Civil Service position, provided a full range of clerical and administrative services for the post Aviation Safety Office.
- Wrote articles for safety bulletins and newsletters; prepared written correspondence.
- Provided clerical support and assistance to the Aircraft Accident Investigation Team.

**PERSONAL**   Excellent personal and professional references are available upon request.

Date

Exact Name of Person
Exact Title
Exact Name of Company
Address
City, State, Zip

**PHYSICIAN ASSISTANT**     Dear Exact Name of Person: (or Dear Sir or Madam if answering a blind ad):

With the enclosed resume, I would like to make you aware of my credentials and experience as a Board Certified Physician Assistant and make you aware of my interest in exploring employment opportunities with your organization.

In addition to graduating with honors from Yale University's AMA-approved, fully accredited Physician Assistant Program, I hold a B.H.S. in Allied Health as well as a B.S. with a concentration in Cellular Physiology and Microbiology. I received numerous scholarships while completing my undergraduate education, and I was elected to many leadership positions which included President of the Physician Assistant Class of 2002 Society and Vice President of the Student Body at Yale. I excelled academically and among the honors I received was the Top Graduate Award.

Currently I am working full time in orthopaedic surgery while also handling part-time responsibilities at an urgent care facility and at a rural emergency medicine facility. I also have experience in a family practice environment and in a specialized urologic setting. I am skilled at general surgery and orthopaedic surgery.

If you can use an accomplished and respected young Physician Assistant to join your organization, I hope you will contact me to suggest a time when we might meet to discuss your needs and how I might serve them. Thank you in advance for your time.

Sincerely,

Stewart May

Alternate Last Paragraph:
I hope you will write or call me soon to suggest a time when we might meet to discuss your needs and goals and how my background might serve them. I can provide outstanding references at the appropriate time.

# STEWART MAY

1110½ Hay Street, Fayetteville, NC 28305  •  preppub@aol.com  •  (910) 483-6611

**OBJECTIVE**    To benefit an organization that can use a Physician Assistant experienced in family practice, urgent care, internal medicine, CVT surgery, as well as general and orthopaedic surgery.

**EDUCATION**    Earned **B.H.S. in Allied Health** while also completing the AMA-approved fully accredited **Physician Assistant Program,** Yale University, New Haven, CT, 2002.
Earned **B.S.,** concentration in cellular physiology and microbiology with a chemistry minor, Yale University, 1999.
- **Leadership:** Vice President of the student body at Yale in 1998; President of the Senate in 1999; President of the Physician Assistant Class of 2002 Society.
- **Academic Honors:** Received Cognitus Psycho **Top Graduate** Award; Omicron Delta Kappa National Leadership Honor Society, 1999-02; Dean's List, 1997-02.
- **Scholarships:** Yale College Incentive Scholarship 1996-97; Scholar Athlete—Football, 1999-00; Memorial Award, 1998-02; Fred Clark Memorial Award, 1999; Methodist Church Award, 1998-99; "Iron Man" Soccer Award, 1996.

**Certification in Cardiopulmonary Resuscitation and Emergency Cardiac Care**, 2001-03.
Trained in Surgery at Norwalk/Yale University in Vascular/General Surgery.

**CERTIFICATION**    Board Certified Physician Assistant; received Special Recognition in Surgery on AAPA Board Exam.

**MEMBERSHIPS**    Member of Physician Assistants in Orthopaedic Surgery; past member, American Academy of Physician Assistants; Past President, Tri-Beta Biological Society

**EXPERIENCE**    **Handle simultaneous responsibilities,** New Haven and Smithfield, CT (2000-present):
**ORTHOPAEDIC SURGERY.** Cape Fear Orthopaedic, New Haven, CT. In this full-time job, handle responsibilities which include clinical orthopaedics managing up to 30 patients daily; am on call every 3rd and every 4th weekend. ED call includes triage, both pediatric and adult orthopaedics as well as fracture reduction, amputation repairs, and foreign body removal. Function as first assistant in all orthopaedic procedures.
**URGENT CARE.** Northside Urgent Care, New Haven, CT. In this part-time position of approximately 30 hours per month in outlying urgent care, obtain physician support by telephone as needed. Manage low-to-moderate acuity problems such as lacerations, occasional common colds, allergies, and dermatologic problems as well as college sports orthopaedic injuries.
**EMERGENCY MEDICINE.** Johnston Memorial Hospital, Smithfield, CT. In this part-time position up to 40 hours per month, work in main ED servicing in a rural community. Am involved in management of chest pain while assisting with trauma cases including intubation fraction stabilization, dislocation reductions, and all other ED situations.

**FIRST ASSISTANT, UROLOGY.** Connecticut Private Industry Council Position, New Haven, CT (1995-99). Was selected for this full-time paid position by Deepak Smith, M.D., and the Industry Council to observe and participate in all aspects of the urologic practice. Was First Assistant on all office cystoscopies, vasectomies, and cystometrograms, and spent more than 250 hours each summer in the operating room.
- Improved computer tracking of cancer patients; performed office microscopic analysis of urine, sperm, and fluids expressed as a result of STDs.
- Presented a disease process weekly; selected to represent the Private Industry Council in documentary presented to The President of the U.S. in 1997.

**PERSONAL**    Can provide excellent references on request. Outgoing and adaptable individual.

## ABOUT THE EDITOR

Anne McKinney holds an MBA from the Harvard Business School and a BA in English from the University of North Carolina at Chapel Hill. A noted public speaker, writer, and teacher, she is the senior editor for PREP's business and career imprint, which bears her name. Early titles in the Anne McKinney Career Series (now called the Real-Resumes Series) published by PREP include: *Resumes and Cover Letters That Have Worked, Resumes and Cover Letters That Have Worked for Military Professionals, Government Job Applications and Federal Resumes, Cover Letters That Blow Doors Open,* and *Letters for Special Situations*. Her career titles and how-to resume-and-cover-letter books are based on the expertise she has acquired in 20 years of working with job hunters. Her valuable career insights have appeared in publications of the *"Wall Street Journal"* and other prominent newspapers and magazines.

# PREP Publishing Order Form

You may purchase any of our titles from your favorite bookseller! Or send a check or money order or your credit card number for the total amount*, plus $3.50 postage and handling, to PREP, Box 66, Fayetteville, NC 28302. If you have a question about any of our titles, feel free to e-mail us at preppub@aol.com and visit our website at http://www.prep-pub.com

Name: _____

Phone #: _____

Address: _____

_____

E-mail address: _____

Payment Type:  ☐ Check/Money Order   ☐ Visa   ☐ MasterCard

Credit Card Number: _____ Expiration Date: _____

Check items you are ordering:

☐ $16.95—REAL-RESUMES FOR FINANCIAL JOBS. Anne McKinney, Editor

☐ $16.95—REAL-RESUMES FOR COMPUTER JOBS. Anne McKinney, Editor

☐ $16.95—REAL-RESUMES FOR MEDICAL JOBS. Anne McKinney, Editor

☐ $16.95—REAL-RESUMES FOR TEACHERS. Anne McKinney, Editor

☐ $16.95—REAL-RESUMES FOR CAREER CHANGERS. Anne McKinney, Editor

☐ $16.95—REAL-RESUMES FOR STUDENTS. Anne McKinney, Editor

☐ $16.95—REAL-RESUMES FOR SALES. Anne McKinney, Editor

☐ $16.95—REAL ESSAYS FOR COLLEGE AND GRAD SCHOOL. Anne McKinney, Editor

☐ $25.00—RESUMES AND COVER LETTERS THAT HAVE WORKED.

☐ $25.00—RESUMES AND COVER LETTERS THAT HAVE WORKED FOR MILITARY PROFESSIONALS.

☐ $25.00—RESUMES AND COVER LETTERS FOR MANAGERS.

☐ $25.00—GOVERNMENT JOB APPLICATIONS AND FEDERAL RESUMES: Federal Resumes, KSAs, Forms 171 and 612, and Postal Applications.

☐ $25.00—COVER LETTERS THAT BLOW DOORS OPEN.

☐ $25.00—LETTERS FOR SPECIAL SITUATIONS.

☐ $16.00—BACK IN TIME. Patty Sleem

☐ $17.00—(trade paperback) SECOND TIME AROUND. Patty Sleem

☐ $25.00—(hardcover) SECOND TIME AROUND. Patty Sleem

☐ $18.00—A GENTLE BREEZE FROM GOSSAMER WINGS. Gordon Beld

☐ $18.00—BIBLE STORIES FROM THE OLD TESTAMENT. Katherine Whaley

☐ $14.95—WHAT THE BIBLE SAYS ABOUT... *Words that can lead to success and happiness* (large print edition) Patty Sleem

☐ $10.95—KIJABE An African Historical Saga. Pally Dhillon

_____ **TOTAL ORDERED (add $3.50 for postage and handling)**

*PREP offers volume discounts on large orders. Call us at (910) 483-6611 for more information.*

THE MISSION OF PREP PUBLISHING IS TO PUBLISH BOOKS AND OTHER PRODUCTS WHICH ENRICH PEOPLE'S LIVES AND HELP THEM OPTIMIZE THE HUMAN EXPERIENCE. OUR STRONGEST LINES ARE OUR JUDEO-CHRISTIAN ETHICS SERIES AND OUR BUSINESS & CAREER SERIES.

Would you like to explore the possibility of having PREP's writing team create a resume for you similar to the ones in this book?

For a brief free consultation, call 910-483-6611
or send $4.00 to receive our Job Change Packet to
PREP, Department Medical, Box 66, Fayetteville, NC 28302.

**QUESTIONS OR COMMENTS? E-MAIL US AT PREPPUB@AOL.COM**

Made in the USA
Lexington, KY
27 February 2014